D1111727

Senator Joe McCarthy

Books by Richard H. Rovere

Howe and Hummel:
Their True and Scandalous History
The General and the President
(with Arthur M. Schlesinger, Jr.)
Affairs of State: The Eisenhower Years
Senator Joe McCarthy
The American Establishment and Other
Reports, Opinions, and Speculations

Richard H. Rovere

SENATOR JOE McCARTHY

Foreword by Arthur M. Schlesinger, Jr.

UNIVERSITY OF CALIFORNIA PRESS
Berkeley • Los Angeles • London

University of California Press
Berkeley and Los Angeles, California

University of California Press, Ltd.
London, England

First California Paperback Printing 1996

This book was originally published in a hardcover edition by Harcourt, Brace, Jovanovich in 1959. It is here reprinted by arrangement.

SENATOR JOE MC CARTHY

Library of Congress Cataloging-in-Publication Data

Rovere, Richard Halworth, 1915–1979
    Senator Joe McCarthy / Richard H. Rovere ; foreword by Arthur M. Schlesinger, Jr.
       p.   cm.
    Includes index.
    Originally published: New York : Harcourt, Brace, Jovanovich, 1959.
    ISBN 0-520-20472-7 (pbk. : alk. paper)
    1. McCarthy, Joseph, 1908–1957. 2. Legislators—United States—Biography. 3. United States. Congress. Senate—Biography.
I. Title.
E748.M143R62   1995
973.921′092—dc20
[B]   95-40975
                                            CIP

1 2 3 4 5 6 7 8 9

The paper used in this publication meets the minimum requirements of American National Standard for Information Sciences—Permanence of Paper for Printed Library Materials, ANSI Z39.48–1984. ∞

for Ann

Contents

Foreword by Arthur M. Schlesinger, Jr.   ix

What He Was and What He Did—1   3

What He Was and What He Did—2   45

Early Days   75

Great Days   119

Last Days   232

Those Days Seen from These Days   255

Author's Note   272

Index   273

Foreword

We Americans like to see ourselves as matter-of-fact, level-headed, practical-minded, no-nonsense, down-to-earth people, not easily flustered or rattled or panicked. We think we are all from Missouri: "You have to show me."

Most of the time most of us probably are that way. But the historical record also suggests that from time to time some of us become frightened by vague and shadowy menaces, haunted by the fear that somewhere a hidden group of evil men is pulling strings that will decide our destiny. From the start of the republic we have been recurrently subject to conspiratorial panics. Adam Weishaupt and the *Illuminati* agitated jittery Americans in the first decade of independence, and the legacy of that eighteenth-century Bavarian crowd still agitates the Reverend Pat Robertson two centuries later. This propensity to believe in the existence of sinister forces plotting in secret to stamp out our liberties has been sufficiently chronic in the American experience for the historian Richard Hofstadter to write about "the paranoid strain in American politics."

Once the season of paranoia is over, we look back with a certain disbelief at our spasms of irrationality. Later generations reading about Joe McCarthy must wonder what in the world their ancestors had been smoking in the 1950s. Could

that many Americans really have fallen for a cynical demagogue like Joe McCarthy? Could an eminent senator like
Robert A. Taft, voted by the Senate in 1957 as one of the five
greatest senators in American history, really have urged Mc-
Carthy on? Could a revered president like Dwight D. Eisenhower and an eminent secretary of state like John Foster Dulles
really have handed McCarthy a de facto veto over State Department appointments? Could Bill Buckley really have called Mc-
Carthyism "a movement around which men of good will and
stern morality can close ranks"?

Yet all these things did take place. And lest later generations be tempted to preen themselves on their superior cool,
let them consider the conspiratorial fantasies that terrify many
of their own contemporaries and drive some to such horrors
as the Oklahoma City bombing of 1995. The phenomenon that
Richard Rovere describes in this wise and illuminating book
is not just history, something finished and over. Paranoia re-
mains an ever-present possibility amidst the tensions and ran-
cors of American life.

America has always suffered its quota of demagogues. A
century and a half ago James Fenimore Cooper identified the
demagogue as the perennial threat to democracy. But most of
our demagogues have been local nuisances. McCarthy, Rovere suggests, was our first national demagogue. His success
was made possible by the nationalization of politics brought
about by the New Deal, the Second World War, and the Cold
War, and by the nationalization of communications brought
about by radio and television.

It was also made possible, of course, by Stalinism—by the Soviet dictator's murderous tyranny, by his purges and his *gulags*, by his network of agents and spies around the world, by the obedience of national Communist parties (China and Yugoslavia excepted, the CPUSA included) to his will, and by the reluctance of some good-hearted Americans ever to say a word against the Soviet Union and communism.

And it was made possible by McCarthy's own demagogic talents. He was a black Irishman, lowbrow and roughneck, restless and reckless, with a certain animal vitality, coarse charm, broad humor, and amusing impudence. He had a con man's instinct for improvisation and publicity and a bully's instinct for weakness and fear. He was not, as Rovere emphasizes, a true believer. He was not a man of principle. He had no great program to offer; indeed, he was conspicuously uninterested in the social and economic problems of the time. His ambition was not to be in the White House; it was to be in the headlines. In Rovere's valuable distinction, he sought not power but glory. He was an alley fighter who relished confusion and trouble and tumult, "a species of nihilist," Rovere writes, ". . . an essentially destructive force, a revolutionist without any revolutionary vision."

The postwar years offered McCarthy a fertile field. After the grim ordeals of depression and war, the American people expected a time of peace and security. They yearned, as they had yearned after the First World War, for what Warren G. Harding, in winning the 1920 presidential election, had called "normalcy." This time, victory, instead of bringing normalcy, was plunging the republic into new dangers. Many Americans were both frightened and angry. What had gone wrong? Who were responsible for the new crisis? The fearful and the mad were tinder for McCarthyism.

But fear and anger would not by themselves have been enough to produce McCarthyism. Demagogues like Martin Dies and J. Parnell Thomas, successive chairmen of the House Un-American Activities Committee, had been working the anti-Red side of the street for years without much impact on the country. McCarthy himself came late to the issue. In 1947 the *Saturday Evening Post*, the favorite magazine of the American middle class, ran an article about him entitled "The Senate's Remarkable Upstart." McCarthy was studying Russian, the article noted; "his friends insist that he has hopes ultimately of . . . charming Stalin in his own language." He stumbled into the issue almost inadvertently in 1950. And his lucky break came when North Korea invaded South Korea and President Truman decided to enter the Korean War.

That war began four months after McCarthy seized upon the issue in Wheeling, West Virginia, in February 1950. Other senators did not take the Wheeling speech very seriously and supposed that the troublemaker could be disposed of without too much trouble. But the Korean War transformed popular emotions. It changed McCarthy's crusade from an evanescent sideshow into a national movement. With Communists killing American boys in Korea, why should American Communists be left free to do their dirty deeds at home? And who was protecting them?

Lengthening casualty lists gave McCarthy an ever more eager audience. Disloyalty to the nation was a damaging charge, and loyalty a difficult thing to prove. His role in bringing about the defeat of senators who had scoffed at his scattershot methods—Millard Tydings of Maryland and William Benton of Connecticut—scared most other senators into expedient silence. J. Edgar Hoover, the powerful and unscrupulous director of the Federal Bureau of Investigation and a McCarthy ally, surreptitiously fed him gossip from FBI files. The federal loyalty program, instituted by President Truman to protect national security against espionage, had its share of abuses from the start; in the early Eisenhower years, it turned into a heresy hunt, driving patriotic government workers from their jobs on the basis of unsupported accusations from unidentified sources. "We're kicking the Communists and fellow-travelers and security risks out of the Government . . . by the thousands," boasted Vice President Richard M. Nixon. Road-company McCarthys sprang up in states and cities across the land, employing guilt by association, secret informers, loyalty oaths, blacklists, and other forms of intimidation. It was a dispiriting time in the nation's history and left behind a litter of broken lives. The great judge Learned Hand spoke for many Americans: "I believe that that community is already in process of dissolution where each man begins to eye his neighbor as a possible enemy, where nonconformism with the accepted creed, political as well as religious, is a mark of disaffection, where denunciation, without specification or backing, takes the place of evidence."

McCarthyism was a national shame and a national outrage. It was not, however, as Rovere makes clear, a national reign of terror. The McCarthyites were vindictive and sometimes fanatical, but their power was far from absolute. Of the two Joes, Stalin was incomparably the worse. Many Americans in politics, the press, the pulpit, and the universities freely condemned McCarthy and his works—and with no harm to themselves. And McCarthy himself overreached. Roy Cohn and David Schine of his staff made him an international laughingstock when they jaunted to Europe to purge the United States Information Agency libraries of books by left-wingers, including Dashiell Hammett, author of thrillers such as *The Maltese Falcon* and *The Thin Man.*

The Korean War had made McCarthyism possible. In July 1953 that war came to an end. The fears and frustrations it had generated began to subside. McCarthy meanwhile pursued his search for Communist spies—he never found even one, by the way—into the United States Army itself. After trying in vain to appease McCarthy, the Army finally fought back. In the spring of 1954 the Army-McCarthy hearings took place in Washington. For seven weeks television brought the hearings to the nation, the audience amounting at times to twenty million people. After thirty-five days of the grating voice, the sarcastic condescension, the irrelevant interruptions ("Point of order, Mr. Chairman, point of order!"), and the unsubstantiated accusations, McCarthy, the professional destroyer, finally destroyed himself.

He also came close to destroying, or at least discrediting,

anticommunism. As Winston Churchill remarked to President Eisenhower, "McCarthy has spoiled a good cause." His wild charges and the excesses that followed in his wake strengthened those who opposed any criticism of communism or the Soviet Union. "Anti-anticommunism" became fashionable in some circles. McCarthy and his gusher of lies made it much harder for liberal anticommunists, like the author of this book (and the author of this foreword), to offer reasoned and factual criticism of Stalin and his agents and dupes.

In retrospect, McCarthy may in the end have helped the Communists more than he hurt them. Communism was a threat *to* America, but it was never a threat *in* America. McCarthy diverted energy and concern from a real external danger to a phoney internal danger. In so doing, he unwittingly served Soviet purposes. Richard Condon saw the paradox, and in his wonderful baroque thriller *The Manchurian Candidate*, vividly filmed by John Frankenheimer, the McCarthy-like character, a Red-hunting senator, turned out to be controlled by a Soviet secret agent.

A word about the author of *Senator Joe McCarthy*. Richard H. Rovere was born in Brooklyn, New York, in 1915 and died in Poughkeepsie in 1979. He went to Bard College, and in the desperate years of the Great Depression joined the Communist movement and wrote for the *New Masses*. But he was too independent a man and mind to stay long with the Communists. He departed in 1939 and thereafter was a leading and outspoken anticommunist liberal.

In 1944 he joined the *New Yorker*, where for thirty years he wrote the "Washington Letter." His writing was notable for its grace, fastidiousness, and lucidity, and his coverage of politics was dispassionate and analytical, marked above all by ironic detachment. He had his own strong private feelings, but his code required him to distance himself from the passions and personalities of his time. He used to say that he liked a ringside seat when he could get one, but he did not want to be in the ring or in anyone's corner. He saw himself reviewing Washington as drama critics reviewed Broadway theater.

He brought to public affairs a well-stocked intelligence, as suggested by the range of literary allusion in *Senator Joe McCarthy*. Too much political writing today is garrulous, overwrought, and self-serving. Too little has anything like Rovere's urbanity, elegance, and wit. In this book readers will find not only a dazzling account of a bad patch in the nation's history but a model of the way political books ought to be written. And one must hope that this brilliant reminder of a squalid past will help inoculate our occasionally distraught society against paranoid relapses in years to come.

Arthur M. Schlesinger, Jr.

Senator Joe McCarthy

 *What He Was*
and
What He Did
—1

The late Joseph R. McCarthy, a United States Senator from Wisconsin, was in many ways the most gifted demagogue ever bred on these shores. No bolder seditionist ever moved among us—nor any politician with a surer, swifter access to the dark places of the American mind.

The major phase of McCarthy's career was mercifully short. It began in 1950, three years after he had taken his seat in the Senate, where he had seemed a dim and inconsiderable figure. It ended in 1954, when the Senate passed a resolution of censure against him. That was three years before his death at the age of forty-eight. Both his rise and his

3

fall were accomplished with breath-taking speed. At the start of 1950, he was a jackstraw in Washington. Then he discovered Communism—almost by inadvertence, as Columbus discovered America, as James Marshall discovered California gold. By the spring of the year, he was a towering figure, and from then on, except for a few brief weeks early in that summer, no man was closer than he to the center of American consciousness or more central to the world's consciousness of America. He filled, almost to the letter, the classic role of the corsair of democracy, described twenty-four hundred years ago by Aristophanes, who in *The Knights* had Demosthenes describe the future of an incredulous sausage-seller in whose very coarseness and vulgarity the great connoisseur of both irony and integrity discerned "a promise and an inward consciousness of greatness":

> Now mean and unregarded; but tomorrow
> The mightiest of the mighty, Lord of Athens. . . .
>
> The sovereign and ruler of them all,
> Of the assemblies and tribunals, fleets and armies;
> You shall trample down the Senate under foot
> Confound and crush the generals and commanders.

Through the first part of the decade, McCarthy was all of these things, and then he found the Senate and the generals and commanders rising up against him, and he collapsed. His decline was more difficult to account for than his ascent. He suffered defeats but not destruction. Nothing of a really fatal consequence had happened. He was in a long and sweaty rumble before television cameras in the spring; in the late summer, a Senate committee recommended that he be censured; and in the winter he was censured—or, in the language of the resolution, "condemned" for conduct that "tended to bring the Senate into dishonor and disrepute." But other Senators, less powerful than he, had been censured and gone on to greater triumphs—among them, an earlier Senator from Wisconsin, Robert M. La Follette, whose son and namesake McCarthy had defeated in 1946. (In the year of McCarthy's death, the Senate voted the elder and censured La Follette one of the five greatest men ever to grace the chamber, the other four being Henry Clay, Daniel Webster, John C. Calhoun, and Robert A. Taft.) Still he had five years on stage, and he was at stage center almost all of that time. He walked, then, with a heavy tread over large parts of the Constitution of the United States, and he cloaked his own gross figure in the sovereignty it asserts and the powers it distributes. He usurped executive and judicial authority whenever the fancy struck him. It struck him often.

He held two Presidents captive—or as nearly captive as any Presidents of the United States have ever been held; in their conduct of the nation's affairs, Harry S Truman and Dwight D. Eisenhower, from early 1950 through late 1954, could never act without weighing the effect of their plans upon McCarthy and the forces he led, and in consequence there were times when, because of this man, they could not act at all. He had enormous impact on American foreign policy at a time when that policy bore heavily on the course of world history, and American diplomacy might bear a different aspect today if McCarthy had never lived. In the Senate, his headquarters and his hiding place, he assumed the functions of the

5

Committee of the Whole; he lived in thoroughgoing contempt of the Congress of which he was a member, of the rules it had made for itself, and—whenever they ran contrary to his purposes—of the laws it had enacted for the general welfare.

At the start of 1950, McCarthy was an empty vessel to the general public outside Wisconsin. There he was known as a cheap politician of vulgar, flamboyant ways and a casual approach to the public interest. It is unlikely that one in a hundred Americans knew of his existence. He was a voice making no sound in the wilderness. Then, on February 9, 1950, he made a speech in Wheeling, West Virginia, in the course of which he said that the Department of State was full of Communists and that he and the Secretary of State knew their names. Later there was some dispute (there was always dispute whenever he said anything) as to whether he had stated that there were 205, 81, 57, or "a lot" of Communists, but the number was of slight importance alongside what he insisted was the fact that Communists "known to the Secretary of State" were "still working and making policy." A Senate committee was immediately appointed to look into his startling assertions. It was the first of five investigations, held by four different committees, to be concerned exclusively with the problem of whether Senator McCarthy was telling the truth about others or, *mutatis mutandis,* others were telling the truth about Senator McCarthy. In the spring of 1950, only the first question was considered. Through March and April and May, when Communist power in the Far East was being mobilized for the war in Korea, life in Washington, political life in the United States, seemed largely a matter of determining whether American diplomacy was in the hands of traitors.

Little of importance was learned except that McCarthy had little of importance to say. He had been talking through his hat; if there were Communists in the State Department, he did not know who they were. Nevertheless, he had cued himself in. The lights played over him. Eyes were upon him. The show was his. Within a matter of weeks, his name was known and heard everywhere, and his heavy, menacing countenance was familiar to newspaper readers, to moviegoers, to television viewers everywhere. Henceforth it would be hard to find anyone who was *un*aware of him.

And he became, quickly, an eponym. Barely a month after Wheeling, "McCarthyism" was coined by Herbert Block, the cartoonist who signs himself "Herblock" in the Washington *Post*. The word was an oath at first—a synonym for the hatefulness of baseless defamation, or mudslinging. (In the Herblock cartoon, "McCarthyism" was crudely lettered on a barrel of mud, which teetered on a tower of ten buckets of the stuff.) Later it became, for some, an affirmation. The term survives both as oath and as affirmation—not very usefully as either, one is bound to say—and has far broader applications than at first. Now it is evocative of an almost undifferentiated evil to a large number of Americans and of a positive good to a somewhat smaller number. To the one, whatever is illiberal, repressive, reactionary, obscurantist, anti-intellectual, totalitarian, or merely swinish will for some time to come be McCarthyism, while to the other it means nothing more or less than a militant patriotism. "To many Americans, McCarthyism is Americanism," Fulton Lewis, Jr., a radio commentator and the official McCarthyite muezzin, said. Once the word caught on, McCarthy himself became intrigued with it. "McCarthyism is Americanism with its sleeves rolled," he told a Wisconsin audience in 1952, and, sure enough, there was the eponym, with his hairy arms bare to the biceps. That year he published a book of snippets from his speeches and his testimony before committees, and it bore the modest title of *McCarthyism: The Fight for America*. There is injustice as well as imprecision in both meanings; if patriotism can hardly be reduced to tracking down Marxists in the pastry kitchens of the Pentagon or the bindery of the Government Printing Office, neither is the late Senator's surname to be placed at the center of all the constellations of political unrighteousness. He was not, for example, totalitarian in any significant sense, or even reactionary. These terms apply mainly to the social and economic order, and the social and economic order didn't interest him in the slightest. If he was anything at all in the realm of ideas, principles, doctrines, he was a species of nihilist; he was an essentially destructive force, a revolutionist without any revolutionary vision, a rebel without a cause.

It is pointless, though, to quarrel with words. They acquire a life and a history of their own, and we have little choice but to accept them and seek understanding. It is simply a measure of McCarthy's impact on our society that he stamped with his name a whole cluster of tendencies in American life—some of them as distant as the stars from any concern or responsibility of his. Once, Brooks Atkinson, the theater critic of the New York *Times*, held McCarthy and McCarthyism responsible for a bad season on Broadway. He said McCarthy had driven all good playwrights to silence or triviality. And in the New York *Herald Tribune* for May 25, 1952, at the height of that green season in which college boys are in the habit of laying siege to college girls' dormitories, the following headline appeared:

RABBI BLAMES MC CARTHYISM IN COLLEGE RAIDS
He Says Danger of Voicing Dissent on
Big Issues Makes Campus Restless

This was madness, of course, and if it can be said that the Rabbi in question* would have been the sort to blame the rape of the Sabines on the lack of outing clubs, bowling alleys, ceramics classes, and square dances in Alba and Lavinium, it was nevertheless a tribute to McCarthyism's actual force and impact that this divine conceived his extraordinary theory. It was an even greater tribute to it that such a newspaper as the *Herald Tribune* would regard this particular sermon as worthy of notice in its sober pages.

In time, the whole world took notice of Senator McCarthy. "In all countries they know of him, and in all tongues they speak of him," Adlai Stevenson said after a trip to almost all countries. in 1953. In Western Europe as well as in Eastern,

---

* The story stated that the rabbi "attributed the current dormitory 'raids' by college students to 'McCarthyism,' which, he said, makes serious discussion and dissent on major issues dangerous. 'A vast silence has descended upon young men and women today in the colleges of our country, and they find an expression for their bottled-up energies in foolish and unseemly "raids" upon dormitories.' " And more of the same.

9

in much of Asia and Africa, in Latin America and the An-
tipodes, McCarthy and McCarthyism stood for all that was
held to be evil in American foreign policy and for much that
was found to be disagreeable in American life. In many
places, McCarthy was looked upon as being, in and of himself, an instrumentality in the affairs of nations. The *Times*
of London, a journal of almost spectacular sobriety, observed
once that "the fears and suspicions which center around the
personality of Senator McCarthy are now real enough to
count as an essential factor in policy-making for the West."
Therefore, it went on, with fierce British logic, "McCarthy
has become the direct concern of the United States' allies."
The *Times* made him sound as though he were nuclear fission
or massive retaliation, and it was by no means alone in its
estimate of him. Sir Winston Churchill became sufficiently
exercised to write an eloquent anti-McCarthy passage into
Elizabeth II's Coronation speech.

From a distance, McCarthy may have looked, by some odd
reversal of optical principles, larger than life and of greater
consequence than he ever really was. But he was large and
consequential enough in those years, and he was, in any case,
the first American ever to be discussed and described as being
himself a menace to the comity of nations and the strength
of alliances. He was the first American ever to be actively
hated and feared by foreigners in large numbers.

In Washington and in all the country west of Washington,
he was a fertile innovator, a first-rate organizer and galvanizer
of mobs, a skilled manipulator of public opinion, and something like a genius at that essential American strategy: pub-

licity. He was by no means the first man to use Senatorial immunity or the investigative power of Congress for selfish and unworthy ends, but he was surely the cleverest; he did more with them than any other man had done before him. And he exploited the American party system in brilliant and daring ways—while being himself beyond partisanship, beyond all the established values of the system and all of its established practices. He was a Republican who had started as a Democrat and had made his first run for office as a supporter of Franklin D. Roosevelt. He became, *pro forma,* a Republican in 1939 and as such won election to the Senate, seven years and a World War later. He brought himself to national attention in 1950, in the weeks after the Wheeling speech, by accusing the Democratic administration of conniving with and being supported by Communists. ("The Democratic label is now the property of men and women who have . . . bent to the whispered pleas from the lips of traitors . . . men and women who wear the political label stitched with the idiocy of a Truman, rotted by the deceit of a [Dean] Acheson, corrupted by the red slime of a [Harry Dexter] White." I fear I shall subject the reader to a good deal of unpleasant rhetoric.) The Democratic years, he said, when they were almost over, had been "twenty years of treason." Then his own party took office, with Dwight Eisenhower as President. McCarthy proclaimed the end of subversion in government. But intimations, allegations, accusations of treason were the meat upon which this Caesar fed. He could never swear off. He accused the administration he had helped bring to power of a "weak, immoral, and cowardly" foreign policy, of "appeasement, retreat, and surrender" before Communism, and of having "perpetrated a fraud on the American people." By early 1954, he had extended treason's reign to "twenty-one years."

It tends now to be forgotten that McCarthy was almost as successful in immobilizing the Truman administration as he later was in demoralizing the successor government. Truman denounced McCarthy, though more frequently and more boldly after he had left the White House than before, but he could never ignore him or disregard his large presence on Capitol Hill. McCarthy's attacks on Truman ("The son of a bitch ought to be impeached," he told a press conference in 1951, after Truman's recall of General of the Army Douglas MacArthur from his Far Eastern commands) and on the executive branch under Truman forced the administration into a series of defensive actions that used up vast stores of time, energy, and credit with the public. Dean Acheson, Truman's Secretary of State, spent a large part of 1950 and the ensuing years explaining to Elks, Moose, Women Voters, Legionnaires, Steel Workers, and the rest that he was not corrupt, that he was opposed to Communism, and that he did not hire traitors. To prove its virtue, the State Department hired John Foster Dulles and fired a number of career officers McCarthy had been attacking. When Acheson was not fending off blows before Congressional committees, he was conducting American foreign policy, which became largely a matter of assuring allies and potential allies that McCarthy really wasn't running the show in Washington, despite contrary appearances. It was difficult. "No American official who has represented this government abroad in great affairs, not even Wilson in 1918, has ever been so gravely injured at home," Walter Lippmann wrote in 1950.

The Truman administration had to be defensive and cautious, for it knew, as the Republicans at first did not, that McCarthyism was a bipartisan doctrine. It penetrated large sections of the Democratic Party and led to much disaffection (or, better perhaps, it fed on an already burgeoning disaffection). "How do people feel about McCarthy these days?" the Republican Senator from Massachusetts, Henry Cabot Lodge, Jr., asked the Democratic Governor of Massachusetts, Paul A. Dever. "Your people don't think much of him," Dever said, "but I'm afraid mine do." The Gallup Poll once tested his strength in various occupational groups and found that he had more admirers among manual workers than in any other category—and fewest among business and professional people. If the Democratic President, from the relative safety of the White House, could be relatively free with denunciations, many other Democrats found it imprudent ever to join him. Paul Douglas, of Illinois, the possessor of the most cultivated mind in the Senate and a man whose courage and integrity would compare favorably with any other American's, went through the last Truman years and the first Eisenhower years without ever addressing himself to the problem of McCarthy. Senator John Kennedy, of Massachusetts, the author of *Profiles in Courage,* a book on political figures who had battled strong and sometimes prevailing winds of opinion and doctrine, did likewise. Maurice Tobin, Truman's Secretary of Labor, once went to a Veterans of Foreign Wars conven-

13

tion with an anti-McCarthy speech in his pocket; sensing a pro-McCarthy climate of opinion, he left it in his pocket and talked of other matters.

In 1952, there were many people not much enchanted by the Republican Party who favored it on the ground that if the Democrats were maintained in power, they would be forever at McCarthy's mercy. The Democrats would be driven on to further demonstrations of their anti-Communist zeal, and some of these had already been ridiculous. In 1951, for example, in the course of the Senate hearings on Far Eastern policy, Dean Acheson and his immediate predecessor, General of the Army George Catlett Marshall—both of them under savage attack by McCarthy—testified that they would never so much as *consider* the recognition of Communist China or support of its admission to the United Nations. They assured the Senate that the very idea of recognition was so abhorrent to them and to other American diplomats that it was never even *discussed* in the Department of State, which simply was not the truth. Pressed further, they made a pledge, which they were in no position to keep, that the United States would never offer recognition. Deception, stupidity, stubbornness, and a commitment in perpetuity—these were the lengths to which McCarthy and McCarthyism drove these intelligent men.

On this account, many people felt that the threat he posed could be better handled by his own party. "It is this newspaper's hope and belief that McCarthyism would disappear overnight if Eisenhower were elected," the Washington *Post* said on March 24, 1952. The hope and the belief were ill-

14

founded. Eisenhower was elected, and within two months Mc-
Carthy was harvesting surrenders on every hand, and the
Post was begging the administration to remember "that the
voice of McCarthy is not the voice of America." To a degree,
though, events did seem to justify the *Post*'s view. In 1953,
for example, the administration negotiated an armistice in
Korea that the Democrats would almost certainly have been
unable to accept—because it would have given McCarthy
additional grounds for impugning their loyalty. "I would
have been crucified for that armistice," Harry Truman said.

The paralysis Harry Truman suffered, though, was as nothing compared to that which in a short time overcame President
Eisenhower, who had to suffer it in silence, at least through
his first two years in office. Eisenhower had been forced into
a large surrender even before he was elected. He had from
the start looked upon McCarthy as a cad, a guttersnipe, and
he had planned a small gesture of defiance and dissociation.
He would go into McCarthy's Wisconsin and speak a few
warm and affectionate words about his old chief and patron,
General Marshall, whom McCarthy had all but called a
traitor. ("A man steeped in falsehood . . . who has recourse
to the lie whenever it suits his convenience . . . [part of] a
conspiracy so immense and an infamy so black as to dwarf
any previous venture in the history of man . . . [one in
whose activities can be seen] a pattern which finds his decision
maintained with great stubbornness and skill, always and in-
variably serving the world policy of the Kremlin.") Learning
of Eisenhower's plans to dispute this view of Marshall—and
trembling at what they were certain was the prospect of Mc-

15

Carthy's fury—the party leaders in Wisconsin and half a dozen other Republican politicians pleaded with him to omit that part of his speech, which he did. (In fairness, the President did, on other occasions, stoutly defend General Marshall.) McCarthy's victory was made sweeter by the fact that he himself had played no part in gaining it. He had let it be known that Eisenhower could say whatever he pleased about Marshall and that he, McCarthy, couldn't care less. He even offered to remove himself from the Eisenhower campaign train in Wisconsin if that would make the General feel any better. But so great was the fear of him that Eisenhower gave in, even though McCarthy had magnanimously said that this would not be necessary.

In 1953, the very thought of Joe McCarthy could shiver the White House timbers and send panic through the whole executive branch. I remember once, in about the middle of that year, calling upon one of the President's assistants, a man who seemed to me then, as he does today, to be well above the average in courage and candor. I had gone in search of enlightenment on a number of things, most of them as unrelated to McCarthy as it was possible for anything to be in those days. We had a friendly enough talk and toward the end of it I brought up Topic A—and of course offered the customary assurances that I would not make use of anything he said in such a way as to embarrass him or make his life more difficult than it already was. At the mention of McCarthy, his whole manner and expression changed; though he did not move from his chair or put his palms together, he assumed, figuratively, and on his face quite literally, a sup-

16

plicating mien. I have no record of the exact words he used, but I have a painfully vivid memory of them. "Don't ask me," he said. "For God's sake, please don't ask me to discuss this. Not now. I'll help you as much as I possibly can, I'll talk about anything else you want. Anything. Just don't press me on this. Don't even ask me why I don't want to talk about it. Maybe someday we can talk it all over, but not now. Accept my word that my reasons are good." I have not before or since seen a grown man in a responsible position behave in such a fashion. I had the feeling that if I had made an issue of it, I might have persuaded him to see what he could do— in exchange for my promise not again to say "McCarthy" in his presence—to get me an ambassadorship or even to declassify the recipe for the hydrogen bomb. The mere mention of the Senator from Wisconsin, the mere possibility of being compelled to discuss him, had reduced this sturdy man to jelly.

McCarthyism rampant managed, for a time, to make politics in America seem almost entirely a matter of idiotic chatter about "loyalty risks" and "security risks." In the early part of the Eisenhower administration, a visitor from another civilization would have been forced to conclude that in the United States the measure of political virtue was the number of unworthy civil servants a government managed to dismiss. The proudest boast the administration's apologists could make was that in the first four months 1,456 federal workers had been dropped under the "Eisenhower security program." Reporting on his first year's stewardship, in his 1954 State of the Union message, the President announced a grander

17

total—2,200. And the Democrats, instead of raising a standard to which people of elementary common sense and decency might repair, boasted that they had done just as well or better when they were in power. The parties seldom argued over the number of gifted people brought into the government; the test was how many rotten apples each had been able to find. "We're kicking the Communists and fellow travelers and security risks out of the Government . . . by the thousands," the Vice-President of the United States said. It happened to be a fact that not one certifiable Communist had been disclosed as working for the government—though quite possibly there were a few. But this was not the worst of it. The worst was that McCarthy and McCarthyism had led us to think that the health of the state was war against clerks of dubious patriotism.

Back in those melancholy days, many people not easily given to alarm feared that a day might come when McCarthy would not be breaking the laws but proclaiming them. World War II was not far in the past, and comparisons with Adolf Hitler came readily to mind. "When I think of McCarthy, I automatically think of Hitler," President Eisenhower's banker brother, Arthur, once said, to the consternation of the White House. "McCarthy's methods, to me, look like Hitler's," Eleanor Roosevelt wrote. Joseph C. Harsch reported in 1953 that when Germans thought about McCarthy, they found "a release from [their] own sense of guilt about Hitler," and in Düsseldorf, Hjalmar Schacht, Hitler's financial prestidigitator, said to John Emmet Hughes, an adviser to Eisenhower, "Perhaps now you realize it is not so easy for a people to get rid of a demagogue just by wishing him to go away—no?" The comparisons were natural and not wholly without justice. Like Hitler, McCarthy was a screamer, a political thug, a master of the mob, an exploiter of popular fears. He used the fear of Bolshevism as Hitler used it, with the difference that Hitler described Communism as a revolutionary menace to the state, while McCarthy described it as a conspiracy that had already achieved some of the ends it prized the most. McCarthy was not anti-Semitic, but in his demonology the Democratic leaders, the liberal intelligentsia, and a supposedly decadent Eastern aristocracy played the accomplice role that Hitler assigned to the Jews.

To be sure, there were points, and crucial ones, at which contrast was more striking than comparison. Hitler had a program for the coming millennium; McCarthy had no program for tomorrow morning. Hitler's aim was to win control of the machinery of the state; it is still arguable as to whether McCarthy was up to anything of quite this magnitude. He never encouraged direct action by his followers; he did not organize uniformed groups or even raggle-taggle street fighters. Politically, he never tried to organize outside the existing party structure, and there are reasons for supposing that he never intended to do so. But he built within the system a large and dedicated following. It was larger than that of any demagogue of the past and the first movement of its kind ever to be national in scope. Though this country has produced many demagogues of proficiency, none of them, before Mc-

19

Carthy, had more than a regional or sectarian power.* Huey Long of Louisiana seemed on the verge of winning a national following when Dr. Carl A. Weiss's bullet found him in 1935, and Father Charles E. Coughlin of Michigan might have led a formidable movement if he had not been silenced by his ecclesiastical superiors at the start of the war. But neither of them made it, and neither of them had anything like McCarthy's influence on American life and institutions.

Because McCarthyism had no real grit and substance as a doctrine and no organization, it is difficult to deal with as a movement. Adherence was of many different sorts. There were those who accepted McCarthy's leadership and would have been happy to see him President. There were others who were indifferent to his person but receptive to what he had to say about the government. There were others still who put no particular stock in what he had to say and even believed it largely nonsense but felt that he was valuable anyway.

McCarthy drew into his following most of the zanies and zombies and compulsive haters who had followed earlier and lesser demagogues in the fascist and semifascist movements of the thirties and forties. At a typical McCarthy rally, there would be, seated in the front rows, thanks to early arrival,

---

* In *The American Democrat*, published in 1828, James Fenimore Cooper wrote as if a demagogue was almost by definition a spokesman for a local interest against the common good. The only types he discussed—in a generally brilliant essay—were "the town demagogue" and "the county demagogue."

numbers of moon-struck souls wearing badges or carrying placards identifying them as Minute Women of the U.S.A., Sons of I Shall Return, members of the Alert Council for America, the Nationalist Action League, We the Mothers Mobilize, the Republoform, and so on. They knew all the words of "Nobody Loves Joe but the Pee-pul," and if this anthem was sung, their voices, generally on the shrill or reedy side, would be heard above the rest. But this was really the least part of it. McCarthy went far beyond the world of the daft and the frenzied—or, to put the matter another way, that world was greatly enlarged while he was about. Into it came large numbers of regular Republicans who had coolly decided that there was no longer any respectable way of un-horsing the Democrats and that only McCarthy's wild and conscienceless politics could do the job. He built, as Samuel Lubell pointed out in *Revolt of the Moderates,* a coalition of the aggrieved—of men and women not deranged but deeply affronted by various tendencies over the preceding two or three decades: toward internationalism, and, in particular, toward closer ties with the British; toward classlessness; toward the welfare state. There were Roman Catholics, par-ticularly those of Irish descent, who saw in this aggressive Hibernian the flaming avenger of their own humiliations of the past and who could not believe that the criticism he pro-voked was based on anything but hatred of his Church and his name. To these and many others he was a symbol of re-bellion. And beyond all this, he simply persuaded a number of people that he was speaking the essential truth; he sent

21

up such vast and billowing clouds of smoke that many men and women who were not abnormally gullible became convinced that there must be a fire beneath it all.

In his following, there were many people who counted for quite a bit in American life—some because of wealth and power, some because of intelligence and political sophistication. He was an immediate hit among the Texas oilmen, many of whom were figures as bizarre and adventurous in the world of commerce and finance as he was in the world of politics. They liked his wildcatting style, and they liked him, and they hurried to contribute up to the legal limit to any campaign he approved, to shower him with Cadillacs and other baubles, and to compete for his presence at their parties, their hunts for white-winged doves, and other exotic entertainments favored by people whose income for a week may exceed that of many men for a lifetime. And there were intellectuals and intellectuals *manque* whose notions of *Realpolitik* had room for just such a man of action as McCarthy. Some of them, like James Burnham, John Chamberlain, Max Eastman, and William F. Buckley, Jr., were far from being fools. (Buckley, the editor of the *National Review,* linked the worlds of money and intellect; his father was in oil, and he was in writing, and in a book that makes an interesting souvenir of the period, *McCarthy and His Enemies,* which he wrote with L. Brent Bozell, he and his co-author made the breath-taking assertion that "McCarthyism . . . is a movement around which men of good will and stern morality can close ranks.") At any rate, the fools and the non-fools contributed mightily to his following, which *was* mighty, and there was a time when just about

22

everyone who depended upon the favor of the people lived in fear of him because they believed that a hostile word from him would be a marching order to millions.

In January 1954, when the record was pretty well all in and the worst as well as the best was known, the researches of the Gallup Poll indicated that 50 per cent of the American people had a generally "favorable opinion" of him and felt that he was serving the country in useful ways. Twenty-one per cent drew a blank—"no opinion." The conscious, though not necessarily active, opposition—those with an "unfavorable opinion"—was 29 per cent. A "favorable opinion" did not make a man a McCarthyite, and millions were shortly to revise their view to his disadvantage. But an opposition of only 29 per cent is not much to count on, and it was small wonder that his contemporaries feared him. It was a melancholy time, and the Chief Justice of the United States was probably right when he said that if the Bill of Rights were put to a vote, it would lose.

☞ For three of his five great years, McCarthy was a first-term Senator on the minority side of the aisle. He had no committee assignments of any importance. His seniority was negligible. He had no special rank or position within his party. He was not known to have any unusual mandate from the voters of Wisconsin, and in any case Wisconsin, though an ornament of the republic, is not quite a first-rate power in politics. These facts seem to go a long way toward settling the question of whether he was a man of really first-class abilities or just a mediocrity who chanced to be thrust upward by a current of the times. What power he had in those first three years, he generated, it seems to me, almost wholly within himself. He was not the only man riding that current; there were a half-dozen others in the Senate and a great many more outside it. But it was McCarthy who had mastered it and given it his name *before* he had any significant power in government or in party affairs. More or less on his own, he was able to make himself a central issue in the 1952 Presidential campaign, to make himself known on every continent, and even to make the New York *Herald Tribune* mistake him for a force of nature.

On January 3, 1953, his own party took office, and he found himself, technically and temporarily, a member of the government rather than of the opposition. From then on, the situation became slightly more complicated.

When the Republicans organized the Senate, McCarthy, who was just beginning his second term, became chairman of the Committee on Government Operations and of its Permanent Subcommittee on Investigations. Thereafter, the chairmanship was the principal pinion of his power, though far from its principal source. The Committee had broad statutory power to investigate the functioning of every part of the executive branch. McCarthy would doubtless have seized the authority anyway, but it was better and easier to have the law on his side, and, also, the Committee had a staff and appropriations, which he was able to use effectively.

One of his most striking instruments was a secret seditionist cabal he had organized within the government. This was a network of government servants and members of the armed forces ("the Loyal American Underground," some of the proud, defiant members called themselves) who, in disregard of their oaths of office and the terms of their contracts with the taxpayers, reported directly to McCarthy and gave him their first loyalty. There were members of the State Department, the Federal Bureau of Investigation, the Civil Service Commission, and other agencies who supplied him with information they had withheld from those to whom they were by law responsible. There were Army officers who acted upon his instructions rather than upon those of their superiors and their commander in chief, the President. Promised McCarthy's protection, they ran the risks of court-martial, and these were sometimes large. In one well-documented case, the subject of reams of testimony in the Army-McCarthy hearings of 1954, an officer in Army Intelligence, or G-2, turned over to McCarthy parts of a communication from the FBI to G-2 relating to security matters in the Army Signal Corps radar laboratories. On the face of it, this was a violation of the espionage laws, which make it a crime to deliver such information to unauthorized persons and a crime, too, for unauthorized persons deliberately to receive such information. During the hearings, an ingenious effort was made—not by McCarthy, but in his behalf—to prove that he was, by virtue of his position as a Senator, an authorized person, but the argument had more ingenuity than soundness, and at all odds he had turned the material over to members of his staff, two members of which had sought and been refused clearance to examine classified material.

McCarthy himself was unconcerned with the question of

whether he or his informant had violated the laws. His interest was in keeping his organization intact, and he was able to make good on his promises of protection. So far as is currently known, no one was ever betrayed by him, or by anyone connected with him, for the delivery of information. In the hearings this colloquy took place:

SENATOR DIRKSEN [Everett Dirksen, of Illinois]: Senator McCarthy, is it unusual or extraordinary for confidential documents to come to you either as chairman of the Senate Permanent Investigation Subcommittee or as an individual Senator?

SENATOR McCARTHY: It's a daily and nightly occurrence for me to receive information from people in government.

SENATOR DIRKSEN: And that's true of many agencies of government?

SENATOR McCARTHY: That is true. Very true.

Nothing was ever true merely because McCarthy said it, but for this boast there was ample confirmation. And beyond this, McCarthy, now openly the seditionist, said:

I will continue to receive information. . . . That will be my policy. There's no power on earth can change that. Again, I want to compliment individuals [who] give me information even though some little bureaucrat has stamped it "secret" to defend himself. . . . None of them, none of them will be brought before a grand jury because of any information which I give. . . . I would like to notify two million federal employees that it is their duty to give us the information they have about graft, corruption, Communists, and treason, and that there is no loyalty to a superior officer that can tower above their loyalty to their country. . . . I just will not abide by any secrecy directive of anyone.

26

What He Was and What He Did

L'état, c'est moi, legibus solutus, and I Am the Law. He
and the country were one and the same, synonymous and in-
terchangeable, and not in his view only, but in that of many
people who had been given sizable public trusts. In the Mc-
Carthy years, the United States government often seemed, as
Senator Stuart Symington, of Missouri, once said, "a bloody
sieve."

It may well be that the Communists, who provided an excuse and a putative adversary for the McCarthy underground,
had at one time a network larger than his and of even darker
intent. But his was unique in our time and perhaps in all our
history for the loyalty it gave one man.*

"I just will not abide by any secrecy directive of anyone."
Of course he would not, for there was no authority outside
himself. No directives on secrecy or anything else had any
force in his system of non-values. Men might be duly elected
or appointed to fulfill responsibilities fixed by the Constitu-

* "Loyalty" is not, perhaps, the word to be applied to every one of
his collaborators. Some undoubtedly were malcontents, injustice-
collectors, who tattled to him in order to get revenge on certain colleagues. And fear was the spur in some cases. That is to say, there
were people feeding McCarthy information who were not, properly
speaking, McCarthyites but who felt that co-operation was a kind
of job insurance. Some had seen how weak the executive agencies
were in protecting themselves against McCarthy's offensives, and
they reasoned, as bureaucrats will, indeed as human beings of almost
every sort will, that discretion was the better part of valor—or that
collaboration was better than valor. As James Reston of the New
York *Times* wrote, government officials are accustomed to "identifying themselves with the people who protect them, and if they
cannot count on protection from the heads of their own departments,
they seek it through association with the McCarthys."

tion or by statute; their credentials might be in perfect order; they might be empowered by the President of the United States to speak in his behalf—but to McCarthy they had no power save that which he chose to accord them or that which they were able to wrest from him. At the start of the Army-McCarthy hearings in 1954, it suited his purpose to contend that the Secretary of the Army, the Counselor to the Department of Defense, and the Counselor to the Department of the Army pretended to an authority they did not have. Before the first witness had been called, he raised his first "point of order," which was that the brief that had been described as "Filed by the Department of the Army" was falsely labeled. It was only, he said, the work of a "few Pentagon politicians attempting to disrupt our investigation [and] naming themselves the Department of the Army. . . . The Department of the Army is not doing this. It is three civilians in the Army, and they should be so named." He did not contend that someone other than Robert Ten Broeck Stevens was the true Secretary of the Army or that the President's appointment of Stevens had been in some way nullified; he simply stated that the fact that a man holds his position by the designation of the chief magistrate, with the concurrence of the Senate, which is the way it is prescribed in the basic charter of American liberties, was a matter of no concern to him. He said:

I maintain it is a disgrace and a reflection upon every one of the million outstanding men in the Army to let a few civilians who are trying . . . to hold up an investigation of Communists [there was no such investigation taking place] label themselves as the Department of the Army.

28

And such was the power of this subversive that Senator Karl Mundt, of South Dakota, ruled that the question of whether the Secretary of the Army could speak for the Department of the Army might properly be set aside until the Secretary took the witness stand.

☞ "The Army today," Hanson Baldwin, the military editor of the New York *Times,* had written on February 28, 1954, "is a far call indeed from the tough units that sailed from the ports of England to the assault on Fortress Europe a decade ago. Its morale is depressed; discipline and efficiency leave much to be desired." And he went on, "Whether President Eisenhower realizes it or not, Senator McCarthy is now sharing with him command of the Army." This was hyperbole; the President could have ordered the Army into combat, and McCarthy could not have done so. There was more truth than poetry in it, though; McCarthy was not authorized to receive military secrets, but he got them when he wanted them, and no one did much of anything about it. He had the power to bring the Secretary of the Army to his knees when the Secretary wished the favor, or wished to avoid the disfavor, of McCarthy's committee, and the history of the relationship between the two men revealed a little of how it happened that McCarthy got away with denial of the Secretary's authority. Once, for example, when McCarthy and his agents had been stamping around in the Fort Monmouth laboratories, Stevens sent McCarthy a wire that read in part, "WILL CALL YOUR OFFICE TO OFFER MY SERVICES IN TRYING TO ASSIST YOU IN CORRECTING ANYTHING THAT MAY BE

29

WRONG." He who abdicates is lost when there is a McCarthy about. In McCarthy's most celebrated campaign of harassment, when he was trying to make a patsy of Brigadier General Ralph Zwicker, an old comrade-in-arms of the President, former Chief of Staff of the Second Infantry, and one of the heroes of the Battle of the Bulge, McCarthy forced Stevens to change his position from the bold declaration that

I have directed [General] Zwicker not to appear before Senator McCarthy on Tuesday in New York. . . . I cannot permit the loyal officers of our Armed Forces to such unwarranted treatment

to

If the Committee decides to call General Zwicker . . . General Zwicker will be available.

The "unwarranted treatment" to which Stevens decided to subject General Zwicker after all was such talk as this by McCarthy:

You are a disgrace to the uniform. You're shielding Communist conspirators. You're not fit to be an officer. You're ignorant. You are going to be put on public display next Tuesday.

Between his first and second statements, Stevens—the holder of a proud office, graced in the past by James Monroe, John C. Calhoun, Lewis Cass, Edwin M. Stanton, Ulysses Grant, Elihu Root, William Howard Taft, and Henry L. Stimson—had lunched with McCarthy, the Vice-President, and several other Senators. "Stevens," McCarthy was reported to have said later, "could not have given in more abjectly if he had got down on his knees." (Under oath, at the Army-Mc-Carthy hearings, he denied ever having said this. His denials were as meaningless as his avouchments, and reputable journalists heard him.) The *Times* of London, when it got word of this affair, echoed Hanson Baldwin. "Senator McCarthy," it said, "achieved today what General Burgoyne and General Cornwallis never achieved—the surrender of the American Army."

It went on all the time in 1953 and early 1954. McCarthy had the Chief of Intelligence, Major General Richard C. Partridge, before the Permanent Subcommittee on Investigations, and in an executive session, with McCarthy the only Senator present, questioned by the Chief Counsel, Roy M. Cohn. (They wanted to know why someone in Partridge's office had listed a book by Corliss Lamont, a writer sympathetic to Communism, in the bibliography of a G-2 study of *Cultural and Psychological Traits of Soviet Siberia*. They also wanted to know on what authority the author had said that the Siberian masses were not likely to become anti-Communist soon.) The General displeased McCarthy and Cohn, which was a way most generals had at the time; McCarthy said he was "shocked beyond words" (words were one thing he was never shocked beyond) by the way the officer had testified and that he considered him "completely incompetent" for the job. Robert Stevens was at the hearing, and General Partridge shortly thereafter found himself a divisional commander somewhere in Europe.

On the other side of the gleaming coin, there was Major General Kirke Lawton, commandant at Fort Monmouth,

31

New Jersey, a Signal Corps installation that McCarthy had been investigating. General Lawton co-operated with McCarthy. Stevens had been considering a change of post for General Lawton. He asked McCarthy if this would be agreeable to him. McCarthy said no. General Lawton kept his post.

The President shared with McCarthy the command of many parts of the government, and the President did realize it. In the first few months of 1953, three heads of the International Information Administration came and went because McCarthy wished it so. In June of that year, he sent Roy Cohn and G. David Schine, a youth with a vast fund of ignorance of Communism and many other subjects who became the Committee's "Chief Consultant," to Europe to inquire into "subversion" in American agencies there, and after that the agencies wore a very different look. The President appointed John Foster Dulles as Secretary of State; McCarthy appointed Scott McLeod as the State Department's Personnel and Security Officer; and in the early days it was pretty much of a tossup as to whether Dulles or McLeod, who had prepared for a diplomatic career as an FBI agent in Manchester, New Hampshire, and had worked briefly in the Washington office of Senator Styles Bridges, had more influence in departmental affairs. Dulles was free to write speeches warning the Russians to behave themselves; he could hold all the conferences he wished with Chiang Kai-shek; but when it came to appointing ambassadors and hiring and firing Department officers, he cleared everything

32

with McLeod, who cleared everything with McCarthy. This was particularly the case after McCarthy had objected to the appointment of Charles E. Bohlen as United States ambassador to the Soviet Union. McCarthy claimed that Dulles and the President had gone over McLeod's head in giving this job to Bohlen. The President and the Secretary very much wanted Bohlen's confirmation by the Senate, so Robert A. Taft, of Ohio, still at that time the most influential Republican on Capitol Hill, got the confirmation through for them—but only after arriving at an understanding that there would be no more appointments offensive to McCarthy.

When McCarthy had a mind to, he constituted himself an agency for the conduct of foreign relations. On March 28, 1953, he announced that he had, in his capacity as chairman of the Permanent Subcommittee, "negotiated" an "agreement" with Greek shipping interests that would result in depriving Communist nations of goods that had up to then been delivered to their ports by two hundred and forty-two freighters and thus would "have some of the effects of a naval blockade." He also announced that he was moving toward another agreement with certain other shipping interests in London. He said he had made his first agreement without the consultation or advice of anyone in the State Department because "I don't want interference by anyone." When Harold E. Stassen, then head of the Foreign Operations Administration, complained that this sort of thing "undermined" the authority of the Secretary of State and other qualified officials, which it patently did, the President

33

said that Stassen was certainly entitled to his opinion but that he didn't share it. (The President took refuge in a nicety of diplomatic theory. He told his news conference that McCarthy could not have been "negotiating" because he had nothing to negotiate with—nothing to cede, nothing to withhold. He overlooked the fact that McCarthy could, and did, negotiate with the power of investigation. According to one of his committee colleagues, Senator Mundt, the shipowners had thought it better to give McCarthy his triumph than to be "hauled down here and have the whole thing ventilated.") The jubilant McCarthy thereupon lunched with the Secretary of State—there was always a lot of lunching to be done—and after coffee they issued a joint statement in which the two agreed that what McCarthy had done was "in the national interest."

And so things went in those days. McCarthy made the rules himself, and nothing delighted him so much as demonstrating this. "Wasn't that a classified document you were reading?" a reporter once asked. "It *was*," McCarthy said. "I declassified it." One day, when he was displeased with the way things were going in a hearing of the Senate Appropriations Committee, he seized the gavel from the startled chairman and carried on for the rest of the session. The chairman did not protest. In the Senate in the early fifties, hardly anyone ever protested against anything McCarthy did. Hardly anyone dared refuse approbation. In February 1954, there was exactly one man in the Senate, William Fulbright, of Arkansas, who found it possible to cast a vote against an appropriation of $214,000 for the Permanent Subcommittee.* Everyone then knew that the Subcommittee had destroyed much and accomplishd nothing of value. Both McCarthy and his enemies outside the Senate insisted that the vote on appropriations be regarded as a vote of confidence. Though it is doubtful if there were more than three or four men in the Senate who had any confidence in him or felt toward him anything but distaste, distrust, and fear, eighty-five members of that great deliberative assembly voted "Yea" on the motion to give him what he wanted in the way of money.

The truth is that everyone in the Senate, or just about everyone, was scared stiff of him. Everyone then believed that McCarthy had the power to destroy those who opposed him, and evidence for this was not lacking. Evidence was not conclusive either, but politicians cannot afford to deal in finalities and ultimate truths; they abide, by and large, by probabilities and reasonable assumptions and the law of av-

---

* Senator Fulbright's "Nay" took courage. Seen from this vantage point in time, it also illustrates one of the basic rules of politics. For in 1957, when Governor Orval Faubus of Arkansas defied the Constitution and the Supreme Court by using the National Guard to keep Negro children from Central High School in Little Rock—an act of which Fulbright could not possibly have approved—he did not speak up against Faubus. Coming from Arkansas, Fulbright was about as safe as a man could be from McCarthy. Great as McCarthy's fame was, it had probably not spread very wide in Arkansas, where outsiders in general are seldom thought to be very interesting or impor-tant. But Fulbright could have been hurt by an Arkansas demagogue, and he was as quiet about Faubus as most of his colleagues had been about McCarthy three years before. The rule seems to be that there is a demagogue for every man to fear

erages, and there was nothing unreasonable, in 1954, in assuming that McCarthy held enormous power in his hands when it came to the question of deciding who should and should not sit in the United States Senate.

In 1950, just a few weeks after McCarthy's Wheeling speech, Millard Tydings, of Maryland, had accepted the chairmanship of the committee that was to inquire into McCarthy's charges against the State Department. Tydings was a titan in the Senate; no man seemed better established there than he, a Maryland patrician, a man of enormous wealth, a member of the inner circle of the Senate. In 1938, Franklin D. Roosevelt, then at the very apex of his career, had tried to get Tydings, a reactionary, as Roosevelt saw it, defeated. Roosevelt failed wretchedly. But McCarthy, a nobody in 1949, threw his weight against Tydings in 1950, and, lo, Tydings lost. (Of course, the methods were somewhat different. Roosevelt went into Maryland and tried to persuade the voters to choose another man. McCarthy stayed in Washington and sent agents into Maryland spreading the word that Tydings was pro-Communist.) That same year, McCarthy went gunning for Scott Lucas, of Illinois, the Democratic floor leader. Lucas was defeated. Tydings' role as McCarthy's chief adversary passed to William Benton, of Connecticut, who had placed before the Senate a resolution calling for McCarthy's expulsion. McCarthy was not expelled; Benton was, though, by the voters. With Lucas gone, Ernest MacFarland, of Arizona, became the Democratic floor leader. McCarthy campaigned against him. MacFarland was defeated.

There were other examples, every one of them impressive.

After the 1952 elections, it was believed in the Senate that McCarthy was responsible for the presence there of eight men—which meant that he was responsible for the absence of eight others. It was not merely a question of his political force, his ability to rally opposition and support; he drove one man—Raymond Baldwin, of Connecticut—out of active politics simply by pouring upon him more abuse than he felt called upon to bear.

McCarthy himself was re-elected in 1952—as it happened, by a quite unimpressive majority—and when he took his seat on January 3, 1953, it had been borne in upon all his colleagues that he was a bad man to cross.

The Senate on that day might have saved itself a good deal of grief—or it might have caused itself a good deal more —by refusing to seat him or by questioning his right to be seated. For either course, there were ample grounds. In 1952, the Rules Committee's Subcommittee on Privileges and Elections, in pursuance of the resolution Senator Benton had submitted, had looked into certain aspects of McCarthy's private and political conduct and had come up with data which created an almost overpowering presumption that he was a crook as well as a rascal. Substantial sums of money he had collected for "the fight for America" had gone into a personal checking account and had gone out again without ever purchasing any sinews for the struggle against Communist subversion; some of it was traced to an Appleton brokerage firm which had bought soybean futures for McCarthy, and some of it was traced to the account of an assistant to McCarthy, Ray Kiermas, who refused to say where it had gone after that. He would not say whether some of it had gone back to McCarthy. While a member of the Senate Banking Committee in 1948 and of a Joint Committee on Housing, McCarthy had accepted $10,000 from the Lustron Corporation, a fabricator of prefabricated houses, which was a steady petitioner for funds from the Reconstruction Finance Corporation. The fee was paid by the president, Carl Strandlund, who covered some of McCarthy's race-track bets, and the $10,000 was said to be compensation for an article McCarthy had signed in a brochure published by Lustron; McCarthy wrote parts of the Housing Act, one of the provisions of which gave the RFC additional funds and authority to make a loan of $7,000,000 to Lustron early in 1949. McCarthy invested the $10,000 from Lustron in the common stock of Seaboard Airline Railroad, which was also indebted to the RFC. In time, the RFC disposed of its Seaboard Airline Railroad holdings, and the stock rose sharply, with McCarthy the gainer by $35,000. He was on a sugar subcommittee of the Banking Committee. The Pepsi-Cola Corporation wished extra sugar, which was then being rationed. McCarthy had an unsecured loan of $20,000 from the Washington lobbyist for Pepsi-Cola. The day after he accepted the loan, McCarthy denounced the rationing that prevented the company from going into full production. And there was much more; there seemed fairly clear proof of violations of tax and banking laws and of regulations on commodity trading, and of bribery.

Perhaps these matters and several others could have been explained away, but whenever the Subcommittee made an appointment with McCarthy to come in and explain, he failed to show up. He refused on five separate occasions: "I don't answer charges, I make them," he said. He said the Subcommittee was a tool of the Communists. He insulted three successive chairmen of the Subcommittee. (That chairmanship was easily the least sought-after in Senate history.) He was technically as well as morally in contempt of Congress. It was thought by some that on the opening day of Congress in 1953, there might be one man in the Senate willing to come forward with the suggestion that McCarthy just had no right to be there. The decisive moment came. McCarthy entered the chamber with the senior Senator from his state, Alexander Wiley; the clerk announced him. The Vice-President stood ready to swear him. No voice was raised. He was sworn.

☞ It was a striking feature of McCarthy's victories, of the surrenders he collected, that they were mostly won in battles over matters of an almost comic insignificance. His *causes célèbres* were *causes ridicules*. The Secretary of the Army groveled before him and offered up General Zwicker as a sacrifice in the course of a lunatic controversy over whether an Army dentist named Irving Peress was properly raised from captain to major. It mattered not at all, except to the paymaster, what rank was held by this obscure jawsmith whose length of service had qualified him for a majority, but McCarthy claimed that in Peress's promotion he had found "the key to the deliberate Communist infiltration of our armed forces." Why was a chief of G-2 removed? Because of a bibliographical citation in a study of Siberian folk-ways, which the chief of G-2 had never seen. Why did heads roll in the International Information Administration and the Voice of America? Because a pair of callow, shallow youths named Cohn and Schine found on I.I.A. library shelves such items as detective stories by a pro-Communist writer and because a young woman employee of the Voice of America testified that she had received from a fellow employee a suggestion for a weekend's recreation that seemed to her not altogether wholesome.*

Yet the antic features of McCarthyism were essential ones. For McCarthyism was, among other things, but perhaps foremost among them, a headlong flight from reality. It elevated the ridiculous and ridiculed the important. It outraged common sense and held common sense to be outrageous. It confused the categories of form and value. It made sages of screwballs and accused wise men of being fools. It diverted attention from the moment and fixed it on the past, which it distorted almost beyond recognition.

The reality it fled, while madly professing to be the only doctrine that faced it, was a terrible one. Only a Communist or an idiot could have denied that the Communist threat to the United States was real and great. The whole Western world was imperiled, in those days as in these, by the thrust of Soviet power, which, just before McCarthy erupted, had been augmented by the emergence of China as an ally of the

---

* What dire offense from am'rous causes springs,
  What mighty contests rise from trivial things!
          —Alexander Pope, *The Rape of the Lock*, 1714.

Soviet Union and by the Russian mastery of nuclear weapons
In the early part of the decade, the threat seemed more directly a military one than it does today, and within a few
months of McCarthy's first appearance as a national figure,
it was established by shellfire and tramping armies in Korea
that Communism was willing to risk military aggression and
war. Communist power in the world was the central reality
for the United States in early 1950. The problem we faced,
as the most powerful anti-Communist nation in the world,
was to form and lead an alliance capable of resisting the
Soviet thrust and to find strategies of resistance that would
not lead to general war and universal destruction.

McCarthyism ignored this reality and fostered the illusion
that what was at most an aspect of it was the whole of reality.
"There is only one real issue for the farmer, the laborer, and
the businessman—the issue of Communism in government,"
McCarthy said in a campaign speech in 1952. He even insisted that the struggle against world Communism was a diversion from the struggle against the domestic conspiracy.
Speaking, in 1951, of our intervention in Korea, he said, "So
the administration which would not fight Communism at
home undertook to prove to the American people that it
was willing to fight Communism abroad." This sort of talk
would have been nonsense at any time; in 1951 and 1952,
it was asinine. In the thirties and early forties there had been
a formidable Communist movement in this country and a
Communist apparatus within the government. It was unquestionably the government's business to break up the apparatus and to combat the movement. By 1950, this had been

41

fairly effectively done—if, in fact, it had not been overdone. Alger Hiss was convicted in 1950 for committing perjury about his activities thirteen years earlier. He had been out of the government since 1946. The atom spies had mostly been apprehended by the late forties. An employee-security system had been in operation since early in the war, and it had been considerably tightened up under the Truman administration. The FBI had just about abandoned its concern with bank robbers and white slavers to turn its full force on Communism. The Communist Party, moreover, was in an advanced state of disintegration—partly because of a spreading disillusionment among its members, partly because the government was locking up its leaders. If the conspiracy was still in any way effective, its effectiveness eluded McCarthy, who, with all his helpers in the FBI and his agents in G-2 and his Loyal American Underground, could find nothing more exciting than a Major Peress, a citation of Corliss Lamont in a bibliography, a girl who had heard talk of unwedded bliss in a propaganda agency, a novel by a Communist on a library shelf, and an ex-Communist here and there in some minor agency. He did no better than that.

Probably its effectiveness *did* elude him. Here and there, no doubt, there were, and in all likelihood still are, Communist agents in the government. Communism is, after all, an international conspiracy, and it has managed in the past to penetrate even such security-obsessed governments as those of fascist Germany and imperial Japan. It would be astonishing if a government employing two or three million people harbored no Communists at all. But the damage that agents can do is limited in any case, and in our particular case steps had been taken long before McCarthy came along to uncover as many agents as possible and further to limit the damage any remaining ones could do. If McCarthy uncovered any additional ones, he seemed unaware of the fact himself, and he certainly did nothing to restrain any that remained.

But even if McCarthy had done far better, McCarthyism would still have been trading in dangerous illusions. It was insisting, as Philip Rahv once pointed out, that Communism was a danger, not *to* the United States, but *in* the United States, when in truth it was just the other way about. It was focusing attention on the spy rather than on the power for whom the spy spies, on the Communist or ex-Communist dentist in the United States Army rather than on the Red Army, combat-ready and nuclear-armed. Indeed, most of its votaries opposed all reasonable efforts to deal with these matters. Not Stalin and Khrushchev with their legions and their satellites and the billions of souls within their empires, not the gathering economic strength of Communism, not the devastating appeal of its propaganda in those parts of the world where bread is still scarce and there are no pop-up toasters at all—not any of this were we to dread but Irving Peress and his promotion to major. At the time when 50 per cent of the American people were said to look upon him with favor, his rallying cry was "Who Promoted Peress?"

It had to be this way, for the demagogue, the seditionist, the master of the mob needs his enemy close at hand, familiar, manageable. McCarthyism could never have hoped to score off Stalin or Khrushchev, but it could stick pins into Major Peress, General Zwicker, and Robert Stevens. Hitler was once asked if he wished the destruction of the Jews. This was in the days before he succumbed utterly to desperation and madness. "No," he said, "it is essential to have a tangible enemy."

 *What He Was
and
What He Did
—2*

"The true theatre of a demagogue is a democracy," James
Fenimore Cooper wrote in *The American Democrat*. Where
public opinion has no force, there can be no role for a
misleader of opinion. The Athenians had demagogues on every street corner; they gave us the word, and they defined
and redefined it. In *Orestes*, Euripides said that the demagogue was "a man of loose tongue, intemperate, trusting to
tumult, leading the populace to mischief with empty words."
In *The Knights*, Aristophanes wrote: "The qualities necessary
to a demagogue are these: to be foul-mouthed, base-born,

45

a low mean fellow." And, on the ravages of demagogy and its flight from reality, Thucydides wrote:

The meaning of words had no longer the same relation to things but was changed by them as they thought proper. Reckless daring was held to be courage, prudent delay was the excuse of a coward; moderation was the disguise of unmanly weakness; to know everything was to do nothing. Frantic energy was the true quality of a man. . . . He who succeeded in a plot was deemed knowing, but a still greater master in craft was he who detected one.

McCarthy, then, was of the classic breed. For all the black arts that he practiced, his natural endowments and his cultivated skills were of the very highest order. His tongue was loose and always wagging; he would say anything that came into his head and worry later, if at all, about defending what he had said. There has never been the slightest reason to suppose that he took what he said seriously or that he believed any of the nonsense he spread. He trusted to tumult and seemed to know, intuitively, most of the secrets of its manufacture. "Looking at you, Senator McCarthy," Joseph L. Welch, the Army's counsel in the Army-McCarthy hearings once said, "you have, I think, sir, something of a genius for creating confusion—creating a turmoil in the hearts and minds of the country." Noise, confusion, tumult—these were the end products of the political process as he saw it. I doubt very much if power—in the sense of office, authority, control—seemed terribly important to him. He revealed no lust or greed for power; he never seemed—to me at least—to be consciously moving toward the American summit, the

Presidency. What he lusted for was glory. He once told a friend that he expected to "end up either in the White House or in jail." He was the sort who could have seen as much of a future in one place as in the other. He had use for power, of course, but he was rather like Napoleon, who saw power as his "violin"—the instrumental source and amplifier of the music he made. To McCarthy, as to Napoleon, conquests were more precious than the self-aggrandizing uses to which they might be put. "The morrow of every victory is an anticlimax," Albert Guerard wrote of Bonaparte. "There must ever be new prodigies." It was thus with McCarthy.

The prodigies were of tumult, which signalized victory and the finish of every campaign. He would drop anything the moment he had exhausted its possibilities for mischief. Beyond mischief, he never accomplished anything. He never really completed any of his campaigns, and some that he announced he never even began. He would speak of Communists "with a razor poised over the jugular vein of this nation" in defense plants, in the Army, in radar laboratories. But he would stop talking and stop investigating the moment the headlines began to diminish in size and number, thus leaving our jugular in as much danger as before. He once said that the "worst situation" of all existed in the Central Intelligence Agency. He had reason to believe there were more than 100 Communists there. He was going to "root them out." The problem got a bit sticky. No one wanted McCarthy's investigators loose in the C.I.A. The President announced that a commission headed by General Mark Clark would look into the problem. Nothing ever came of the Clark

47

investigation. McCarthy could easily enough have overcome the resistance to his own and raised hell anyway, but he sensed that the victory would be a bit costlier than most—that it would take much energy and effort without any promise of a high yield. "I guess I'll skip it," he said, and the "worst situation" continued to prevail—perhaps to this day.

This sovereign of the assemblies was "foul-mouthed," all right, and "a low mean fellow," and he wanted no one to think otherwise of him. He was a master of the scabrous and the scatological; his talk was laced with obscenity. He was a vulgarian by method as well as, probably, by instinct. He belched and burped in public. If he did not dissemble much, if he did little to hide from the world the sort of human being he was, it was because he had the shrewdness to see that this was not in his case necessary. He seemed to understand, as no other politician of his stature ever has, the perverse appeal of the bum, the mucker, the Dead End kid, the James Jones–Nelson Algren–Jack Kerouac hero to a nation uneasy in its growing order and stability and not altogether happy about the vast leveling process in which everyone appeared to be sliding, from one direction or another, into middle-class commonplaceness and respectability. (I am not altogether satisfied that this appeal is strongest in these circumstances. But one can observe, I think, that the seditionists in societies that are rank with inequality and injustice tend toward austerity and asceticism, *e.g.,* Robespierre and Lenin, Gandhi and Fidel Castro; in circumstances more nearly resembling ours, one finds Hitlers and Mussolinis. Where the powers that be are relatively decent, the indecent makes a large appeal.) Sometimes, when he found himself among Gold Star Mothers or before a Catholic Youth Organization, he would get a shave, perfume his breath, scrub up his language, slick down what remained of his hair, and lay on the particular kind of charm that in my youth and his was identified by respectable ladies of a certain class as that of "a nice Catholic boy." But there was always a note of self-mockery, a kind of hamming of this part. In general, the thing he valued was his reputation for toughness, ruthlessness, even brutality. He didn't mind at all having it get around Washington that he had threatened to "kick the brains out" of Robert Stevens if the Secretary of the Army didn't get in line on the Zwicker case. He once said to a Wisconsin crowd, "If you will get me a slippery-elm club and put me aboard Adlai Stevenson's campaign train, I will use it on some of his advisers, and perhaps I can make a good American of him." He boasted of how he had been instructed by some old North Woods scamp named Indian Charlie to go straight for an adversary's groin whenever he was in serious trouble.

And this sort of thing was always well received by his followers. They were pleased with the thought that their leader had had so sage a mentor; those who might have suspected that Indian Charlie was pure fiction and that McCarthy had never needed instruction in going for the groin would have been pleased with the turn his inventive gifts took.*

* It may have been ever thus, but if so, the fact was not universally appreciated. In 1940, James Thurber published a short story, "The Greatest Man in the World," about an aviator named Jack Smurch,

As McCarthy's detractors saw it, one of his great disservices to the republic was an effort to fasten upon it a suffocating "conformity." He was the enemy, they said, of character, of originality, of independence, of dissent, of adventurous thought. And so, in general, he was. Though McCarthyism was not a doctrine in any real sense, it called for doctrinal judgments of others. It created, or at any rate greatly heightened, an atmosphere in which dissent was itself a suspicious circumstance, requiring explanation and apology. But it is putting the matter the wrong way about to say that McCarthyism sought to *impose* conformity. It had no such positive goal as this; but, seeking tumult, it victimized nonconformists and thus induced a large measure of conformity and orthodoxy.

It is ironic in any case that this Typhoid Mary of conformity was himself a rebel by nature, a flouter of conventions and orthodoxies. In his time, he was the least con-

---

a former garage mechanic who had circled the globe nonstop in a small plane. He was on his way to becoming a national idol, like Charles Lindbergh and Admiral Richard E. Byrd. Unlike them, though, he was a low-life—a crude, ugly, stupid, snarling, grasping stinker. He was such a misfit for the heroic mold that the elite of our society, including the President of the United States, felt that the public would be terribly hurt when it learned, as inevitably it would, the awful truth about Smurch. Smurch was summoned to a meeting in New York, and at a signal from the President, he was pushed from a ninth-story window by the secretary to the city's mayor. The point of the story, which is more benign than Thurber perhaps realized, was that the American people would not accept a man who was demonstrably a mucker and a bum. Yet in 1954, only 29 per cent disapproved of McCarthy, a card-carrying Smurchite.

formist of politicians. He followed no leader and stamped with no herd. He was a chronic oppositionist, a dissenter for dissent's sake; he had to depart every majority and to attack every authority. He never thought positively. He denounced the very institutions that are customarily thought of as the fortresses of American conformity: the Army, the Protestant clergy, the press, the two major parties, the civil service. And of course he attacked by his very existence the conformities of American politicians. He never affected the pieties of a Dwight Eisenhower. He made little pretense to religiosity or to any species of moral rectitude. He sought to manipulate only the most barbaric symbols of "Americanism"—the slippery-elm club, the knee in the groin, and the brass knuckles, but never motherhood or the love of a man for a cocker spaniel, blueberry pie, or honest toil or the bitch goddess. He was inner-directed. He was closer to the hipster than to the Organization Man. He reached the heights at a time when the rules of politics were being rewritten by public-relations and advertising men, opinion samplers, professional elocutionists like Robert Montgomery, and the moguls of television. While his contemporaries were slavishly adapting themselves to the ways urged upon them by these people, McCarthy paid no attention to any of it. He didn't want the world to think of him as respectable. He encouraged photographers to take pictures of him sleeping, disheveled, on an office couch, like a bum on a park bench, coming out of a shower with a towel wrapped around his torso like Rocky Marciano, or sprawled on the floor in his shirt sleeves with a hooker of bourbon close at hand.

51

Where other politicians would seek to conceal a weakness for liquor or wenching or gambling, McCarthy tended to exploit, even to exaggerate, these wayward tastes. He was glad to have everyone believe that he was a drinker of heroic attainments, a passionate lover of horseflesh, a Clausewitz of the poker table, and a man to whom everything presentable in skirts was catnip. (When a good-looking woman appeared as committee witness, McCarthy, leering, would instruct counsel to "get her telephone number for me" as well as the address for the record.) His drinking prowess, until the last year of his life, was in fact notable. He could "belt a fifth," as it was put in his set, between midnight and five A.M., catch a couple of hours of sleep, and be at his office at eight or nine, ready for a hard day's work leading the populace to mischief with empty words. His devotion to horse racing was real; he was a fixture at Pimlico and Laurel and Bowie during the season, and one often saw him, during slow moments in hearings, running over the day's form sheet while Roy Cohn confounded and crushed the generals and commanders. He was said to be a brilliant poker player, and was, in any case, a frequent one. And if the sexual aggressiveness he displayed at social gatherings was a true measure of his prowess, it, too, was notable.

☞ "McCarthy," Joseph and Stewart Alsop wrote on December 3, 1953, "is the only major politician in the country who can be labeled 'liar' without fear of libel." The generalization was a bit too broad; there have always been politicians who would put up with the most terrible indignities, who

would see their characters viciously assailed and their good
faith held up to derision, rather than have their truthfulness
put to the test under strict rules of evidence. But McCarthy
was surely the champion liar. He lied with wild abandon; he
lied without evident fear; he lied in his teeth and in the teeth
of the truth; he lied vividly and with a bold imagination; he
lied, often, with very little pretense to be telling the truth.
"Over his grave," Thomas Griffith wrote in *The Waist-High
Culture,* "should be written the simple epitaph: THE TRUTH
WASN'T IN HIM." I am not sure that he was a pathological
liar—which means, I take it, a compulsive liar, a man with
an almost aesthetic preference for untruth, one who will lie
even in circumstances where there is no possible gain in lying,
no possible loss in telling the truth. He appeared to be obsessed, as I shall later point out, with the whole subject of
lying and truthfulness, but I know of nothing to suggest that
he ever lied except with calculation.

This, however, he did ceaselessly, and almost from the
outset of his career. In his first successful campaign, in 1939,
he ran for a Wisconsin judgeship against a man who was
sixty-six. McCarthy was just short of thirty-one at the time.
He made age the issue, and sharpened the issue by giving
his opponent an extra seven years. In speeches and campaign
literature, he said the man was seventy-three. Now and
then, he advanced him to eighty-nine. The man's true age
was a matter of record, of course, but McCarthy didn't care.
His own age was a matter of record, too, but he lopped off a
year in order to qualify as the youngest Circuit Court judge
in Wisconsin's history. Campaigning after the war, he would

affect a limp, itself a lie, and explain that he was carrying "ten pounds of shrapnel" in his leg. He carried no shrapnel; in fact, it would have been just about impossible for anyone to carry ten pounds of it about. The first eight words that brought him to national attention were a lie. "I have here in my hand a list . . ." he said, holding aloft a piece of paper which he maintained, according to reporters who were there, contained the names of 205 Communists in the State Department. He denied, subsequently, that he had used that figure, but he had lied before he even got to the figure. He didn't hold a list at all; what he held, he later claimed, was a letter written in 1947, by Secretary of State James Byrnes to Representative Adolph Sabath, of Illinois, which dealt in statistical terms with State Department personnel matters. It contained no names except those of the sender and the receiver; it made no mention of Communism or Communists. To be sure, one has no certain knowledge that he *was* holding up the Byrnes letter; that was his story. It might have been a laundry list or a bill from his bookmaker or the notes for his speech.

McCarthy had some decent instincts—who doesn't?—and probably some yearnings of his own for lace-curtain, wall-to-wall respectability. He was able to overcome the decent instincts with conspicuous ease when he wished to, but he did not always wish to. He could be engaging. The ranter, the accuser, the screamer, the fanatic, the plot detector—this character was for display purposes only. He did not have the cool, motiveless, abiding malignity of an Iago. Away from the platforms and the hearing rooms—even as short a distance away as the Senate floor—he was full of bonhomie, and never more so than with his enemies, or, since they were not really enemies at all, his pincushions. He could accuse a man of shielding Communists in the morning and in the afternoon meet and greet him on the floor, give him a wink and a manly hug, and flash to the press galleries what Murray Kempton called "that delinquent choir boy's smile." Kempton once described such a scene involving Ralph Flanders, of Vermont, whose demand for McCarthy's censure by the Senate brought to an end the long period in which that body lived in mortal fear of him:

Without a moment's unease, Joe McCarthy said, "Hi, Ralph," and threw a blue-serge arm around the shoulder of this old man who had accused him of trying to wreck the Republican Party and had been commended [that morning] by the President of the United States. Flanders giggled a little and said that he was glad to see Joe . . . and McCarthy said with a smile and a trickle in his throat that he'd been looking up Flanders' record.

The further he got from the hearing room, the more he abandoned even the transparently mock sincerity of the public character. "Senator McCarthy, when did you discover Communism?" a young woman asked him at a cocktail party given for him in 1950 by Frederick Woltman of the Scripps-Howard newspapers. "Two and a half months ago," McCarthy answered without a moment's hesitation.

His show of conviviality with Senator Flanders was not very winning, and the show of candor at the cocktail party was only a trifle more ingratiating than would be that of a burglar who acknowledges burgling to be a way of life. But McCarthy did have it in him to be a friend and a loyal one.

55

Had he not been, he could have escaped the condemnation by the Senate that marked the end of his influence in that body. According to several persons who participated in his defense, there existed for a time the possibility of avoiding the issue of censure by a compromise. This would have involved nothing costlier than a small speech of apology by McCarthy to some of those he had called "handmaidens of Communism" and a pledge of better behavior in the future. Had he agreed to do this, the White House would have urged, on prudential grounds, the withdrawal of the censure resolution, and there is no doubt that it would have been withdrawn. Half the Republicans voted against the resolution in the end, and many who voted for it would have been happy to have been relieved of that unpleasant duty. The terms of a compromise had been worked out by McCarthy's lawyer, Edward Bennett Williams; they were acceptable to the Republican leadership in the Senate, and the Democrats were known to be unwilling to vote a censure without substantial Republican support. McCarthy had no principles to be outraged by compromise; an almost complete moral vacuum, he could have made an apology as easily as he gave insult. (He had already admitted the possibility of error. "It has been said that I am the cause of disunity in the country and in my party," he told the Watkins Committee, which held hearings on the resolution of censure. "There is disunity, and perhaps my activities have been part of the cause.") But he refused to accept the compromise because he knew it would hurt his two great supporters in the Senate, William Jenner, of In-

56

diana, and Herman Welker, of Idaho, who believed in his mission far more than he did. Jenner and Welker had worked night and day not simply to avoid censure but to gain vindication for McCarthy, and McCarthy gave the emissaries of compromise the explanation that he could not accept it because his friends would feel let down.

"That fighting Irish marine," Welker once said of McCarthy, "would give the shirt off his back to anyone who needs it—except a dirty, lying, stinking Communist. That guy he'd kill." Welker was capable of more hate than McCarthy, as well as of more ideology. McCarthy had no wish to kill Communists, and he might very well, in certain circumstances, have given one the shirt off his back. There is a case on record of a proffered act of charity to a man he had just handled brutally in a hearing. Having learned that his victim not only bled from the wounds he had inflicted but was also desperately in need of money, McCarthy sought the man out and said that he might be able to give him a hand with his financial problems. The man of course refused—no doubt thinking that McCarthy sought to rob him of his pride as well as of his good name. In fact, McCarthy wanted neither; he wanted only the tumult occasioned by the session on the witness stand, and that he already had.

James A. Wechsler, the editor of the New York *Post,* came closer to the truth than Welker when, speaking of his impressions of McCarthy after several days as a witness before the Permanent Subcommittee, he said that he sensed an element of impatience and disappointment in McCarthy's furies. "I had the feeling," Wechsler said, "that he really wanted me to understand his point of view. He seemed to be saying, 'Look, bud, you've got your racket, and I've got mine, and this is it. There's no need for you to be such a wet blanket.' "

The world took McCarthy seriously, as indeed it should have, but he never really took himself seriously. He was the leader of a fanatical movement, and he gave his name to a fanatical doctrine, but he was no kind of fanatic himself. It is conceivable that in his later days he began to believe what he was saying and to imagine himself truly persecuted by his enemies; at times, during the Army-McCarthy hearings, he would fly into fits of what appeared genuine hysteria. He may by then have cast his spell over himself. But even this is doubtful. Mostly, his hysteria was for the birds. He was capable of going into a tantrum before the television cameras and screaming "Mr. Chairman, Mr. Chairman, point of order, point of order"—and then making a beeline for the Gents' Room, the objective he had had in mind when he began his diversion. Why not put nature into politics? He would tear passion to tatters—saying he could bear no more of this "farce," which made him "sick, sick way down inside" —and stage a walkout that would take him no farther than a corner of the room outside the sweep of the television cameras, there to observe calmly and be amused by the commotion he had caused. He often timed his walkouts for the newspaper deadlines. He knew when all of them were, and if the serious business of ferreting out Communists was producing little for the reporters to report, he would throw some kind of scene that would bring the hearing to an end or would at least get him out into the corridors, where he would quickly dish up something, generally something outrageous.

If he came to believe his own lies and to hate and fear his detractors as they hated and feared him, he did so only sporadically. If he fell under his own spell, the spell quickly passed. He was, to be sure, a prince of hatred. The haters rallied round him; at a word from him, their hate glands would puff and swell—fresh supplies of venom would flow into their venom sacs. But this most successful and menacing of all our apostles of hatred was himself as incapable of true rancor, spite, and animosity as a eunuch is of marriage. He just did not have the equipment for it. He faked it all and could not understand anyone who didn't. When he ran into Dean Acheson in a Senate elevator, he thought it cold and unfriendly of Acheson to respond to his "Hello, Dean," with clenched teeth and a crimson forehead. When, in the course of the Army-McCarthy hearings, he sank to what even Roy Cohn knew to be the very bottom of the pit of moral degradation—by trying to meet a powerful attack by Joseph Welch with a counterattack that was a wholly gratuitous smear on a young friend and associate of Welch's who had nothing whatever to do with the case—he was baffled by the way everyone shrank from him and cleared the path before him as before a leper (Unclean! Unclean!) as he left the Caucus Room. They had all been on Welch's side when he addressed McCarthy:

59

Until this moment, Senator, I think I had never gauged your cruelty or your recklessness. . . . If it were in my power to forgive you for your reckless cruelty, I would do so. I like to think that I am a gentle man, but your forgiveness will have to come from someone other than me.

When, later, McCarthy at last found someone who would speak to him, he held out his hands, palms upward, and said, "What did I *do?*" He knew what he had said, of course, but I genuinely believe that he did not know what he had *done.* In his mind, there was an almost total severance between words and their meanings. This was so even when he spoke the truth. A year or so before he died, he met at a Washington party a former drinking companion, a government servant he had publicly betrayed and ruined. He went up to this man and within the hearing of the astonished guests asked why they had not seen each other in months. "Jeanie was talking about you the other night," he said. "How come we never see you? What the hell are you trying to do—*avoid* us?" The man was speechless.

I am trying to suggest—it is a perilous as well as a difficult undertaking—that there was to this ogreish creature a kind of innocence that may be one of the clues to his triumphs and his failures. Basically, of course, he was a great sophisticate in human relationships, as every demagogue must be. He knew a good deal about people's fears and anxieties, and he was a superb juggler of them. But he was himself numb to the sensations he produced in others. He could not comprehend true outrage, true indignation, true anything.

There was the legendary case of a celebrated English journalist,* a man who had convinced himself at his desk in London that McCarthy was a great beast at large in the world—a monster that had to be destroyed, and right away, in the name of human decency. He appointed himself a St. George, grabbed up his typewriter, and boarded the first transatlantic plane he could make. He was to write a series of articles so powerful that McCarthy, exposed at last, would immediately be crushed. Naturally, he had to see the dragon. In Washington, he phoned McCarthy's office and asked for an appointment. To his surprise—for one expects to have trouble getting an audience with the most terrible man in the world—he got one right away. Bracing himself, reminding himself that violence never solves anything and that a McCarthy hurled from a Senate Office Building window might be a martyr stronger in death than in life, he went up to Capitol Hill. He was shown in immediately, and the conversation began something like this.

MCCARTHY: Come on in. They tell me you're a hell of a reporter. Have a drink?

CELEBRATED ENGLISH JOURNALIST: Senator McCarthy, I think you should know that I despise you and everything you

* This story has gone the rounds at the Members' Bar of the National Press Club in Washington many times. I recently had a letter from the English journalist about whom it is generally told advising me that it was not an accurate representation of his experience with McCarthy. I accept this and print the story nevertheless; I would do so even if it were wholly apocryphal, for it is surely in character for McCarthy, and many reporters, myself included, had experiences a good bit like the one described.

61

stand for. It is only fair for me to tell you that I think you are the greatest force for evil in the world today.

McC: No kidding. How about the drink? What'll you have? I've got bourbon and—

CEJ: I have just told you, Senator McCarthy, that I loathe and detest you. I am here to expose you. It will get you nowhere to try to be kind to me. When I leave here . . .

McC: We can talk later. Now what about . . . ?

CEJ: I will start talking now. I wish only to warn you fairly that you can expect no quarter from me. I have observed your career for several years now, and in my opinion—

McC: For chrissake, are you going to have a drink or aren't you? Let's settle that first.

CEJ [Nearly dehydrated]: If it is clearly understood that I am under no obligations, that I am retracting not one word of what I have said about you, that your hospitality will not gain you my good opinion, I will, thank you, accept a drink. I will, if you please, have some whisky, with perhaps just a dash of soda.

McC: Good. Want ice?

The interview then began and proceeded without interruption for an hour or so. The Londoner could not put a question without telling McCarthy what a foul and poisonous creature he was. McCarthy could not answer without offering some more whisky with perhaps just a splash of soda. Both were loaded almost to the muzzle when McCarthy was reminded that he had a dentist's appointment. He invited St. George to come along, and the interview went on insofar as it was possible with McCarthy's great jaw clamped open, and a dentist with trembling hands worked over McCarthy's cavities and tried to keep his head in an atmosphere blue with the talk and quavering with the fumes of the bourbon he had consented to allow the patient to use as a rinse. Back in McCarthy's apartment, the interview still continued, in a much degenerated form. It carried over to the next morning. Finally it ended; the Englishman wrote his articles; they burned with moral outrage, but they weren't quite so powerful an assault on McCarthy as they had been planned to be. He was not destroyed.

McCarthy was, then, human; he wanted to be liked. It was difficult to satisfy this desire, but not impossible. Many of those who despised his role and fought him bitterly were able to see him as essentially a rogue and to get along quite well with him. One such was John Hoving, who had covered McCarthy in Wisconsin as a reporter on the Milwaukee *Journal* and had later been an official of Americans for Democratic Action. "Without a doubt, Senator McCarthy is one of the most cynical men I have ever known," Hoving once wrote. "[Yet] I like him quite a lot and enjoy being with him." Sooner or later, though, most of those who found themselves liking McCarthy and marveling at their ability to do so began regarding themselves as somehow morally flawed. For the public role, they had in the end to concede, overwhelmed the private one, and this man was, one had to tell oneself, not a rogue but a rattlesnake. Moreover, the mucker pose became increasingly dominant in both roles, and it was not charming, and one despised oneself if one found anything charming in it.

In my own case, I had known him slightly before his emergence as a national figure and rather well in the first year or

63

two after he had become one. I was never able to like him much, but I found it instructive and often amusing to talk with him. Sometime in 1951 or 1952, I found it impossible to sustain this taste. Revulsion had by then replaced—or, better perhaps, excluded—amusement, and thereafter, although I never missed a chance to watch him at work, I never sought a chance to be with him, and I could not help shrinking and looking away when he greeted me, or, as he so often did with all correspondents, gripped my shoulder as he walked past the press tables in the hearing room.

McCarthy's particular style, I have often thought, owed a great deal to that of a certain kind of American athlete: the kind who earns and revels in such sobriquets as Killer and Slugger; who looks ugly and talks ugly and wants to deceive no one on this score; who attaches enough importance to winning the Goddamned game to throw spitballs and rabbit punches and do a little Indian Charlie work with elbows and knees in the clinches and pileups. It was not, I imagine, without some such image in mind that he acquired his swaggering, shoulder-heaving walk and his ballplayer's slouch; that he cultivated a five-o'clock shadow with almost cosmetic care; and even that, in 1951, he changed his signature and all his listings from "Joseph R. McCarthy" to "Joe McCarthy." (The name, as it happened, was that of a former manager of the New York Yankees; there is no reason to believe, though, that he sought a specific identification with this particular Joe McCarthy.) He liked to be known as a politician who used his thumbs, his teeth, and his knees, and I suspect he understood that there is a place for a few such men in our moral universe. Our ideas and ideals of sportsmanship may be no lower than those of most people,* but they exist in an ambiance with our ideas and ideals of success, and they thus include an appreciation of Leo Durocher's famous maxim, "Nice guys finish last," and a certain tolerance—particularly in the ninth inning and the fourth quarter and maybe even in the eighth chukker—for mean, low-down bastards who win.† Senator John Bricker, a former Y.M.C.A. official and for many long years the plumed knight of Ohio conservatism, was not being in the least un-American when he told McCarthy in the Senate cloakroom in 1950, "Joe, you're a dirty son of a bitch, but there are times when you've got to have a son of a bitch around, and this is one of them." McCarthy, it was said at the time, was mightily pleased.

---

* "When the rules of the game prove unsuitable for victory, the gentlemen of England change the rules."—Harold J. Laski.
† A. J. Liebling, a student of such problems, has advised me that the tolerance for dirty players is much greater in team sports than, for example, in boxing. From a vast knowledge of the subject, he tells me that while there have been a good many baseball players who have been admired despite, if not because of, their low tactics, the dirty fighter is generally despised by the fans. McCarthy, of course, had no team loyalties, but those who admired him thought of him as being on *their* team, and some, at least, made the kind of identification I have in mind. In the Memorial Services held in the House of Representatives after his death, Emmet Byrne, of Illinois, began his eulogy with these words: "Goodbye, Joe. You were always in there swinging and taking your cuts at the ball. Mickey Mantle tries for the fences, but he strikes out too. . . . When you reach the pearly gates, I am sure your batting average will measure up and please St. Peter."

☞ Was he, then, merely an ignoble savage? Did he destroy men and the truth with no trace of guilt or remorse? Did he create tumult to no purpose? Was he deranged? A psychopathic personality?

He was never, so far as I am able to learn, under direct psychological or psychiatric observation—except, perhaps, in his very last days, which he spent in circumstances as yet not satisfactorily explained. There was, though, a widespread interest in his behavior among psychiatrists, and at least two of the more eminent among them were sought out and asked to observe him as closely and as thoroughly as possible, with a view to suggesting any strategies of combating him that might seem effective in the light of their findings. Not for political reasons, but for professional ones (no psychiatrist wishes to be associated with a diagnosis not made from a direct study of the subject and not authorized), their notes have never been published. One study, which I have had described to me, stressed the elements of classical paranoia in McCarthy's actions: life was a series of conspiracies, the most fiendish of which were directed at him; no one acted except from base motives; delusions of persecution were manifest and were accompanied by delusions of grandeur. The psychiatrist's recommendation was that McCarthy's adversaries attempt, antitherapeutically, to lay bare the paranoid reaction by prodding, goading, and taunting him ceaselessly.

The second study, written in 1954, contains the following passages:

What He Was and What He Did

The significant thing about McCarthy is the extraordinary intensity of his neurotic drives. . . . The key to understanding is the recognition of his basic insecurity, self-doubt, and self-contempt. [His] brash, ruthless, and insatiable drive to power is the way he has taken to compensate for underlying feelings of insecurity and unworthiness. . . . He has a shrewd and apparently excellent intellect and, until recently, the asset of extraordinary physical stamina.

[He] has developed a facility for being "charming." [Some] highly neurotic individuals are able to turn on a gush of good will, which conceals their inner doubts, hatreds, and feelings of unworthiness.

. . . Truth and justice are recognized by him only when they serve his ends. When they do not serve his ends, they are unrecognized or cleverly distorted "to make the worse appear the better reason." This seems to be overtly a shrewd opportunistic maneuver but basically is a sinister neurotic trait.

Although at times, McCarthy seems to have gone beyond the borders of sanity, he has a remarkable resilience. His power to protect himself against emotional breakdown [is] very striking. Out of his insecurity and need to be right, he has developed ideas of greatness (in the psychotic, these become "delusions of grandeur"). McCarthy has seen and portrayed himself as the savior of his country. . . .

When intellectual devices—rationalizations—fail, McCarthy is able to fall back on physical illness. This may be real or exaggerated in his mind. Illness gives him a chance to temporarily withdraw, if the going is rough. . . . Fatigue is his enemy.

. . . McCarthy is now on a downgrade course. With the resilience of his mental makeup, he is unlikely to become overtly insane. It is more likely that he will become a prey to physical ailments. Alcohol may be used increasingly to allay anxiety. Secondary toxic effects from any such sedentary measures would tend to reduce efficiency, impair judgment, and might lead to mental and physical collapse. This form of alcoholism, if it should occur, is the desperate type, to reduce acute feelings of disturbance.

[However] one possibility of further real trouble with Mc-Carthy is that if he has, during this interval, recovered sufficiently mentally and rested up physically, he may try a shrewd comeback into public favor. He is capable of trying to do this under certain conditions, namely if his ardent followers can give him sufficient reassurance . . . or indications of support from one or another . . . factions also striving for power.

Many people were firmly convinced that he was a homosexual. The evidence was wholly circumstantial, and some of it was not even that: a member of his staff had been picked up as a sodomist in Lafayette Park; a journalist got a story from a Marquette coed of his reluctance, as a suitor in his college days, to be anything but verbal; one untried affidavit describing a homosexual encounter with McCarthy in a Wisconsin political meeting some years before McCarthy came to Washington;* the apparent compulsiveness and hostility

* This came into the possession of Herman Greenspun, a former New York lawyer, a former press agent for a Las Vegas, Nevada, gambling house, and in the early fifties the publisher of the Las Vegas *Sun*. In a speech in Las Vegas in 1951, McCarthy had spoken of Greenspun as a "confessed ex-Communist." McCarthy said this was a slip of the tongue, which it probably was; he had meant, he said, to call Greenspun a "confessed ex-convict," which Greenspun was, having been convicted in 1950 of violating the Neutrality Act by running guns to Israel. Greenspun swore vengeance upon McCarthy and attempted to get it by publishing stories about him as a "disreputable pervert." McCarthy never commented upon Greenspun's charges, a fact that did *not* lend any added weight to the charge. (No politician in his senses would advertise such charges by attempting to repudiate them.)

of his pawing of women at parties. Certain of his enemies did their best to get more evidence, but they failed, and in the absence of further data, we are left, in point of fact, with no data at all.

☞ There is no doubt about McCarthy's self-preoccupation; whether or not it was obsessive, it was surely excessive. There was a gorgeous instance of its excessiveness once on the Senate floor when a speech on a subject of large importance to him was being delivered and listened to attentively by most of his colleagues. It was a moment for him to take with high seriousness. What he took seriously, though, was an envelope that had reached his office without anything on it but the necessary postage and a picture of him clipped from a newspaper and pasted to the envelope. While the speech was in progress, he moved from desk to desk, putting a hand on the shoulder of each seated colleague and displaying this new evidence of the celebrity he had attained.

And there was no doubt that he was full of bodily afflictions commonly associated with an afflicted psyche. He was

---

But he did try to silence Greenspun. He called to the attention of the Post Office Department a column in the Las Vegas *Sun* predicting his assassination: "Senator Joe McCarthy has to come to a violent end. Huey Long's death will be serene and peaceful compared with the demise of the sadistic bum from Wisconsin. Live by the sword and you die by the sword. Destroy people and they in turn must destroy you. The chances are that McCarthy will be laid to rest by some poor innocent slob whose life and reputation he has destroyed. . . ." Greenspun was indicted for mailing "matter . . . tending to incite murder or assassination." He was acquitted.

a mass of allergies. His hands trembled incessantly. His stomach ailments were unending. "He had a flaming belly all the time," one of his closest friends said. He had bursitis, troubled sinuses, and was accident prone.

Certainly no one who tried to see McCarthy whole could doubt that he was in some meaningful sense aberrant, even if he seemed in no meaningful way disabled or out of touch with the realities he needed (as a demagogue leading a flight from reality) to be in touch with. It would be hard to maintain a faith, even one heavily salted with skepticism, in the values of our civilization if we did not regard a wholly contemptuous and destructive attitude as somehow psychopathic.* Yet to many of us who watched him in Washington over the years, the extraordinary thing about his behavior was his composure. He was prodded, he was goaded, he was taunted, and he never really went to pieces, though he sometimes pretended to do so. Whatever he did he did for an effect that he seemed either to have calculated or intuitively to have appraised with soundness. My own view was that

* The late Robert Lindner wrote, in *Rebel Without a Cause,* a definition of the psychopathic personality that has certain points of interest in connection with McCarthy: "[The] psychopath is a rebel without a cause, an agitator without a slogan, a revolutionary without a program: in other words, his rebelliousness is aimed to achieve goals satisfactory to himself alone. . . . All his efforts, hidden under no matter what disguise, represent investments designed to satisfy his immediate wishes and desires. The psychopath, like a child, cannot delay the pleasure of gratification; and this trait is one of his underlying, universal characteristics. . . . He cannot wait upon the development of prestige in society; his egoistic ambitions lead him to leap into headlines by daring performances."

whatever the wellsprings of his behavior and whatever tributaries fed them, he could be described as a true cynic and a true hypocrite. This seemed to me to make him a rather special case. True cynics—"those canine philosophers," as St. Augustine called them—are very rare, and true hypocrites are even rarer. Cynicism requires a disbelief in the possibility of sincerity, and most men, at least in our kind of society, find it necessary to insist upon their own sincerity. As for hypocrisy, one cannot practice it without acknowledging the fact to oneself; to be a hypocrite, a man must *see* a hypocrite whenever he faces a mirror. And such is the human capacity for self-deception that almost every sinner born of woman has some device for convincing himself that his base acts serve in some perspective some sort of good. Dr. Johnson once observed that there are few wrongs in this world that do not have, in the eyes of their perpetrators, enough right in them to keep the wrong in countenance. Thus, it seems to me, that very few men can fairly be charged with hypocrisy even when it is apparent to all the world that their practices balance most unfavorably against their preachments. Only in a very loose sense, for example, could one say that Dwight Eisenhower was being hypocritical when, after forty-odd years as a non-churchgoer, he went into politics and took up regular worship. The President, we can be sure, was not blind to the construction that might be placed upon this change in his Sunday-morning habits. But we may be just as sure that it never crossed his mind that this revealed cynicism or hypocrisy. All kinds of good reasons were available to him as a justification—for instance, that it was incumbent

71

upon him, as a President who had always had an abstract conviction that religion was a good thing, to set for the nation, as a parent sets for a child, an example somewhat better than his own earlier conduct.

I cannot, though, find the right in McCarthy's acts that might have kept the wrong in countenance. In the case of the true believers in McCarthyism, it is easy enough to see the rationalizing processes. To the bat-haunted Minute Women of the U.S.A., to the Texas millionaires, to the China lobby, to the "hard" anti-Communist intelligentsia of New York, the destruction of Communist power was a sacred, or, at any rate, a splendid, mission, and McCarthy, as they always said, was "doing something." To Robert A. Taft and the Republicans who encouraged McCarthy in Congress, the nation stood in need of new leaders and defenders, and McCarthy was "doing something" about that. But to McCarthy everything was profane. I know of nothing to suggest that he ever for a moment really thought the government was riddled with Communists; had he really believed this, had he really cared, he would not have abandoned investigations merely from ennui or because of their failure to produce the headlines he had expected. He was a political speculator, a prospector who drilled Communism and saw it come up a gusher. He liked his gusher, but he would have liked any other just as well.

In the mirror, McCarthy must have seen and recognized a fraud. But it cannot be said with any assurance that he paid no price at all for the corruption of the spirit. He lied with poise and spontaneity, but he was obsessed with the problem of truth and falsehood. He was morally indecent, but the idea of decency seemed everlastingly and hauntingly on his mind. No man was ever quicker than this super-Munchausen to call another a liar, generally with amplifying adjectives, as when he called the publisher Henry Luce a "debased, degraded, degenerate liar." He found as much mendacity as Communism, and one of his favorite gambits—going at least as far back as 1949, which was *before* he struck Communism —was to challenge anyone who got in his way to take a lie-detector test. Sometimes, he would volunteer to demonstrate his own veracity by taking such a test himself, or in tandem with a critic. (It was often observed that he made his offers secure in the knowledge that he could lie with such cool aplomb as to outwit the machine; others said that if he ever actually submitted, he would fracture the whole apparatus, and its flying parts would be a menace to anyone nearby.) His challenges were never accepted, and so far as is known he never experimented with a lie detector himself.

A. C. Bradley, the Shakespearean scholar, once wrote of Macbeth that "He has never . . . accepted as the principle of his own conduct the morality which takes shape in his imaginative fears." Putting aside the question of fear, McCarthy's imagination was surely full of the shapes of the morality he rejected. He said that "mud, slime, filth, and moral squalor" characterized his opponents in 1952. It could be argued, of course, that his appeals to this alien morality were pure rhetoric—that when he spoke of the monitoring of telephone calls, a common practice in his own office, as "the most indecent and dishonest thing I have heard of," he was

73

simply playing tricks of a debasing nature upon the language. But the same words turned up with suspicious regularity: "completely indecent and improper," "indecent and illegal under the laws," "vicious," "dishonest and vile," "dishonest, grossly dishonest," "vile and scurrilous"—all of this in an outburst over the use by others, against him, of a technique he used every day, against others. And he was always making demands upon others "in common decency, in common honesty"—in the instant case, a demand that Senator Symington take the witness stand at the Army-McCarthy hearings. Offended, he was always "sick, Mr. Chairman, sick deep down inside."

 *Early Days*

In his speeches, in his interminable testimony, in interviews, and in the handful of things he wrote for publication, McCarthy often spoke of himself and of the meaning of his own life. He found himself endlessly interesting, and he would always summon his fanciest, gamiest rhetoric when his subject was McCarthy. (He favored the third person and often referred to himself as "McCarthy.") In the opening pages of *McCarthyism: The Fight for America,* he recalls in seeming tranquility what he says were his thoughts when, a month after his Wheeling speech, he made his way to the first session of the Tydings Committee:

When the inter-office buzzer across the room on my desk sounded, it seemed as though only ten minutes had passed since I had stretched out on the leather couch in my office after a night's work.

Actually, an hour had passed since I had asked my office manager to wake me at 10:15.

It was now 10:15 a.m.

This was March 8, 1950.

In fifteen minutes I was due in the Senate Caucus room to begin testifying before the Tydings Committee. . . .

I quickly shaved and checked through my briefcase to see that the documents, photostats, and other exhibits were all there. . . .

As I walked down the long marble corridors to the Senate Caucus room, I wondered if I would be able to accomplish what I had set out to do. . . .

In the back of my mind there was faintly echoing the chairman's statement, "Let me have McCarthy for three days in public hearings and he will never show his face in the Senate again." [Senator Tydings denied ever having said this or anything like it.]

The picture of treason which I carried in my briefcase to that Caucus room was to shock the nation and occupy the headlines until Truman declared war in Korea. . . . [To McCarthy, even a war against Communism might be just a publicity stunt, an attempt to steal the headlines, and the anti-Communist issue, from McCarthy.] As I walked toward the hearing room, many things crossed my mind. For example, in a few seconds I relived the first trip which I had taken in the rear seat of an SBD to divebomb Japanese anti-aircraft on the then southern anchor of the chain of Japanese Pacific defenses at Kahili on the southern tip of Bougainville. . . .

As we flew over the Japanese airfield on Ballale island that morning, a few minutes before our break-off for the dive through

Kahili's anti-aircraft fire, there crossed my mind the thought: "McCarthy, why are you here? Why isn't it someone else?" . . . But then I remembered the next thought which I had as my pilot —I believe it was little Johnny Morton—cracked his flaps and I saw the red undercover as the dive bombing brakes opened up. My thought was: "Hell, someone had to do the job. It might as well be me."

In a split second my thoughts shifted from the Pacific to the Arizona hills and I found myself riding a long-legged black mule rounding up cattle in the hills and canyons of the rim-rock country beyond Young, Arizona. It was on the ranch of Kelly Moeur, father of one of the less retiring and modest Marines of my acquaintance. . . .

Ten saddle-sore days which I spent on that desolate but friendly cattle ranch, played a most important part in my anti-Communist fight. . . .

The best place to lay the plans for this fight, I decided, was in the lonely relatively uninhabited rim-rock country of Arizona. . . .

The planning was made infinitely easier by my contact with real Americans without any synthetic sheen—real Americans who are part of the Arizona hills—real Americans like J.K.'s mother and his father, Kelly Moeur, like Rillabelle, old Jim Sands, and Old Jack with the hounds, whose last name I cannot recall. . . .

So it was that I walked into the huge, red-carpeted Caucus room on that Wednesday morning more than two years ago.

Rillabelle and Old Jack with the hounds, whose surname escaped him, sound suspiciously like Indian Charlie. But what seems revealing about this passage and all the reminiscent ones in his speeches is that McCarthy's mind never went back to childhood and youth. In *McCarthyism,* the only reference to his early life and to his family is the non-

committal and absurd contention that "I came to know the
Pacific and the coast of Asia almost as well as I knew Dad's
farm when I was a boy." This is surely a curious circumstance. As a rule, the American politician who wishes to
construct myths about himself dwells extensively on his
childhood—especially if it was, as in McCarthy's case, a
childhood on the farm, with the days spent in walking to a
one-room country school and returning home for long hours
behind the plow. Harry Truman, who had such a background, spends so much time on it in his first volume of
Memoirs that one wonders if he is ever going to make his
way back into the twentieth century and Washington. Mc-
Carthy mentions his Arizona friend's mother and father, but
he never, so far as I have been able to learn, said or wrote
anything about his own. Nor did he ever say—as almost any
politician would who could—how much fun it was and how
splendid for the development of character to have been
brought up in a family of nine children, a family that had,
indeed, started in a log cabin.

A biographer addicted to the modern canons might conclude from this that McCarthy's childhood was a bad, sad
memory and that he did not wish to refresh it by discussing
it. It might further be concluded that he lived part of his
childhood in his later life and that even that experience
was so impoverished that he was compelled to construct
fantasies about himself. Whatever the explanation, it seems
a fact that he preferred not to discuss his early years. In
any case, we have no accounting from him of his childhood
or, for that matter, of any part of his life before World War

II. What we have are only a few vital statistics, a few memories drawn from neighbors by enterprising journalists, and a few facts drawn from the public record of his beginning years in Wisconsin politics.

When McCarthy died on May 2, 1957, it was reported that he was forty-seven years old, having reached that age the preceding November. He sometimes gave his birth date as November 9, 1909, sometimes as November 14. In the *Congressional Directory* and *Who's Who in America,* it is set down as November 14, 1909. The records of Grand Chute Township, where he was born to Timothy and Bridget McCarthy, establish it as November 14, 1908.

He was the fifth of nine children, and his parents farmed one hundred and forty-two acres near Grand Chute, in Outagamie County in east-central Wisconsin on the north shore of Lake Winnebago. His home was about a hundred miles north of Milwaukee and about eight north of Appleton. The McCarthy farm was in the middle of a section known locally as "the Irish Settlement"—an island of Hibernians in a sea of farmers of predominantly German and Dutch ancestry. Timothy McCarthy was half Irish, half German. He was native born. His wife, who had been Bridget Tierney, was an immigrant, all Irish. Both were Roman Catholic, and both were said to be intensely pious. They were literate, but not, evidently, a great deal more than that. The land they worked, and the land all about in that part of the state, was poor; it had been farmed to near-exhaustion by those who had bought it from the federal government at $2.50 an acre in the middle of the last century. The McCarthys were poor, but, although

79

the land was unyielding and the children numerous, the family prospered enough to move, just before Joseph's birth, from a log cabin to a clapboard house.

It seems to be the testimony of those who knew McCarthy as a child that he was an awkward boy and not very appealing in a conventional way. He was teased a good deal, they say, and did not take well to it; he was too shy to be able to recite in school. His mother, it is said, sensed his difficulties, and in researches on McCarthy it is frequently asserted that the fifth child was Mrs. McCarthy's favorite and that he was a victim of overprotectiveness, which is cited by some writers as the principal source of his adult behavior. In *The Crucial Decade,* Eric F. Goldman wrote:

. . . the McCarthys were a struggling brood of nine, and Joe was the ugly duckling, barrel-chested and short-armed with thick eyebrows and heavy lips. Mother Bridget McCarthy threw a special protective wing around the shy, sulky boy, and when the rough testing came, he sought out her big warm apron. "Don't you mind," she would console. "You be somebody. You get ahead."

Joe took heed. He would get back; he would show everybody. The shy sulkiness turned into a no-holds-barred ambition.

Perhaps it is all true. But even if it were just as Mr. Goldman sets it down, it would still leave unanswered the large question of how it happened that out of all the millions of boys who sought out big warm aprons and were admonished to "be somebody," only one became Senator Joe McCarthy. It is universally conceded nowadays that the tree inclines the way the twig is bent. The difficulty is that twigs are never straight to begin with and are bent back and forth a good deal and often end up as wavy as a blackthorn. Also, with human beings, the bending is a largely hidden process; very little of it is done on sunlit days in the presence of witnesses with total recall, with the consequence that very often a skilled psychoanalyst with a patient only a few feet away and eager, at least in his conscious mind, to make the journey back to childhood finds the whole affair hopelessly elusive.

In the little that is known of McCarthy's childhood and youth, there is nothing that is singular enough in nature to account for this singular man. We may assume as facts his unattractiveness (though short arms and a barrel chest, large eyebrows and heavy features do not in themselves make a child unattractive to others, and McCarthy in manhood seemed a common enough physical type) and his rejection by his peers. Two early biographers, Jack Anderson and Ronald W. May, did scrupulous field work for their book *McCarthy: The Man, the Senator, the "Ism,"* and the Grand Chute neighbors they interviewed insisted that these were the facts. We may assume, too, that he felt a certain self-pity because of his limited opportunities. On February 20, 1950, he read this into the *Congressional Record:**

* The passage was in what he claimed was the text of his maiden speech on Communism, the one he delivered in Wheeling on February 9. However, he had earlier said that he had spoken from notes, and by the next morning the notes were gone. It is conceivable— indeed, it is probable—that someone on his staff wrote this between February 9 and February 20 and that he inserted it without ever having said it or even read it. It was quite clear, as I shall show later

The reason why we find ourselves in a position of impotency . . . is the traitorous actions of those who have been treated so well by this nation. It is not the less fortunate or members of the minority groups who have been selling this nation out but rather those who have had all the benefits the wealthiest nation on earth has had to offer—the finest homes, the finest college educations, and the finest jobs in the government that we can give. This is glaringly true of the State Department. There the bright young men who are born with silver spoon in their mouth [sic] are the ones who have been worse [sic].

There seems, in any case, to be scarcely any doubt that toil was his lot; the life the McCarthys lived called for labor from everyone, and there is no reason why McCarthy's brothers and sisters and their neighbors should remember him as a hard and uncomplaining worker if in fact he had been a laggard in the barns and fields. It would be more difficult for others, particularly brothers and sisters, to be sure that he was his mother's favorite and that she mothered him more than the others. But even if we accept as revealed truth all that had been said and all that may be assumed about his early life, we are still lacking any necessary background for a demagogue of genius. Adversity and rejection may scar the soul or enlarge it or have no identifiable consequences. He could have grown up shy, awkward, compulsively industrious, too much mothered in what we can picture as the meager conditions of life in Grand Chute in the twenties and been something very different from what

---

on, that most of what he put into the *Record* on February 20 was as unfamiliar to him as to everyone else. Nevertheless, this does sound in character.

he turned out to be: an Outagamie County farmer like his father, a respectable dentist in Appleton, a priest, a Communist functionary, a burglar, a respected public servant in the great Wisconsin tradition, or Joe McCarthy. At this point in time, no mysteries can be penetrated by speculations about the early years.

Certain facts are more or less beyond dispute. He attended Underhill Country School and did well enough—despite a reported inability to recite normally—to skip a grade. When he was fourteen and had just finished grammar school, he became a full-time chicken farmer. Using some money he had earned at odd jobs, he acquired a flock of fifty, which he raised on land rented from his father. Before long, he had ten thousand chickens, a new chicken house, and a truck for trucking the chicks to Chicago. When he was nineteen and prospering, a sad thing happened. He fell ill of pneumonia—contracted, so the story goes, from too much time spent in moist coops in good weather and bad—and was compelled to hire some local boys, who lacked his dedication to the welfare of the fowl. They were careless. Disease spread. Laying hens and broilers were wiped out. McCarthy faced the choice of starting all over again or quitting the poultry business. He quit.

He left Grand Chute for Manawa, a town of some five thousand about twenty miles distant. There he found employment as the manager of a grocery store, part of a chain named Cashway. (With his near-birth in a log cabin and his storekeeper past, he might have claimed a small share in the Lincoln tradition, but he never did.) Apparently, he did well and was much liked in Manawa, and he was urged by some leading citizens to resume his schooling so that he might be ready for even larger callings than the local Cashway management. Two months short of twenty, he enrolled in Little Wolf High School, and in one year completed the scholastic work of four. His determination made a large impression on the principal, who devoted much of his own time to tutoring McCarthy, and he made McCarthy's feat of acceleration the subject of his commencement address. ("We never graduated a student more capable of graduating.") The following fall, he enrolled as an engineering student at Marquette University, a Jesuit institution in Milwaukee. After two years, he abandoned engineering for law. He supported himself and paid his tuition by working as a dishwasher and pie-baker in the Pfister Hotel, a gas-station attendant, a pick-and-shovel man on a road-construction gang. His academic record seems to have been average. He was president of his class, though, and a varsity boxer, and when he was in law school, he was the college boxing coach.

Upon graduation, he hung a shingle in Waupaca, a potato market town and the seat of Waupaca County, just west of Outagamie. He shared offices with a dentist, but the dentist, according to Anderson and May, did most of the business. The records show only four cases for his nine-month stay there. He reported earnings of $777.81 for 1935. He made ends meet, they say, with his poker winnings. He next took a job, at fifty dollars a week, with an attorney named Michael Eberlein, whose practice was in Shawano, still another county seat—this one north of Outagamie. Eberlein was a Repub-

lican, and McCarthy was, by an inheritance he then chose
not to reject, a Democrat, and in their bipartisan collaboration they followed an old tradition—honored to this day,
probably, in every county seat north of the Mason and
Dixon line—of law firms working both sides of the street.
McCarthy became chairman of the Young Democratic Clubs
of Wisconsin's Seventh District and ran as a Democrat for
District Attorney. To no one's surprise, he lost the election,
but he did a good deal better than his supporters had expected. It was a three-way election, with the candidate of
the La Follette Progressives expected to win, which he did,
and with McCarthy expected to come in behind the Republican. McCarthy did better than the Republican.

He went back to work for Eberlein—it was now the firm
of Eberlein & McCarthy—and stayed for the next three
years. No biographer has accounted for this period, which
begins with a McCarthy who might, for all that we know of
him, be almost any young lawyer in any county seat with
enough of an interest in politics to take over as head of a
club and, for the sake of the publicity and party advancement,
run for an office he knew he could not win; and which ends
in 1939, with the essential McCarthy the world came to
know just about fully formed—fully enough, at any rate,
to run a campaign, as a Republican, on the same principles
as his later ones and to abuse power in ways that later became familiar.

One imagines these years to have been rather bleak ones
—particularly if McCarthy harbored any dreams of an in-
cendiary future. His gifts as an attorney were never very

striking; the life of a small-town lawyer offers rewards of many sorts to men of a certain temperament, but it is hard to suppose that McCarthy would ever have much appreciated its satisfactions. Law offers a quick approach to politics, but McCarthy in Shawano in his late twenties, even with a determination to scale the heights, even with large dreams, could not sensibly have thought his prospects very bright. What, after all, would have been a reasonable expectation, a supportable hope, for the head of the Young Democrats of Wisconsin's Seventh District? Election to the state legislature perhaps, and, given time and luck, the House of Representatives someday. As for the Senate or the Governorship—there were, after all, seventy-one counties in Wisconsin and in each county seat, at a conservative estimate, a half-dozen McCarthys. Even granted the "no-holds-barred" ambition whose origins Mr. Goldman thought he could trace to Bridget McCarthy's large, warm apron, even granted that he had been an Iago, "subtle in his designs," as Dr. Johnson wrote, and cunningly "studious of his interests and his vengeance," it is difficult to picture him exercising his subtlety and his studiousness in Shawano.

The period is, at all events, pretty much of a blank. We know that it saw his emergence as a Republican, but of the conversion itself, if conversion is the word, we know nothing. ("It was an advantage," he once said, "to be a Republican with a Democratic name.") It has also been established that Michael Eberlein had wanted to run for the judgeship that McCarthy won and that he felt a deep sense of betrayal when, just as he was about to announce his candidacy, McCarthy announced *his*. But by the time anyone grew interested enough in McCarthy to inquire into his back-country days, they were far behind him; the past was irrecoverable, the truth—if it could ever have been known—was hidden. McCarthy was a large figure in the nation and a giant in Wisconsin politics, and there were few people who would discuss him freely. Michael Eberlein would not talk about him because he was a prisoner in the judgeship McCarthy had won in 1939 and had left in 1946, upon his election to the Senate. Eberlein had got the job with McCarthy's support.

☞ What is surely clear is that somewhere between birth and thirty, which was his age when he ran for Circuit Judge in Wisconsin District 10, and tacked seven years on his opponent's age, McCarthy had become liberated from the morality that prevailed in his environment, in his time, in his profession. It was not the fact that he lied that revealed this; there are men and women positively enslaved by the prevailing morality who lie with metronomic regularity; it was McCarthy's surpassing boldness, in some ways even the grandeur of his falsehoods, that set him and them apart from ordinary misrepresentation. The Alsops were mistaken in saying he was the only politician who would not sue for libel if he were called a liar, but they would have been right if they had said he was the only politician of his time who would unashamedly persist in misrepresenting a simple truth even when the truth was accessible to everyone and when everyone could see what he was doing with the truth. "The present Judge, Edgar V. Werner, was born in 1866," one piece of McCarthy literature said. "Even though he is willing to sacrifice himself, the job of circuit judge is too exacting for a man of his age." It was a matter of record that this was not the case, that Judge Werner was not seventy-three—or, as McCarthy sometimes made it, eighty-nine—but sixty-six.* The ordinary, unliberated liar would not have attempted anything quite so bold, if for no other reason than that he would have feared being trapped in untruth. After all, Judge Werner's real age was verifiable—a matter of public record. The ordinary liar would have reasoned that a man who falsifies a simple and relevant figure that is in the public record is bound to be exposed and hurt by the exposure. If such a man had wished to use the age issue in a campaign such as McCarthy's against Judge Werner, he would have gone about it in a less direct fashion. He might, for example, have spread the rumor that Judge Werner suffered from some ailment that placed him on the verge of death, or he might have intimated that the Judge's recent conduct had shown a growing senility. The rumor or the intimation would have been a lie no less deplorable than

* There is a peculiar bit of arithmetic here. If Judge Werner was sixty-six in 1939, he was born, probably, in 1873. McCarthy told the voters of District 10 that Judge Werner was seventy-three. If that had been so in 1939, the judge would have been born in 1866. I have no evidence for this—and no one else, to the best of my knowledge, has suggested it—but it would not have been unlike McCarthy to have noticed the neat possibilities for getting everyone mixed up with 66, 1866, 73, 1873.

McCarthy's direct falsehood, but it would have been a lie that no one could nail down. The truth in such matters is unascertainable; it cannot be proved that a man does *not* have a fatal disease or that he is *not* moving toward senility.

McCarthy, obviously, worried about none of this. He knew that often, particularly in the short run, truth crushed to earth simply burrows underground and out of sight. It was not until after he had won the judgeship that word of his deception got around, and by then, probably, nobody much cared. The election was in the past, and people weren't much impressed to hear that McCarthy had misstated his opponent's age. They had chosen youth. They would have done so, probably, if McCarthy had given his true age, which was, on Election Day of 1939, just a few days short of thirty-one, but he wished the distinction of being the youngest Circuit Court judge in the state's history, so he arranged to get it by making himself twenty-nine. (Later, he was to claim that he had been only twenty-eight.) Judge Werner's supporters got up a petition to have the election voided on the ground that McCarthy had won it by fraud and deception and on the further ground that he had violated the state's corrupt-practices law by campaign spending in excess of the statutory limit. But McCarthy had won his judgeship, and nothing ever came of the petition.

His campaign slogan, incidentally, had been "Justice is Truth in Action."

He graced the bench for something over four years, but these were divided, almost in the middle, by a little more than two years of military service. Taken all in all, his comportment as a judge revealed that emancipation from convention which characterized him in his 1939 campaign and in his behavior as a United States Senator. One of his early cases was to become a classic one for students of judicial misconduct. The state Department of Agriculture sought from Judge McCarthy an injunction against the Quaker Dairy Company of Appleton to force compliance with a marketing law. McCarthy granted a temporary injunction. Three days later, he suspended his own order, for reasons he never put in the record. Then, when the case came to trial before him, he dismissed the state complaint with the argument that the law the state was trying to enforce would be off the books in six months. This was true; the legislature had adjourned without re-enacting the marketing law, which had a statutory expiration date. Judge McCarthy simply undertook to advance the expiration date. He also said that he was dismissing the complaint on the ground that enforcement of the law, which is supposed to be no respecter of persons, would work a "hardship" on the defendant. His opinion was appealed. When the record of the case reached the state Supreme Court, it was found to be incomplete. McCarthy, it was discovered, had ordered his court reporter to take out and destroy parts of the statement he had made from the bench in dismissing the complaint.

The content of the missing parts is unknown. Asked why he had destroyed them, he said, "Because they weren't material." The court's horrified reaction to both the grounds for the dismissal and the destruction of a crucial part of the record is of a piece—almost tiresomely of a piece—with many subsequent documents on McCarthy. The court said, in part:

We are cited no authority and we find none which justifies a court in suspending the operation of [the] statute. . . . It must be concluded that the grounds upon which the trial court acted did not constitute a sufficient or legal reason therefore and that this action constituted an abuse of judicial power. . . . [A] judicial officer is required to administer the law without respect to persons so long as it is enforced. Any other course would constitute an infringement upon the powers and functions of the legislature, interfere with the operation of agencies . . . and result in advantage to persons who disobey the law. . . . Ordering destruction of these records was highly improper. . . . We can only say that if it were necessary to a decision, the destruction of evidence under these circumstances could only be open to the inference that the evidence destroyed contained statements of fact contrary to the position taken by the person destroying the evidence.

As a judge, he had only one claim to distinction, and its validity was questionable. The court calendar was choked with untried cases—approximately two hundred and fifty of them, according to him—and he undertook to put an end to the law's delay. In one period of six weeks, he kept his court in session until midnight a dozen times. Within a few months, he had cleared the calendar, and never again fell behind. Justice, though, may not have been advanced by his efforts to accelerate it. He became noted for five-minute divorce judgments. Anderson and May describe one:

He opened the case while he was still making a beeline [up the courthouse steps] for his court.

91

"Are you the lawyer for the plaintiff?" Judge McCarthy asked one of the attorneys striding alongside him.

"Yes," the lawyer answered.

"And are you the lawyer for the respondent?"

"Yes."

"Are these stipulations correct?"

"Yes."

"Is there anything anyone wants to say before we proceed?"

"No."

And within two minutes the proceedings were over. The plaintiff looked up in surprise as she was told she could leave the courtroom. "Am I divorced?" she said.

"Yes," Judge McCarthy announced.

Divorce was a specialty. The Wisconsin laws were fairly rigid, and the state, which has always prized its reputation for governmental good works, had instituted a system for attempting to mend rifted lutes; each court had a divorce counsel, required by law to offer his mediating services to couples whenever a suit for divorce had been filed. McCarthy got the job for his campaign manager, a lawyer and taxi-owner named Urban P. Van Susteren.* But the Judge found that more could be accomplished when Van Susteren's services were dispensed with, and in time he earned a reputation as a kind of mobile Reno—a circuit judge who worked exceedingly fast and seldom found any obstacles in the statutes,

---

* A fascinating name for a campaign manager but not quite as fascinating, I think, as Loyal Eddy. When I first came upon this in an account of McCarthy's early days, I felt certain that it was an incomplete identification. I supposed it was Loyal Eddy Jones, or something of the sort. But Loyal Eddy it was, with nothing more. And McCarthy had, later on, a bodyguard named Otis Gomillion.

particularly where friends or political supporters were involved. The Milwaukee *Journal* joined the Supreme Court in anguish over McCarthy. Commenting on divorce procedures in his circuit, it said,

Judge McCarthy, whose burning ambition for political advancement is accompanied by an astonishing disregard for things ethical and traditional, is doing serious injury to the judiciary in this state.

☞ McCarthy was thirty-three when the United States entered the war. As a judge, he was exempt from military service. He did not accept the exemption. On June 2, 1942, he wrote the Marine recruiting officer in Milwaukee setting forth his qualifications for a commission, and then followed his letter to Milwaukee, where he advised reporters that, having reached the conclusion that "we can't win the war by letting the neighbors do the fighting," he was eager to enlist as a "buck private." He was, he explained, "more interested in a gun than in a commission." He got a commission before he got a gun. On June 4, he was sworn in as a first lieutenant and instructed to report for training at the Marine base at Quantico, Virginia.* He did not resign his judgeship, but,

* He had some different versions. In a newspaper release he authorized upon his return in 1944, and probably wrote himself, it was said: "Though automatically deferred from the draft, he left the bench and enlisted as a buck private in the Marine Corps. He was sent to an officers training school, where he earned a second [*sic*] lieutenant's commission." In the 1947 *Congressional Directory*, he wrote, "In June of 1942 applied for enlistment in Marine Corps as a buck private and was later commissioned." The following year, in the same publica-

instead, requested his colleagues on the other circuits to take over his duties until his return, which they did, though not without complaint. The chairman of the board of circuit judges had thought it an unusual and unreasonable request. "I am confident," Judge Arnold F. Murphy wrote, "that even though they [the other judges] give their best and I help them that your absence from the bench will be a serious hindrance to orderly procedure in the courts in the three counties of your circuit." McCarthy was not dissuaded. Fitted to a cash-and-carry uniform, he stopped by the courthouse in Milwaukee, where another circuit judge, Gerald Boileau, was holding court and sat on the bench for one last case. Photographers had been alerted. A judge not in robes but a Marine tunic was a novelty. Then he was off for Quantico and the wars.

He was a Marine from June 1942 until December 1944, when he resigned his commission and left the corps. For most of that time, he was an intelligence officer in the South Pacific with Scout Bombing Squadron 235. His major duty was to sit at a desk and interview pilots upon their return from missions, and there is nothing to suggest that he performed this work, or any other assigned to him, with anything short of competence. He was sometimes under enemy fire, and he was never known to lack courage. He invented

tion, he wrote, "In June of 1942 enlisted in the Marine Corps and assigned to Marine aviation." In later years, his *Congressional Directory* biography contained nothing but his birthday—the wrong one—his birthplace, and the year he was elected to the Senate.

a military record for himself, though, that was one more tissue of lies. He claimed several combat wounds. He had none. Long after the war, he got a Purple Heart for a leg injury; his record shows that the leg was broken when he fell down a flight of steps during an Equator-crossing party aboard the seaplane tender *Chandeleur* far from any actual hostilities. He later claimed to have been a gunnery officer—"Known in the Pacific as 'Tail-Gunner Joe,' " his campaign brochures said. He was never a tail gunner; he went along on several strikes and sat in the tail-gunner's seat, the only place for a passenger, and now and then fired the guns, but he was taken along only when little enemy resistance was expected; where resistance was heavy, the pilots wanted trained gunners at the tail gun. (In 1943, according to the Associated Press, he set a record for the number of rounds shot in a single day, 4,700; but that ammunition, it appears, was expended mainly on cocoanut trees on bases safely in American hands.) Running for the Senate in 1944, he said he had been on fourteen missions. In the Senate, in 1948, he claimed seventeen. In 1951, he made it thirty. In 1951 he asked for and in 1952 was given the Distinguished Flying Cross, which is awarded for twenty-five combat missions. According to the Washington *Evening Star* for November 14, 1951, his Marine Corps service record "shows no notation of his having qualified for an aerial gunner's wings or being credited with combat missions."

In his political speeches, when he thought the moment had arrived to jerk a few tears, he told a story about "some

95

of the less pleasant days we spent on the South Pacific islands," from which a few standard and salient details follow:

I was with a Marine dive-bombing squadron . . . and one of my tasks at night after we lost pilots or gunners was to write home to the young wives or mothers. . . . If, as was often the case, I had to explain why [the] body, having been lost at sea, his grave would remain forever unmarked. I might try to tell that unfortunate young woman that the greatest headstone any fighting man could desire would be the vast moon-swept, wind-tossed Pacific Ocean.

I recall one evening particularly. It was after the raid on Rabaul, one of our roughest strikes. A great number of letters had to be written that night. As I sat in my dugout going over them, the Chaplain came in—

And McCarthy, according to McCarthy, asked the Chaplain what sort of consolation to offer. The Chaplain told him to write that "we made the solemn promise that when this gory, bloody mess is over, there will arise a world that will be to some extent cleaner and finer and more decent."

It was all malarkey. He never lived in a dugout. Writing letters was none of his job. He may well have written a few —for he could be a generous and helpful soul as well as a liar—but he could not have written "a great number" in one evening or in the entire war, since the unit he was talking about, VMSB-235, lost, from start to finish, a total of five officers and two enlisted men.

By 1944, McCarthy was in a position to sustain great expectations. He had been two years a Marine and two years a judge. The scandals of his court had received far less publicity than the picture of him as a bundle of energy seeing to it that justice was not denied by being delayed. The Wisconsin press had been supplied with innumerable photographs of the warrior-jurist, generally seated in a bomber cockpit, wearing a flying helmet and grinning broadly. Also, he was moderately rich. Though his gross income from 1935 up to the time of his enlistment, as reported to the Wisconsin Department of Taxation, came to $24,867.05, he had somehow or other managed to put $50,000 into the stock market, and in 1943 netted a profit of $42,353.92. (His salary as a judge had been $8,000, which was three times what he had reported in his best year as a lawyer.) While still in the South Pacific, he decided to enter the Republican primaries in Wisconsin and contest the nomination of Senator Alexander Wiley. There were two obstacles of a legal nature to his candidacy. One was a military ruling that forbade servicemen from speaking on political issues. Another was Article 7, Section 10 of the Wisconsin Constitution, which read: "Each of the judges of the supreme circuit courts shall . . . hold no offices of public trust, except a judicial office, during the term for which they are respectively elected, and all votes [for them] for any office, except a judicial office shall be void." McCarthy overcame these with fair ease and his customary insouciance; he simply paid no attention to them, or very little. He filed, got himself home on a thirty-day pass, and made campaign speeches. He told the Milwaukee League of Women Voters that "I wish I could discuss the importance of oil and the importance of maintaining a strong army and navy . . . but I may not do so.

97

. . . If I were able to speak, here's what I'd say. . . ."
The Wisconsin Secretary of State proposed that the Attorney General take action under Article 7, Section 10.
The Attorney General said he would take the matter under
advisement; the violation, if it was one, would have to be
tried under due process, and that would take more than the
short time remaining before the primaries. McCarthy had
impressive support. His candidacy, the Wisconsin *State
Journal* said, was "a very good sign of a public awakening
to the need of vigorous intellects in high office. Captain Mc-
Carthy is the type impregnated with the mother wit and
quick, penetrating ability, gloved in prudence," etc., etc. He
lost to Senator Wiley, but he came in second in a field of
four, which was good.

He went back to the Marine Corps, and asked for a three-
month leave in which to campaign for re-election as circuit
judge; this was in October 1944, when the war in the Pacific,
in which he had enlisted for the duration, had almost a year
to run. When this request was denied, he turned in his resignation, which was accepted the following February. He
sported his limp for the first time and told the voters of his
three counties that he was "sick, sick at heart" over what
"my boys" would come home to, if they came home. He said
that his prayer each evening in the South Pacific had been,
"O, God, for one more day, spare these, my boys." He was
re-elected circuit judge in 1945, and the following year was
elected to the Senate seat held for twenty years by Robert M.
La Follette, Jr., and for twenty years before that by La Follette's father, perhaps the noblest figure in the flowering of

political idealism in the Middle West early in this century.

☞ Ironies that in retrospect became almost unbearable attended McCarthy's defeat of Robert M. La Follette, **Jr.** The younger La Follette was a man of less outward splendoi and magnetism than his father, but not of less substance. The Catiline looks had gone to his brother, Philip, who served several terms as governor of Wisconsin, and the insurgent fire had died with the father. Robert, Jr., was a gentle and inward spirit; he was also a man of fine critical intelligence and high moral purpose. He and his conqueror were antipodal in specific ways. Civil liberties knew no stouter champion than La Follette. In the thirties, he had been chairman of a Senate Civil Liberties Committee and had conducted an investigation of industrial espionage that was everything a McCarthy investigation was not. McCarthy threw the United States Senate into disorder; La Follette, in the forties, had devoted himself to bringing order into its affairs. Together with Representative (later Senator) A. S. Mike Monroney, of Oklahoma, La Follette had devised most of the structural and procedural reforms under which Congress in McCarthy's time was to function. The Committee on Government Operations, which McCarthy was to chair, was a La Follette invention. (For four years after the 1946 reorganization, it was known as the Committee on Expenditures in the Executive Departments.) The poll of correspondents and political scientists that in the fifties held McCarthy to be the "worst" Senator had in the forties held La Follette to be the "best."

99

It is unsettling to think that in a free election, in what has often been spoken of as one of the most politically civilized communities in the Western democracies, Robert La Follette, Jr., should have been defeated by a scapegrace whose campaign slogan was "Congress Needs a Tail Gunner." It happens to be a fact, though, that there is something about the United States Senate, something about its role in government and its place in American thinking, that makes tragedies of exactly this sort every few years. The Senate offers great scope to men of intellect and imagination. They come to it as ambassadors from rather meager sovereignties, and before long they are likely to find themselves dealing with the affairs of the entire nation and of the great world beyond its shores and borders. If their interests and aptitudes are engaged by their opportunities, they are very likely to alienate—and become alienated from—the provincial politicians upon whose favor they are dependent. The more time they devote to seeking just solutions to national and international problems, the less time they have for dipping into the pork barrel for the people back home, for chatting with constituents who have just come to Capitol Hill from the Washington Monument or the Round Robin Bar at the Willard, or for touring the county seats and market towns at home. They neglect the grass roots; in extreme cases, they find they can no longer bear the sight of the grass roots. In time, someone, not necessarily a McCarthy, but in all likelihood a man of limited perspectives, is bound to come along and point out to the voters that their Senator has been neglecting them and their interests and has become too involved in the life of Washington and other capitals to represent the humble folk who elected him. It happens often that a Senator loses his seat because, primarily, of the distinction with which he has filled it.

This, in essence, was what happened to the younger La Follette. His political circumstances, though, were different from those of most of his colleagues. In 1946, he was seeking, for the first time, the nomination of a major party. In the past, he had been the candidate of the Progressive Party of Wisconsin, an organization whose only assets were its association with the La Follette family and its association, largely through the family, with the heroic period of insurgency. These weren't enough, in 1946, to keep a party going. Philip La Follette had not been in the State House since 1938 (he had been, through the war, an aide to General Douglas MacArthur), and insurgency was not the mood for the moment. The party disbanded early in 1946, and, largely at the urging of Senator La Follette, had voted to make a prodigal's return to its Republican parents. It was Robert A. Taft who was principally instrumental in influencing La Follette to take this course, and although the convention that liquidated the party was not of one mind (some opposed liquidation; some wished to join the Democrats), La Follette prevailed. This placed upon him the necessity of seeking the Republican nomination.

He filed, evidently with not enough appreciation of the fact that powerful Republicans would not be entirely happy to be represented in the Senate by a man noted chiefly for his championship of civil liberties, of organized labor, of the

welfare aspects of the New Deal, and of Congressional reorganization. He was not a shrewd politician; indeed, had he
not borne his father's name, he would, in all probability,
have had to seek fulfillment in some other endeavor. Nevertheless, he had always gone to the Senate with heavy Republican support, and he assumed that those who had supported him under another label would be happy to support
him under their own. Many did, but not enough. While he
stayed in Washington, working for Congressional approval
of his reorganization plan, McCarthy, who had thrust himself upon the anti-La Follette Republicans, went up and
down the state asking why La Follette stayed on his "Virginia plantation" instead of coming home to defend his
record before his own people. He described the La Follette–
Monroney Act as a grab and said it showed only that its author was "making salary increases for Congressmen his chief
concern," which was untrue. He accused La Follette of being
a slacker: "What, other than draw fat rations, did you do
for the war effort while 15,000,000 Americans were fighting
the war and 130,000,000 more were building the sinews of
war?" He asked what good had come of La Follette's service as chairman of the Committee on Labor: "Why have
you failed to do anything to create labor-management
peace?" He discovered that La Follette had a one-fourth interest in a Milwaukee radio station and that his share of the
profits over a two-year period had been $47,339, or about
five thousand dollars more than McCarthy had made in a
single wartime year in the securities market: "HOW DID LA
FOLLETTE GET THAT MONEY? NO REGULATION ON LA FOL-

LETTE'S PROFITS" a campaign tabloid screamed. And so it
went: "This is the type of thing that must be eradicated in
Washington. . . . Connections are considered necessary.
Deals are considered commonplace. The air seems to reek
with intrigue. That is why I believe new blood should be
injected. . . ."

To be precise, tail-gunner blood. A McCarthy flyer read:

JOE McCARTHY was a TAIL GUNNER in World War II.
When the war began, Joe had a soft job as a Judge at EIGHT
GRAND a year. He was EXEMPT from military duty. He re-
signed his job to enlist as a PRIVATE in the MARINES. He
fought on LAND and in the AIR all through the Pacific. He
and millions of other guys kept you from talking Japanese.
TODAY JOE McCARTHY IS HOME. He wants to SERVE
America in the SENATE. Yes, folks, CONGRESS NEEDS A
TAIL GUNNER. Now, when Washington is in confusion, when
BUREAUCRATS are seeking to perpetuate themselves FOR-
EVER upon the American way of Life, AMERICA NEEDS
FIGHTING MEN. Those men who fought upon foreign soil to
SAVE AMERICA have earned the right to SERVE AMERICA
in times of peace.

In the Republican primary, McCarthy won by 5,400 votes
out of 410,000 cast. La Follette led, though narrowly, in the
rural areas, and when this became known on Election night,
it was expected that he would get a commanding majority in
Milwaukee and the other industrial centers, where he had
always been strong. But it was in the working-class wards
that he lost, and it has often been said that he was defeated
because the Communists wanted him out of the way. The
Communists despised Robert La Follette because he was,

like his father, a liberal who regarded Communism as totalitarian. He was thoroughly aware of the Stalinist penetration of the labor movement, which was especially notable in Milwaukee, where Communists controlled the United Automobile Workers and the machinery of the Congress of Industrial Organizations. Neither the Communists nor the C.I.O. did anything to save La Follette's seat. "The people will not mourn La Follette," the *Daily Worker* announced, and McCarthy was reported to have said, when accused of having Communist support, "Communists have the same right to vote as anyone else, don't they?" But the known facts will not sustain the theory that McCarthy owed his nomination to the votes controlled by Communists in Milwaukee. There is no evidence that the Communists instructed their following to enter the Republican primaries or gave McCarthy any assistance beyond their generalized attacks on La Follette.*

McCarthy won the general election with fair ease. His opponent was Howard MacMurray, a scholar from the University of Wisconsin who had served briefly in the House. He was intelligent, courageous, and honest, and McCarthy creamed him, 640,430 to 378,772. On February 24, 1953, Robert La Follette, Jr., shot himself dead in Washington.

In McCarthy's first three years in the Senate, there was little to suggest that he would be—or even aspired to be

---

* This whole question is thoroughly canvassed in a doctoral thesis done at Princeton by Karl Ernest Meyer and titled "The Politics of Loyalty: From La Follette to McCarthy in Wisconsin, 1918-1952." I am indebted to Mr. Meyer for a chance to read his manuscript, from which I have borrowed freely.

—anything more than a competent boodler and a publicity-hungry politician of a quite ordinary sort. He was on the make with all the devices of ambition, and he was unencumbered by any sort of morality. But his ambition did not yet match his capacities.

He made a brisk-enough start in Washington. *Life* magazine chose him, evidently because it felt it had to choose someone, as the subject of a picture story on a freshman Senator, and a young woman trailed him around for a day, doing a regulation *Life* job. At the editors' request, she asked him to tell his first thoughts upon his arrival in the capital. He obliged. "When we pulled into Washington," he said, "I stepped down from the train, took a look around, and said, 'Hell, it's raining.' " His first act was to call a press conference. The boldness of it brought out a few reporters, one of whom said, "Mr. McCarthy, what makes you think a new Senator is important enough to call a news conference?" McCarthy shrugged and said he wanted to say something about the coal strike then in progress: "Let's get down to business. Now about this coal strike, I've got a solution: the Army should draft the striking coal miners. That would solve the problem." Intrigued, the reporters asked what he would do about John L. Lewis, the head of the United Mine Workers, then in his sixties. "Draft him, too," McCarthy said. "When you want me," he told the departing correspondents, "don't hesitate to call me—night or day." He arranged for some Wisconsin cheese to be sent to the National Press Club.

He soon fell in with the seediest lot in Washington—men with their sights fixed not on power in the grand, malevolent sense in which he was to come to know it, but on the fast buck. One of his first friends was John Maragon, a diminutive Greek who had once been a Kansas City bootblack and who was working his way toward notoriety as an influence peddler and the penitentiary as a perjuror. Maragon was a lobbyist for a lobbyist who worked for the Allied Molasses Company, a firm in trouble with the Department of Agriculture for having somehow got hold of a million and a half gallons of sugar-cane syrup which it refined and sold to the Pepsi-Cola Company. Under the rationing orders still in effect, Pepsi-Cola was not supposed to have it. Through Maragon, McCarthy came to know the Pepsi-Cola lobbyist, a sport named Russell Arundel, who enjoyed being known as the "Prince of Outer Baldonia." (He owned an island off Nova Scotia to which he had given this name.) In almost no time, McCarthy achieved the distinction of being the Senate spokesman for Pepsi-Cola. The man the *Times* of London regretted as seriously as any foreigner since Hitler was at one time referred to in Congress as "the Pepsi-Cola Kid," and his principal effort for advancing the general welfare in his first days in Congress was a crusade against sugar rationing. Ignoring Communists in the State Department, untroubled by the fact that the country was in the fourteenth year of the twenty years of treason, he fought like a tiger for full production of soft drinks, and he succeeded in having sugar controls lifted six months earlier than they had been scheduled to end. "The speculators are singing a *Te Deum* in their hearts tonight throughout the country," Charles W. Tobey, of New Hampshire, said on the Senate floor in Mc-

Carthy's hour of triumph. One speculator at least had reason for rejoicing. McCarthy's credit in the Appleton State
Bank had been stretched to the snapping point, and the
examiners were troubled. McCarthy sent the bank a note for
$20,000 endorsed by Russell Arundel, which was all right
for a time. When the examiners went over the books again,
though, they objected to Russell Arundel's note for the reason, as the bank's president, Matt Schuh, put it in a letter to
McCarthy, that "Mr. Arundel hasn't any liquid assets shown
on his statement." Outer Baldonia was an offshore island,
and the shore was Canada's, and a good connection with
Pepsi-Cola wasn't liquid in the examiners' terms.

McCarthy had an even more profitable association with
the real-estate lobby. He had established connections with a
number of enterprising men who saw, in postwar years, large
opportunities in the manufacture and sale of prefabricated
homes—particularly small ones to be sold at relatively low
prices. There was a large cloud on their bright horizon,
though. There was a powerful movement in Congress for
expanded federal financing of low-cost public housing, and
the movement had won a formidable recruit in Robert A.
Taft, an enemy of the welfare state who had nevertheless
come to believe that the federal government simply had to
take a hand in this matter. He had given his support to a
measure known as the Taft-Ellender-Wagner Bill, and it was
a good bet for passage. McCarthy and some other Congressmen who sided in general with the builders proposed the
creation of a Joint Congressional Housing Committee, and
the proposal was adopted. He was not the chairman, but he

assumed the largest role on the Committee, and he conducted most of its investigations; the usual cries of scandal and outrage went up, but they were muted, for the hearings did not attract much attention from the press. It was not until a good deal later that it was learned that McCarthy had become the richer by $10,000 turned over to him by the Lustron Corporation, theoretically in payment, at the handsome rate of $1.43 a word, for an essay entitled *A Dollar's Worth of Housing for Every Dollar Spent;* that the president of Lustron had been bank-rolling McCarthy's wagers at the Pimlico and Laurel tracks; or that another housing man had obligingly allowed him to get out of a crap-game debt of $5,400 by rolling double-or-nothing until the debt was wiped out. For such favors, he performed well. In the end, the Taft-Ellender-Wagner Bill was gutted by amendments, mainly by McCarthy, which amended its public-housing features out of existence.

And so things went. He skipped from issue to issue—from being the fur farmers' friend to demanding investigations of corruption in the name of dead Marines,* from seeking the

* He had a gift for giving words to this sort of piety. One of his early speeches described a visit to some Marines in a veterans' hospital: "One young man, a Marine with both legs amputated, said—I shall try to quote him as nearly verbatim as I can: 'When we were in the Islands and the days were especially rough and the number of dead and injured mounted, and you would lie there at night and listen to the moan of the jungle on the one side and the music of the sea on the other, then the veil between life and death became very, very thin, and very often your good friends who had died that day were much nearer to you than those who still lived, and we knew then and know now that many of those men died because of graft and corrup-

impeachment of the Secretary of the Navy to denouncing the foreign-aid programs just getting under way. There were intimations of the McCarthy to come, but they were faint: once he introduced a bill calling upon labor unions to report to management on Communist workers and calling upon management to fire the offenders forthwith. But Senator Taft thought the idea a terrible one, and McCarthy dropped it. On the other hand, there was this sort of thing—the insertion in the *Congressional Record* of a resolution, probably written by him, adopted by the Green Bay Diocesan Union of the Holy Name Societies at a meeting in the far-off city Shawano, which read in part:

We rejoice in what seems to be the determination of the new Secretary of State [George Catlett Marshall] to set a pattern for American diplomacy which seems to be taking the initiative in China, Korea, Japan, the Middle East, and virtually throughout the world, thus putting Communism on the defensive.

McCarthy's aspirations may have been smaller in those early Senatorial days than a sound precognition or even an appreciation of his own talents might have supported. The essential gifts were already well-developed, the innovations perfected. Writing about McCarthy in a "Letter from Washington" for the *New Yorker* in the early days of his attacks on the State Department, I described one of the most striking innovations as "the Multiple Untruth," a tech-

---

tion which the Senate proposes to investigate.'" A likely story, but he told many such, and he was accounted an earnest young Senator by many.

109

nique comparable in many respects to Hitler's Big Lie. I wrote in part: "The 'multiple untruth' need not be a particularly large untruth but can instead be a long series of loosely related untruths, or a single untruth with many facets. In either case, the whole is composed of so many parts that anyone wishing to set the record straight will discover that it is utterly impossible to keep all the elements of the falsehood in mind at the same time. Anyone making the attempt may seize upon a few selected statements and show them to be false, but doing this may leave the impression that only the statements selected are false and that the rest are true. An even greater advantage of the 'multiple untruth' is that statements shown to be false can be repeated over and over again with impunity because no one will remember which statements have been disproved and which haven't." The technique was not one he had developed for his debut but one that had been in his bag of tricks since his days as a back-country campaigner in Wisconsin. And he had used it in his first days in Congress. In the floor debate over sugar rationing in 1947, he pitched around so many random facts and figures that two New England apostles of reasoned argument, both of whom were to play a part in his eventual downfall, had to complain: "The Senator from Wisconsin," Ralph Flanders said, "has raised questions so fast that I am having difficulty in keeping up with him"; and Senator Tobey: "I point out that the Senator is confusing the Senate of the United States by a heterogeneous mass of figures which will not stand the test of accuracy."

As it happened, I got a taste of his flimflammery the first time I met him, which was about a year before he emerged from the shoddy world of John Maragon, Carl Strandlund, and the Prince of Outer Baldonia. In May of 1949, I was in Washington—reporting on the founding sessions of the North Atlantic Treaty Organization—and in an idle moment I dropped in at a hearing at which testimony was being taken on the alleged mistreatment by Americans of some German S.S. men, members of an outfit prettily called the Blowtorch Battalion, who had been accused of massacring a hundred and fifty United States troops and a hundred Belgian civilians at a crossroads village named Malmédy five years earlier. I had been in the hearing room only a few minutes when McCarthy became involved in an altercation with Raymond Baldwin, a fellow Republican who was shortly to resign—on the ground that suffering McCarthy's abuse was too far above and beyond the call of duty for a Senator in time of peace—to become a judge of the Supreme Court of Errors in his home state.

It was an angry exchange. McCarthy said that the Americans had in fact been guilty of brutal conduct. In this brush with the Army, he claimed that it was coddling, not Communists, but sadists. He said he had proof but that Baldwin, intent for some unexplained reason on protecting the accused men, would pay no attention to it. Baldwin said he wasn't trying to protect anyone. After a while, McCarthy rose from his seat, stuffed a lot of papers into his briefcase, and left the room, saying he would no longer be party to a "shameful

111

farce . . . a deliberate and clever attempt to whitewash the American military," for which, as he later said, Baldwin was "criminally responsible."

Curious about the dispute and at that time ignorant of its background,* I followed McCarthy into the corridor and asked him if he would be kind enough to tell me why he was in such a stew. He said he would be pleased to, and suggested that I go with him to his office. "These documents will speak for themselves." He hefted up the bulging briefcase to give me some idea of the sheer bulk of them. "When you've looked at a few of my documents, you'll agree with me that this is one of the most outrageous things the country has ever known." I said that if this was the case, I would certainly feel privileged to be allowed to inspect them. "You'll see them all right, all right," he said. "I'm not hold-

---

* The background, as it later turned out, was interesting. The Nazis who were doing time or awaiting execution for the massacre wished—as what criminals do not?—to claim a frame-up. They found a champion in a man named Rudolph Aschenauer, a Communist agitator who evidently saw in the Malmédy affair a means of spreading anti-Americanism. By what means we do not know—but probably through pro-Nazis among Wisconsin German-Americans—he got in touch with McCarthy. He gave McCarthy the countercharges of the S.S. men—that their confessions had been tortured from them by lighted matches under the fingernails, by being clubbed in the stomach, by violence upon their sex organs, and so on. McCarthy publicized these charges in the Senate; Aschenauer picked them up from the American Senator and got them into the German press. The Military Affairs Committee found no evidence in support of Aschenauer's charges. McCarthy had been had by a Communist agent.

ing anything back. I'm through with this lousy investigation, and I'm taking my case to the public."

He struck me as being a bit overwrought, but on the whole he seemed an earnest and plausible young Senator. Though he used extravagant language, his tone was restrained, his manner almost gentle. As we walked along through the corridors, he kept talking of the magnitude of his revelations, and although I had wanted—for a starter at least—just a brief résumé of his side of the story, he succeeded in whetting my appetite for the contents of the briefcase.

We reached his office at last and sat down at his desk. He emptied the briefcase and piled up the papers in front of him. "Let's see now," he said as he thumbed his way down toward the middle of the pile, "I've got one document here that's a real eye-opener. Oh, yes, here we are now." He pulled out several pages of photostat paper and handed them to me. "I think the facts will mean more to you than anything I could say."

I read rapidly through what he gave me. Then I read it a second time, more carefully. When I'd finished the second reading, I was certain that the Senator had selected the wrong document. I no longer recall just what was in it, but it was a letter from one Army officer or government official to another, and it didn't seem to me to prove anything about anything. I told McCarthy that as far as I could see, it was a pretty routine piece of correspondence.

"You're certainly right about that," he said. "Don't get me wrong, now. I didn't mean you'd find the *whole* story

there. Standing alone, it doesn't mean much. I know that just
as well as you do. But it's a link in a chain. It's one piece in
a jigsaw puzzle. When you've seen some of these other documents, you'll know what I mean."

This was reassuring. In fact, I felt a bit ashamed of myself for expecting to master a complex situation in a few
minutes. I read the next document McCarthy handed me.
"Now, when you put these two together," he said, "you get
a picture." The second document was mainly a listing of
names. None of them meant anything to me. I tried to think
what connection they might have with the letter I'd just read
or with Senator Baldwin. I tried to "put them together," as
McCarthy had advised, and "get a picture." No picture came.
I confessed this to McCarthy.

"Exactly," he said. "That's exactly my point. Those names
mean nothing to *you*. They didn't mean anything to me,
either, when I began to look into this conspiracy. But they're
going to mean something to you—I can guarantee you that.
I wanted you to have a look at them, because when you've
seen some of the other things I've got here, you'll see how
this jigsaw puzzle fits together. Now just bear those names
in mind."

I tried to bear the names in mind. It was impossible.
Nothing unsticks faster than names you can't associate with
real people. But although it was, I thought, curious that
McCarthy hadn't shown me the documents explaining the
significance of the names before showing me the names themselves, I continued to be impressed by his manner. And the
papers themselves were impressive—not by virtue of their

contents but by virtue of their existence. Photostats and carbon copies and well-kept newspaper clippings have, I think, an authority of their own for most people; we assume that no one would go to the bother of assembling them if they didn't prove *something*.

As McCarthy sat at his desk sorting out the papers, putting some in a stack to his right and some in a stack to his left and consigning others to a filing cabinet behind him, he seemed knowledgeable and efficient. "I'm just trying to put this picture together for you," he kept saying. Two or three times in the course of our interview, he called in a secretary and asked her to fetch him some document that wasn't among those he had taken to the hearing. I wondered as I watched him what had become of the promise to provide a blinding illumination with a single document, but for quite a while I assumed it was my fault, not his, that I wasn't grasping the details very well.

He kept handing papers across the desk to me. "Here are a few more links in the chain," he would say as he handed me more correspondence, more lists, and many pictures of the Germans who had accused the Americans of brutality, of the accused Americans, of Malmédy farmhouses, of Army barracks in occupied Germany. None of them seemed to advance his argument by very much, but then he was no longer claiming very much for them.

At one point he handed me a rather thick document. "I don't want you to leave without seeing this," he said. "Here we have the facts in the Army's own records. This is a transcript of the first hearing on this affair. This is what Baldwin

115

and the administration are trying to cover up. Remember, now, this is from the Army files—its own records."

I read here and there in the Army files, and told McCarthy that, perhaps because of my ignorance, I was unable to see any holes in the Army's case.

"Of course you don't," he said. "Naturally, they're going to make out the best case they can for themselves. You wouldn't expect them to spill the beans in their own records, would you? The whole thing is a pack of lies."

I was beginning to get impatient, though I tried not to show it. I said that as I understood the situation, he, McCarthy, was persuaded that the Malmédy massacre was a fiction of our own military authorities, that Germans had been tortured into confessing acts that had never been committed, and that a Republican Senator, a man with a considerable reputation for probity, was trying to protect the torturers. I was about to go on to say that thus far nothing he had shown me established the truth of all this. But McCarthy interrupted me.

"That's right," he said, in a manner that suggested appreciation of my insight and my gift of summation. "You're beginning to get the picture now. Now I'll show you some of the affidavits we've gathered on this case."

He handed me a stack of affidavits. They were the sworn statements of the S.S. men held as war criminals, and they alleged the most hideous mistreatment by the Americans. It was because these statements were being published in newspapers throughout Germany and, the government had been advised, were being believed by large numbers of Germans

116

that the Senate Armed Services Committee had decided to conduct its own hearings, under Senator Baldwin. Although McCarthy had given the impression of resigning from this group, the fact, as I later learned, was that he couldn't resign, because he hadn't been a member to begin with. He had merely exercised the Senatorial privilege of sitting with the Committee during the hearings, at which he had done most of the talking. He was able to do this, incidentally, only after he had won a long fight to get from Senator Baldwin the right, which isn't normally regarded as part of the privilege, to cross-examine all the witnesses.

After scanning some of the affidavits, I said that while it was entirely conceivable that a Nazi under sentence of death or imprisonment could be telling the truth about his own past behavior, it was at least equally conceivable that he would falsify. I wondered, I said, what McCarthy had in the way of evidence that it was not the convicted Nazis but the Americans who were lying. "You've put your finger on it," he said. "Those are precisely the facts that Baldwin and the administration don't want me to bring out. That's why I walked out of that hearing. They're concealing all the evidence. I've shown you some of the pieces in this jigsaw puzzle, and believe me, when I take this story before the American people, the truth will be forced to come out."

I asked McCarthy if he had anything else he wanted to show me. "Well, I've got the affidavits of the Army people here," he said. "But I guess you can imagine what's in them. Lies from start to finish. Naturally, they're trying to protect themselves. I've got them here if you want to see what's in

117

them." I said I thought I'd skip them. I thanked the Senator for his courtesy and left.

I was not aware then of having been switched, conned, and double-shuffled by one of the masters.

 *Great Days*

No one was more astonished than McCarthy by the furor he raised in February 1950. He was a stranger to the controversies in which he found himself taking part and to the peculiar world of the controversialists. He had trifled a bit with the Communist issue: describing his opponent in the general elections as a "pinko . . . nothing more than a megaphone being used by the Communist-controlled P.A.C."; attempting to discredit public housing by saying the Communists favored it; putting in a bill to have Communist workers in industry sacked. But this was all part of the cant of the day, which he knew well enough; in the late forties, politicians of a certain

119

kind were using "pinko" and "Communistically inclined" in much the way that, in an earlier time, others had used "the interests" and "Wall Street" and others "anarchism" oɪ "alien philosophy." But beyond this playing with nonce words, he had had nothing to say about Communism, and his voting record on the Cold War was that of a man who had not yet conceded its existence.

McCarthy took up the Communist menace in 1950 not with any expectation that it would make him a sovereign of the assemblies, but with the simple hope that it would help him hold his job in 1952. He could not take re-election for granted. In 1946, he had performed a notable feat in bringing an end to the La Follette dynasty in the Senate, but luck as well as good management had played its part. It was a great Republican year. The party had gained thirteen seats in the Senate and fifty-seven in the House of Representatives —the Eightieth Congress was the first since the Hoover administration to come under Republican control. (Thirteen years later, in 1959, the Republican National Chairman, H. Meade Alcorn, recalled it as the only time in three decades in which the party had "won what could properly be called a national party victory.") However, 1948 had brought a strong reaction to 1946. Harry Truman won his stunning victory over Thomas E. Dewey after a campaign in which he had done little but denounce the first Congress in which McCarthy had served as "that do-nothing, good-for-nothing Eightieth Congress." The country gave Truman a Democratic legislature, and in retrospect, the 1946 elections took on a rather freakish look. It was only prudent for a man like

McCarthy, who was capable of prudence in matters affecting his own welfare, to reason that his second run might be harder than his first. He had made some good connections in Washington and had doubtless bettered his own lot, but he had not done much to commend himself to his constituents. They would not be much impressed with his services to Pepsi-Cola or Lustron. His defense of the German principals in the Malmédy affair may have been pleasing to some of the German-Americans in his state, but those people alone weren't of much help. Taking one consideration with another, he had been a rotten Senator—as the correspondents who were soon to vote him "the worst" were even then aware.

Moreover, word of his malpractices and of his chiseling was beginning to circulate in Wisconsin. The Milwaukee *Journal* and the Madison *Capital-Times* dug up the stories of divorce scandals in his court. He had filed no returns with the state Department of Taxation on his stock-market killings in 1943. The Department called this to his attention, and he claimed that he had not been a resident of Wisconsin but a tail gunner in the South Pacific that year; the Department ruled that this was nonsense and forced him to pony up $2,677. In 1949, the Board of Bar Commissioners censured him for violating the state Constitution and its own code of ethics by running for the Senate while holding a judgeship. An examination of the reports of his 1946 campaign committee showed contributions amounting to $18,000 reported as coming from his father, his brother, and his brother-in-law, none of whom, according to their own tax returns, had ever had that kind of money. (And none of whom, for that matter, had ever shown any interest in Joseph McCarthy's political career.) In general, he did not add luster to the Wisconsin tradition of public service.

On January 7, 1950, at the Colony Restaurant in Washington, McCarthy confided to three dinner companions that he stood in need of a dramatic issue for the 1952 campaign. The three were the late Father Edmund A. Walsh, regent of the School of Foreign Service at Georgetown University; Charles H. Kraus, a professor of political science at Georgetown; and William A. Roberts, then a Washington attorney and businessman. None was a close friend of McCarthy's or a close political associate. Roberts was a Democrat and a liberal; the other two had no party affiliations, but it is safe to assume that neither had much in common with McCarthy's kind of politics. What all four had in common was Roman Catholicism, and Kraus had arranged the gathering in order to encourage in a young Catholic Senator a serious approach to serious matters. He had been urging McCarthy to read Father Walsh's recent books, which dealt with the problems of resistance to world Communism, and he was having McCarthy meet the distinguished priest, educator, and publicist for the first time. McCarthy brought up the question of his pressing need of an issue. Roberts suggested that McCarthy come forward as a champion of the St. Lawrence Seaway. McCarthy said he didn't think that would do. He asked the others what they thought about some up-to-date variant of the Townsend Plan—a hundred dollars a month pension, say, to everyone over sixty-five. The others disapproved—too demagogic, they felt. Father Walsh then suggested Communism—its power

122

in the world at large and its capacity for subversion. Mc-
Carthy seized upon the idea at once and at once began, according to one of the participants, to vulgarize. "That's it,"
he said. "The government is full of Communists," he said.
"We can hammer away at them." The group adjourned to
Roberts' office in the DeSales Building, adjoining the Colony,
and continued the discussion. McCarthy was warned of the
dangers of an irresponsible approach to these matters. He
left saying that he wouldn't think of making an irresponsible
approach. Within a matter of months, all three of his companions felt called upon to repudiate him.

Sometime after the dinner at the Colony, McCarthy asked
the Senate Republican Campaign Committee to assign him
to speak on Communists in government and to get him some
bookings for the Lincoln's Birthday weekend—a time as important to Republican members of Congress as the pre-Christ-
mas selling days are to owners of department stores. (Abra-
ham Lincoln did an immense service to his party by being
born at just that time of year when the lines are firmly drawn
and the issues before Congress are, momentarily at least, of
marvelous clarity. Mid-February, when promises have been
made but are far from being due for redemption, is an excellent time for orators from Capitol Hill.) The bookings he
got were not of the best. He was to open at Wheeling, West
Virginia, on February 9 before the Ohio County Women's
Republican Club and then go on to Salt Lake City and Reno
for other meetings.

One of the large advantages enjoyed by a man adept in the
use of the Multiple Untruth is that of appearing to have done

123

a great deal of research when in fact none or very little has been done. The Wheeling ladies who on February 9 heard McCarthy say that he had the names of 205 (or 81 or 57) Communists in the State Depa.tment must have felt that a man who had made such a precise compilation had surely gone to some lengths to get hold of the facts. After all, Madame Chairman had never come up with such exact and important information—nor had Westbrook Pegler or George Sokolsky. There is no reason to believe, however, that between the Colony dinner on January 7 and the Wheeling speech on February 9 McCarthy undertook anything more strenuous than reaching for the telephone a couple of times and scribbling down a few notes. It is known that he called Willard Edwards, a member of the Washington bureau of the Chicago *Tribune* and asked for assistance on a speech about Communists in the government. This was something about which Edwards had written extensively, though not, so far as anyone had observed, with anything like an abundance of detail. In any case, Edwards was co-operative, to the extent of drawing McCarthy's attention to some material on State Department loyalty procedures gathered in the Eightieth Congress by the House Committee on Appropriations and to a letter written on July 26, 1946, by James F. Byrnes, Truman's Secretary of State. The letter from Byrnes was in response to an inquiry from Representative Adolph Sabath, of Illinois, and this now historic document reads in part:

Pursuant to Executive Order, approximately 4,000 employees have been transferred. . . . Of those 4,000 employees, the case histories of approximately 3,000 have been subjected to a pre-

124

liminary examination, as a result of which a recommendation against permanent employment has been made in 284 cases by the screening committee to which you refer in your letter. . . . Of the 79 actually separated from the service, 26 were aliens and therefore under "political disability" with respect to employment in the peacetime operations of the Department. I assume that factor alone could be considered the principal basis for their separation.

From this dusty veteran of the file drawers, with its obsolete statistics, compiled for the predecessor of the predecessor of the then Secretary of State, McCarthy elaborated the myth on which his whole subsequent career was based. He said time and again that the Byrnes letter was what he held aloft before the Wheeling ladies, and probably it was. That letter and some hasty notes, most of which he subsequently mislaid, were all that he had when, according to a report by Frank Desmond of the Wheeling *Intelligencer,* he said:

While I cannot take the time to name all of the men in the State Department who have been named as members of the Communist Party and members of a spy ring, I have here in my hand a list of two-hundred and five that were known to the Secretary of State as being members of the Communist Party and who nevertheless are still working and shaping the policy of the State Department.

Not many sentences spoken in this century have been subjected to quite so much exegesis and controversy as this one. And not many have been less worthy of it. For what McCarthy was reported to have said was not only untrue—it was, on the face of it, utterly preposterous. Why couldn't he have taken the time to have named a few on his list, if he had had a list?

125

And if he had a list, where on earth would he have got it? Who would have given it to him? The FBI? The State Department? Why? Could he have worked it up himself? Conceivably—if the data had existed, which it did not. But if he had had such a list, or even a single name, why on earth, as William Shannon of the New York *Post* once asked, would he have chosen to make his shattering announcement "before a group of Republican ladies in a Triple-I League town?" *
The speech was reported in the Wheeling *Intelligencer* and the Chicago *Tribune;* the Associated Press picked up a couple of paragraphs from Desmond's *Intelligencer* copy, but its bulletin got scarcely any circulation. The only other coverage was in a tape recording, made for rebroadcast over Station WWVA and erased almost immediately following its use. It was not until three days later that the New York *Times* made its first mention of the whole affair.

McCarthy was obviously unprepared to find himself the cause of a major sensation. He had reasoned, one imagines, that by the time the weekend was over and he had spoken in Salt Lake City and Reno as well as in Wheeling, word would have got back to Wisconsin that the state's junior Senator had become a figure of a certain prominence in the ranks of the Communist-hunters. Extravagant representation had always been part of his method, and while it had generally paid off in one way or another, it had never made him a national fig-

---

* Wheeling is not in the Three-I League, but it might be. When the population of Steubenville, Ohio, is joined to that of Wheeling, the urban complex formed by the two makes, according to the 1950 census, the forty-eighth largest metropolitan area in the United States.

ure. He was not prepared to be one now. He had not even taken the simple precaution of keeping the materials for his speech in Wheeling so that he would know for a certainty what he had said there. Frederick Woltman, who befriended him in his early days as a recruit to anti-Communism, recalled how "on a number of occasions—mostly in my apartment in the Congressional [Hotel]—I heard McCarthy and his advisors wrack their brains for some lead as to what he said in that Wheeling speech. He had no copy . . . he could not find the notes. . . . The Senator's staff could find no one who could recall what he'd said precisely. He finally hit on the idea of appealing to ham radio operators in the area who might have made a recording of the speech. He could find none."

All this was some time later. In the immediate aftermath of Wheeling, he simply threw up smoke screens. Although the speech had received slight notice in the press, word of it quickly reached the State Department, which wired him a request for the names he had said he had and promised a prompt investigation of the 205. He panicked in an uncharacteristic way—possibly because he feared that some part of what he had said was actionable—and in Denver, en route to Salt Lake City, he claimed to have been misquoted. He brought his remarks more or less in line with the Byrnes letter and said he had spoken not of 205 Communists but of "205 bad security risks." (Subtracting the 79 whose employment had been terminated from the 284 the screening committee had recommended for discharge did, in a manner of speaking, justify the figure, as of 1946; by the same reasoning, though,

127

if someone checked * and found that all these people were still in the State Department, it could have been maintained that the 205, having survived the years and all security proceedings, had proved to be not bad but good risks.) In Salt Lake City he came up with a new figure and a new version of Wheeling. He told his Salt Lake audience:

Last night I discussed the Communists in the State Department. I stated that I had the names of 57 card-carrying members of the Communist Party.

There was no toying with the statistics in the Byrnes letter that would yield this Heinz Varieties figure, though some reporter reasoned that he might have taken the square root of the Wheeling figure and multiplied it by four for good measure. (The true origin was not to come out for several days. The State Department in 1948 had advised the House Appropriations Committee that of 108 employees whose files the Committee had studied, 51 were no longer in the Department. Thus, in 1948, 57 remained.) Reporters asked if they could see the list. McCarthy said he would show it only to Dean Acheson. Before leaving Salt Lake, he was interviewed on the local radio by a man named Dan Valentine:

MCCARTHY: Last night I discussed the Communists in the State Department. I stated that I had the names of 57 card-

* Actually, someone, Alfred Friendly of the Washington *Post*, did check. In *Harper's* for August 1950, he revealed that 65 of the 205 had been in the State Department the preceding February. I am much indebted to Friendly's heroic labors of analysis for the material in the pages directly following.

carrying members of the Communist Party. . . . Now I want to tell [Acheson] this: if he wants to call me tonight at the Utah Hotel, I will be glad to give him the names of those 57 card-carrying Communists. . . .

VALENTINE: In other words, Senator, if Secretary of State Dean Acheson would call you at the Utah Hotel tonight in Salt Lake City, you could give him 57 names of actual card-carrying Communists in the State Department of the United States—actual card-carrying Communists.

McCARTHY: Not only can, Dan, but will. . . .

VALENTINE: Well, I am just a common man out here in Salt Lake City, a man who's got a family and a son and a job. You mean to say there's 57 Communists in our State Department that direct or control our State Department policy or help direct it?

McCARTHY: Well, Dan, I don't want to indicate there are only 57, I say I have the names of 57.

Dean Acheson wasn't tuned in on Salt Lake that night and didn't telephone the Utah Hotel. But a second Department wire went off in the morning, and, in Washington, Lincoln White, a Department officer said, "We know of no Communist member of the Department and if we find any they will be summarily discharged." The fuss was beginning to build up. McCarthy told the press that if the President would phone him at the Utah Hotel, the President could have the names. But he wired the President something a bit different: "WHILE THE RECORDS ARE NOT AVAILABLE TO ME I KNOW ABSOLUTELY OF ONE GROUP OF APPROXIMATELY THREE HUNDRED CERTIFIED TO THE SECRETARY FOR DISCHARGE BECAUSE OF COMMUNISM. HE ACTUALLY ONLY DISCHARGED APPROXIMATELY EIGHTY." It sounded as if he had mislaid his copy of the

Byrnes letter. The President did not phone. McCarthy went on to Reno and said:

In my opinion the State Department, which is one of the most important government departments, is thoroughly infested with Communists. I have in my hand 57 cases of individuals who would appear to be either card-carrying members or certainly loyal to the Communist Party but who nevertheless are still helping to shape our foreign policy.

He returned from Reno to face a demand, which he was eager to satisfy, that he explain himself before the Senate. He did so, after a fashion, in six wild hours on the floor on the night of February 20, and he kept at it until early summer. Wheeling's 205 gave way to the 57 of Salt Lake and Reno; to the 81 of February 20; to the 10 of the open Tydings Committee hearings; to the 116 of the executive sessions; to 1 when he said he would stand or fall on the single case of Owen Lattimore; to 121 in the closing phases of the investigation; to the 106 of a Senate speech on June 6—of which, he said, at least three were still employed by the State Department. And sometimes, for a change of pace, he had nothing. "Unfortunately, I cannot get the names of those 205 accused persons," he said on a "Meet the Press" interview on April 21, while insisting, of course, that the 205 were "all still working for the State Department." What he meant was that he could not risk giving out names when he was not cloaked in Senatorial immunity; actually, he was by then trading heavily in names on the floor of the Senate. Moreover, he had twice assured the Senate he would resign if he ever refused to say off the floor what he had said on the floor.

☞ The February 20 speech in the Senate made one of the maddest spectacles in the history of representative government. Late in the afternoon, a three-bell quorum call was sounded, and available members of what is often—and with some justice—called the world's greatest deliberative body filed into the chamber to deliberate McCarthy's extraordinary and extraordinarily varied assertions. At the appointed hour, McCarthy appeared, clutching the bulging briefcase that was to become his emblem. He began on a note of relative candor: "I wish to discuss a subject tonight which concerns me more than [any] I shall ever have the good fortune to discuss in the future." He announced that he had penetrated "Truman's iron curtain of secrecy" and that he proposed forthwith to present 81 cases, without identification. The figure 81 was new. What relation did it have, the Majority Leader asked, to the 205 and the 57? "I do not believe I mentioned the figure 205," he said. "I believe I said over 200." But the 81 he was now discussing embraced the 57 and included 24 more cases. Cases of exactly what? "I am only giving the Senate," he said, "cases in which it is clear there is a definite Communist connection . . . persons whom I consider to be Communists in the State Department." But soon enough it turned out that he didn't want it thought that all 81 were *presently* in the State Department. "I may say that I know that some of these individuals whose cases I am giving the Senate are no

131

longer in the State Department. A sizeable number of them are not." And the Senate would be mistaken if it concluded that every last one was a Communist. Some, he said, were not Communists.

Some, in fact, were not anything. Cases 15, 27, 37, and 59 simply never showed up; he skipped them entirely. Cases 21 through 26 were identified only by the fact that they worked for the Voice of America. Cases 1 and 2 and several others worked for the United Nations. Case 3 was the same as Case 4; Case 9 was the same as Case 77. Case 14—who was "primarily a morals case"—turned up in Case 41, of which he was not the principal, and was such a vigorous anti-Communist that Dean Acheson had fired him. Cases 13 and 78 were only applicants for State Department jobs—or had been in 1948. There was nothing on Case 52 except that he was subordinate to Case 16, "who, the State Department files indicate, was one of the most dangerous espionage agents in the Department." Case 12 used to be a Department of Commerce employee, but McCarthy had no idea "where he is as of today. I frankly do not know." Case 62 was "not important insofar as Communistic activities are concerned." Of Case 40, he said, "I do not have much information on this except the general statement of the agency [unidentified] that there is nothing in the files to disprove his Communist connections."

One case was notable, McCarthy pointed out, "in that it is the direct opposite of the cases I have been reading. . . . I do not confuse this man as being a Communist. This individual was very highly recommended by several witnesses as a high type of man, a Democratic American who . . . opposed Communism." Also, the man had never worked for the State Department. This was Case 72 "of those I consider to be Communists in the State Department."

It was a flabbergasting performance, lasting from late afternoon almost until midnight. Senators drifted in and out of the chamber as McCarthy, growing hoarser, redder, and less coherent, shuffled about the idiotic "dossiers" that were spread untidily over two desks and that were plainly as foreign to him as they were to the other Senators.* Scott Lucas interrupted sixty-one times, mainly in a futile effort to make McCarthy straighten out his mixed-up figures. Brien McMahon, of Connecticut, called from a Georgetown party by the sergeant at arms (it was the first time in five years that the sergeant at arms had been instructed to use his powers to "compel" members to come to the floor), appeared in white tie late in the evening and made thirty-four vain attempts to have McCarthy submit to a testing of his claims against reason and evidence—to conduct the debate within the framework of rationality as rationality is codified in the Senate rules. Other Senators tried, too, but it was useless. He would

---

* The source of the "dossiers" was revealed the next day. He was simply reading, obviously for the first time, the files supplied the House Appropriations Committee by the State Department. He took the 57 cases the Department had said were then in its employ and filled them out with some of those who had left the Department in 1948 or earlier. The House Foreign Affairs Committee and the Committee on Expenditures had also studied these on February 20, 1950. The means by which McCarthy had penetrated "Truman's iron curtain of secrecy" might have been explained. Not that this would have mattered much one way or the other—he survived far more damaging revelations.

not explain, he would not amplify, he would not qualify--
yet, and this was always part of his method, he would employ
all the cant of rational discourse, all its paraphernalia, all its
moods and tones and tenses. Cornered on the conflicts in his
totals, he said, "Let's stop this silly numbers game." Asked
if the report in the Wheeling *Intelligencer* was correct, he said,
"I may say, if the Senator [Lucas] is going to make a farce of
this, I will not yield to him. I shall not answer any more silly
questions of the Senator. This is too important, too serious a
matter for that." Confronted with a request for clearer language, he said, "I am afraid that if it is not clear to the Senator
[Herbert Lehman] now, I shall never be able to make it clear
to him, no matter how much further explanation I make."
On the Majority Leader's motion, the session broke up a bit
before midnight.

It had all been rather like dealing with the manifold improvisations of a child too innocent ever to have entertained the
proposition that honesty has its uses even for the dishonest,
yet worldly enough to know how to sow confusion and doubt.
The language and the modes of adult discourse had been inadequate to the challenge.

☞ In the aftermath of Wheeling, or, at the very latest,
in the aftermath of February 20, a great *aura popularis* must
have come shimmering into his field of vision. From this point
on, it could never be doubted that his expectations were, if
not limitless, great. Henceforth, he addressed himself only to
large tasks, to large audiences, in a large manner.

It was not Washington's reaction that emboldened him.

134

That had been, by almost any measure, terrible. In that stupefying evening on the Senate floor, he had had no defenders. A couple of his party comrades—Owen Brewster, of Maine, and Karl Mundt, of South Dakota—had now and then risen to say that the Truman security program was inadequate and that there certainly had been Communists in the government, but no one gave him any real support, and the Republican leadership in the Senate maintained that it would not make a defense of McCarthy's charges a matter of policy. Robert Taft, though he enjoyed anything that discomfited the administration, said he thought McCarthy, whom he knew hardly at all at the time, must surely be daft. "It was a perfectly reckless performance," he said. Kenneth Wherry, of Nebraska, a mortician from Pawnee City who was briefly the Republican floor leader, had dutifully given McCarthy whatever parliamentary advantages it had been within his power to win, but he avoided making common cause with him. In the ranks of the militant anti-Communists which McCarthy sought to join, dismay prevailed. Richard Nixon and the other members of the House Un-American Activities Committee considered him a disaster. In New York, Eugene Lyons, a journalistic éminence grise of the movement, took the view in the *New Leader* that "the luck of the Communists . . . held good" when McCarthy cast himself as the latest Hercules. The earlier stable-cleaners—Martin Dies, of Texas, John Rankin, of Mississippi, J. Parnell Thomas, of New Jersey—had been fools or worse, and now the ultimate fool, a paragon of ignorance and innocence and irresponsibility, had come to succeed them and to make a mockery of true, dis-

135

interested anti-Communism. The masses would be further mis-led, Lyons feared, "but the hooting and whistling of the press and on the air should not be permitted to drown out the facts that those stables need cleaning." Even his syntax went awry as he contemplated the disaster.

But Taft, Wherry, Lyons, and the rest were to see things very differently within a matter of weeks. Once McCarthyism took hold, Taft, the sea-green incorruptible of the Right, encouraged its author to keep on with his accusations on the ground that the law of possibilities could not in the long run fail him. "If one case doesn't work, try another," he told McCarthy. To Kenneth Wherry and the rest of the Republican leadership, McCarthy was, within a matter of weeks, to become pure gold—a partisan with a bipartisan following. And to the veteran anti-Communists like Eugene Lyons, he was to become a great pagan ally—a man of action, a man of the people, a lighter of prairie fires. He was crude, he was unwashed, he was unversed in the theology, but what did any of this matter in so long as he had the ear of the people and was able to be heard when he said the stables needed cleaning?

In almost no time, it became evident that he did have the ear of the people. He gained it at first by the unexpected force of the Multiple Untruth. To those who had been on the Senate floor and in the galleries on the night of February 20, it had seemed that the only thing to be taken seriously about him was his capacity to bore and exhaust his critics; he had shown himself to be not only dishonest, but fatuous—perhaps, indeed, crazy. (Could anything but sheer lunacy lead a man discussing eighty-one Communists to say that one of the Communists was an important example because he was not a Communist?) To thoughtful readers of the thoughtful press, similar conclusions would commend themselves. But the accounts of that night that reached most people were of necessity foreshortened. Few newspapers could print—because few readers would read—reports of a length sufficient to give the true gamey flavor of the performance. Even if they had wished to do so, it would have been difficult to get the reports, for McCarthy's presentation had been so disorderly, so jumbled and cluttered and loose-ended, that it was beyond the power of most reporters to organize the mess into a story that would convey to the reader anything beyond the suspicion that the reporter was drunk. There was a bedlam quality to McCarthy's speeches that seldom got through to those who never read them.

What did filter through, then, to a moderately conscientious reader of a moderately conscientious newspaper was the news that a United States Senator had delivered a long and angry speech giving what he claimed were details on eighty-one persons who he insisted were Communists in the State Department. It would be clear to the reader, of course, that McCarthy's assertions had met with severe criticism—that he had failed to convince many of his peers; it would also be clear that he had revised his figures a good deal over the fortnight that had passed since he first spoke on the subject. But no newspaper could print the truth—because no newspaper could be sure it *was* the truth—that he had failed to identify even one Communist in the State Department. The

137

reader might be advised by a favorite columnist or radio commentator that McCarthy's past record did not inspire much confidence; at the same time, if he sought further enlightenment, he would be reminded that it had been far from impossible for Communists to get into the State Department. Alger Hiss had been convicted just a month earlier, and the Hiss trial had produced the name of at least one other Communist, Julian Wadleigh, who had betrayed Department secrets.

In the circumstances, there were three possible views for the citizen who brought to a consideration of McCarthy's early speeches no very close knowledge of the materials he was dealing with and no prejudices that would overpower judgment altogether. In the first, he could be disregarded on the ground that what he was saying was preposterous. If he knew of 205 or 81 or 57 Communists, why hadn't he, in two weeks, stepped out and named one or two instead of beating around the bush with elastic figures and fishy-sounding case numbers? The man had the look and sound of a fourflusher, and until he produced something, there was no reason to believe he was anything else. In the second view, the evidence could be held to be inconclusive. McCarthy had not yet proved that there were any Communists in the State Department, and at the same time no one else had proved there were none. Obviously, the whole matter called for suspended judgment. In the third view, it was reasonable to give him most of the benefit of the doubt. This he merited because his figures were so large; he might be wrong about even the lowest of his figures, but the chances were against a United States Sena-

tor being *entirely* wrong. Surely he wouldn't dare get up on
the Senate floor and make such large claims if he couldn't
back up *any* of them. Holders of this view would not necessarily be upset by the fact that McCarthy had changed his
totals several times. This was a matter in which accuracy was
difficult to achieve; the Communists, obviously, wouldn't provide the Senator with exact details on their penetration of the
government, and naturally an administration embarrassed as
this one was would try to deny everything. A man trying to
get the facts was up against formidable odds, and he was not
to be held to strict account on every detail. Assume that there
was a small kernel of truth in what McCarthy had said—and
there is generally a kernel of truth in what any man says—
and the situation would be quite alarming enough.

Thus, the Multiple Untruth created for McCarthy an audience he would not have had if he had been a simpler or more
modest liar. If he had said, at the outset, that he knew of *one*
Communist in the State Department or even of three or four,
and if he had failed to prove his case pretty quickly, he would
have lost the suspended-judgment school early in the day and
some of the benefit-of-the-doubt school not long after. But as
things turned out, there was little but gain in the extravagance
of his claims, and even the confusion he bred by repeatedly
changing his story worked to his advantage. It kept the story
alive and lively and made it practically impossible ever to dis-
pose completely of his charges. Moreover, even among those
disposed to deny him the benefit of the doubt, he created an
interest in himself—simply by being such an outrageous fourflusher. His whole approach made it, on the one hand, prac-

139

tically impossible for the press to deny him publicity—and, on the other, impossible for it to provide for its readers any comprehensible accounting of the ratio of truth to falsehood in what he was saying.

McCarthy was never, I think, a truly Machiavellian figure. He had no strategic sense—no cunning that would serve him tomorrow as well as today. He improvised from moment to moment, and some of his improvisations turned out badly. I do not believe it was with any calculated wisdom that he worked out the strategy that paid off so handsomely after the Wheeling speech. He had learned back in Wisconsin that the penalties for a really audacious mendacity are not as severe as the average politician fears them to be, that, in fact, there may be no penalties at all, but only profit. And he had learned that he was the possessor of remarkable gifts as a bamboozler. But if he had thought of the Multiple Untruth as a principle or a strategy of particular utility for this campaign, he would not have done what he was to do within a few weeks and risk his prestige on the single case of Owen Lattimore. But by then he had acquired the momentum of six weeks of tumult—six noisy, confusing, unpleasant weeks in which he had been the central figure in American politics.

☞ He had gained an audience, and from the audience came, very rapidly, a following, and from the following came several things of value—increased support within the party, fear of his retaliatory power, nourishment for his strange ego, and money. In the beginning, the followers came to him from the outermost fringes, where grievances and anxieties were the

140

strongest and the least grounded in reason; where the passion for authoritarian leadership was greatest; where the will to hate and condemn and punish could most easily be transformed into political action. The organized hate groups and the volunteer policers of patriotism fell into his lap. Throughout the war years, they had lacked leaders and spokesmen. McCarthy did not cater to all their manias and phobias; he was not anti-Semitic,* he was not antilabor, he was not by conviction isolationist or reactionary. But these people had been identifying their hatreds with Bolshevism since Bolshevism had come into being, and they were pleased with the thought that a Senator had discovered that the government was crawling with Communists—something they, of course, had always known. They offered him their support and— to what must have been his surprise—they sent him money. It came in the mail, in small amounts of cash, as a rule, but in mounting volume, and one gets something of a picture of the growth and spread of McCarthyism in the first period from the bank-deposit slips and the checking-account statements published in the 1952 report of the Subcommittee on Privileges and Elections. From February through May and June of 1950—from the Lincoln Day lecture series through the Tydings hearings—the dollar bills and the five-dollar bills came tumbling in, accompanied by a few checks and postal

---

* One at least of the professional anti-Semites had no use for him. According to Ralph Lord Roy's *Apostles of Discord,* a Washington oddity named Mrs. Agnes Waters claimed to have "documentation" that McCarthy was "a crypto Jew" and that his real name wasn't McCarthy at all.

141

notes for ten, twenty-five, and a hundred dollars (as well as some odd sums like $2.70 and $38); the money came from Washington, New York, Chicago, Los Angeles, Philadelphia, Houston—and from Columbia City, Indiana; Fort Lee, New Jersey; Hayward, California; Akron, Colorado; Princeton, Minnesota; Centerville, Alabama; and Browning, Montana. As the weeks went on, more substantial sums showed up: $1,000 from Fort Madison, Iowa; $3,000 from Detroit; $7,000 from Washington. When it began to rain a bit, McCarthy sensed the possibility of floods, and before long, he was spreading the word—via Fulton Lewis, Jr., and other sympathetic publicists—that anti-Communists were proving their dedication with contributions "to the hard and costly struggle against subversion."

The big money came from big people, and there were more and more of them. Some of them were merely wealthy men and women who shared the anxieties of the frenetic contributors of $2.70. Others had specialized interests; these were people like Alfred Kohlberg, the New York lace importer who bank-rolled innumerable anti-Communist ventures, or Mrs. Garvin Tankersley, the publisher of the Washington *Times-Herald,* the District of Columbia distributor of the Anglophobia of her uncle, Colonel Robert R. McCormick, the publisher of the Chicago *Tribune.* Others were, like Senator Taft and most of the rest of the politicians now encouraging McCarthy, eager to be of what help they could to anyone making things uncomfortable for the Democrats. And in time there were the preposterously rich Texans who alone perhaps among his more influential supporters were genuinely fond of him as a human being and eager to advance his personal interests.

But his personal interests were of a curious character for a political leader of demonstrated puissance. Followers of high and low estate came to him, offered themselves to him, emptied their pockets at his feet. He thanked them, acknowledged their benefactions, said he needed more assistance— and then he did nothing with it. He never organized, even in the simplest way. If there were "McCarthy Clubs" (and here and there a few organizations bearing such names did spring up), they were started not on his initiative but on someone else's.

As for the money, precious little of it went into the struggle against subversion. Actually, the "struggle against subversion," as conceived by McCarthy, cost very little. Publicity came free. He had little in the way of a staff and needed little. His kind of "research" could get along without much subsidy. There were stories, which he did little to discourage, about a vast network of McCarthy agents feeding him information not only in Washington but in many parts of the world, and color was lent to them by the arrest in Switzerland of a man named Charles Davis, who confessed in a Swiss court to charges of spying on the American minister to Berne, John Carter Vincent. The Swiss court said it had some evidence that he worked for McCarthy, and gave him eight months. But the story never quite added up, and in those early days— as contrasted with the later ones, when he did have a real underground in the government—what he called his "organization" was strictly bogus. Joseph and Stewart Alsop once

143

described the scene in Room 5-A in the basement of the Senate Office Building, which McCarthy used as his anti-Communist headquarters:

A visit to the McCarthy lair on Capitol Hill is rather like being transported to the set of one of Hollywood's minor thrillers. The anteroom is generally full of furtive-looking characters who look as though they might be suborned State Department men. McCarthy, himself, despite a creeping baldness and a continual tremor which makes his head shake in a disconcerting fashion, is reasonably well cast as the Hollywood version of a strong-jawed private eye. A visitor is likely to find him with his heavy shoulders hunched forward, a telephone in his huge hands, shouting cryptic instructions to some mysterious ally.

"Yeah, yeah, I can listen, but I can't talk. Get me? You really got the goods on the guy?" The Senator glances up to note the effect of this drama on his visitor. "Yeah? Well, I tell you. Just mention this sort of casual to Number One, and get his reaction. Okay? Okay. I'll contact you later."

The drama is heightened by a significant bit of stage business. For as Senator McCarthy talks he sometimes strikes the mouthpiece of his telephone with a pencil. As Washington folklore has it, this is supposed to jar the needle of any concealed listening device.

He was a Potemkin, and the followers were credulous Catherines. It was a cheap-John operation, and very little of the money that rolled in rolled out into the coffers of the crusade. The money went into the Joseph R. McCarthy Special Account in the Riggs National Bank in Washington and perhaps into other accounts. The Subcommittee on Privileges and Elections turned up only McCarthy's Riggs cache. (It did note, though, spectacular increases in the cash reserves of Ray Kiermas, McCarthy's administrative assistant, and it noted that McCarthy, in his earlier days, had had many baskets for his eggs.) The money from Akron, Colorado, and all the other home towns went into the Special Account and shortly went out again, either to Wayne, Hummer & Co. or to the account of Henry J. Van Straten, Superintendent of Schools in Appleton, and thence into soybean futures and thence (when the beans were resold) into McCarthy's personal account.

And it left there fast enough—some of it, perhaps, for political purposes and for the specimens who cluttered up his basement headquarters. But more went, one suspects, to bookmakers and poker companions or for more soybean futures.

☞ On February 22, the Senate had, by unanimous resolution, instructed the Foreign Relations Committee, "or any duly authorized Subcommittee thereof," to "conduct a full and complete study and investigation as to whether persons who are disloyal to the United States are or have been employed by the Department of State." In time, this language was to be the cause of much misunderstanding and bitterness; it was said, and not merely by McCarthy and his friends, that the Subcommittee under Senator Tydings had neglected to discharge its broad mandate and, instead, had investigated only the charges brought by McCarthy, who, of course, was not mentioned in the resolution.* The mandate was broad; it

---

* In 1954, the American Committee for Cultural Freedom sponsored a study, *McCarthy and the Communists,* by James Rorty and Moshe Decter, which even-handedly found against both and against the

145

had to be broad to serve as a warrant for looking into the charges he had made. But his charges were the sole occasion for the investigation. No other Senator was saying that the State Department harbored disloyal persons in large numbers. And by the time the Committee (it so overshadowed the parent body that its status as a subcommittee was lost sight of and it was commonly called the Tydings Committee) was set up, it had become clear that all McCarthy's information and misinformation had come from the files of investigations conducted by the House of Representatives in the preceding Congress. No less than four House committees had covered exactly the same ground and had found nothing that would lend any substance to what McCarthy was saying. On the contrary, the man who had headed the investigation for the Committee on Foreign Affairs, a Michigan Republican named Bartel Jonkman, had said on the House floor:

. . . before the Eightieth Congress adjourns, I want the members to know that there is one department in which the known or reasonably suspected subversives, Communists, fellow-travelers, sympathizers, and persons whose services are not for the best interests of the United States, have been swept out. That is the Department of State.

Tydings investigation as well. "The State Department's security program has been lax and frequently ineffective," Rorty and Decter wrote. "With this [the] committee, for partisan reasons, lamentably failed to deal." Partisanship could have played a part. Senator Tydings was a Democrat and wasn't eager to reveal administration weaknesses. However, the Subcommittee was specifically authorized to subpoena records only in cases of persons "against whom charges have been heard."

146

McCarthy, by his own telling, had taken off soon after
February 20 for Arizona and the "ten saddle-sore days" with
"Rillabelle, old Jim Sands, and Old Jack with the hounds." He
was back by March 7 and ready to be sworn as the first witness before the Tydings Committee. He arrived on time with
his burden, the briefcase that contained "the picture of treason
[that was] to shock the nations and occupy the headlines until
Truman declared war in Korea," opened it, shuffled its contents a bit, and read the first case on his list of 81 "card-
carrying Communists" in the State Department—Judge Dorothy Kenyon, a lady lawyer from New York, who had never
worked for the State Department or any other agency of the
federal government for as much as five minutes. She had
held an honorific membership on the United Nations Commission on the Status of Women and had sat on the Municipal
Court in New York City, but had otherwise exercised her
civic-mindedness as a private citizen. An indefatigable doer
of good works, a tireless joiner of organizations professing
worthy aims, she had amassed quite a record for becoming
involved in what turned out to be Communist-front organizations, and she had amassed quite a record for getting out of
them. McCarthy spent a day and a half talking about the
organizations she had joined and no time at all telling about
those she had left.

From early March through early July, the Committee sat,
its members gravely taking testimony that was in time to bulk
up into 1,500 printed pages and more than a thousand of
documentation. The very thought of it is now somehow
chilling—one must look to philosophy for an explanation.

147

"Men are mad so unavoidably," Pascal said, "that not to be mad would constitute one a madman of another order of madness." This was a necessary but certainly mad enterprise. Millard Tydings was chairman of the Senate Committee on the Armed Services. Brien McMahon, who shared most of his burdens, was chairman of the Joint Congressional Committee on Atomic Energy. The Tydings Committee constituted more than one-third of its parent body, the Foreign Relations Committee. In early 1950, there were very few groups of men on this planet whose responsibilities were heavier than those of these men. Whatever the United States did in the world—and it was then doing, or attempting to do, a great deal—had to have their consent and, constitutionally, was supposed to have benefited by their advice. Every season of this decade has been one of crisis, and it is perhaps going a bit too far, and waxing a bit too solemn, to maintain that these months were uncommonly crucial. Yet it is no less than the truth that in those months we were grappling for the first time with the immense fact of the loss of China to Communism; that we were attempting to determine whether our commitment to Western Europe should be underwritten with large and permanent garrisons of American troops; and that we were making the first hydrogen bomb. In all these undertakings, the members of the Tydings Committee had an enormous role to play, yet the mad force of mad circumstances compelled them to sit and listen for days and weeks and months on end to a poolroom politician grandly seized with an urge to glory (and soybean futures) reciting facts that were

148

not facts about State Department employees who were not State Department employees.

McCarthy enacted before the Tydings Committee essentially the same travesty on reason, logic, and evidence he had put on before the Senate on February 20—and was so often to put on in the coming months. Of course he had more time to fill. (He had told reporters that he planned to keep the hearings going into the autumn, so that they would be in the voters' minds on Election Day.) He spent four days testifying on ten people. Although he had said he was going to tell all about the 81 he had discussed in his February 20 speech (or the 66, when omissions and duplications were allowed for), these ten were added starters, as were 25 more he gave the Committee in closed session. He gave names but in nearly all cases no evidence. Where was the evidence? the Committee asked. In the State Department files, McCarthy would say. And Senator Tydings would point out that the resolution creating the investigation empowered the Committee to subpoena records only when charges had been made. "You have left the committee in a rather embarrassing position," Tydings once said. "How do we get the records? We are authorized to get them . . . if you or somebody makes a charge. [He meant, of course, a formal, specific "charge"—not the random accusations McCarthy was making every five minutes.] You say you are not making any charges." And McCarthy responded:

I am not making charges. I am giving the committee information of individuals who appear by all the rules of common sense

149

as being very bad security risks. . . . I am not in a position to file any formal charges. . . . If you want me to charge from the evidence . . .

But what evidence? It was all in the files. In exasperation, Tydings went to President Truman and implored him to let the Committee see the files, despite an executive order discontinuing the practice of releasing personnel files to Congressional committees and despite McCarthy's refusal to place any charges. The President agreed. Immediately, McCarthy called it "a phony offer of phony files." The records had been "raped and rifled," he said. The FBI information had been lifted from them. J. Edgar Hoover was asked to look the files over and see if this was true. He wrote to Tydings and said that "the State Department files were intact" when his staff, at the Committee's request, had inspected them.

Twice, when McCarthy seemed to have strained the Committee's credulity to the point of danger to himself, he announced that he was going to rest everything on one big case —he would be willing, he said, to have the Committee call the whole show off and report him as a faker if the Committee was unimpressed by the evidence he had on a single person. On March 10, he said he would go for broke on the case of a man in "an important post" in the Department. He needed only the weekend to gather and organize the data; he would be ready first thing Monday morning, March 13.

He could not make time stand still. The morning came. McCarthy showed up, briefcase in hand. Rumpled and breathless, he explained to the Committee that he was all ready with his case, but that something terribly important had come up

—a Senate debate on housing. He high-tailed it for the door. A committeeman hailed him back—saying that word had just come up that the housing debate had been postponed. That was good news, McCarthy said, for he had another pressing matter to attend to—some Wisconsin constituents had just come to town and were waiting in his office. He had to see them right away. But the Committee wouldn't let him go. It sat him down and asked for his evidence. He said he would be glad to give evidence and that he had, in fact, four cases he wished to present. One was in the Navy, two were in the State Department, and one, Owen Lattimore, was a professor at Johns Hopkins University.

The Lattimore case—the second one on which he was ready to go for broke, unless Lattimore was the first one as well—was probably the most celebrated of all his cases. He did not pursue it that morning of March 13. He merely said Lattimore was "an extremely bad security risk." But about a week later, he began telling the press that he was on the verge of naming "the top Russian espionage agent" in the United States. "I am willing to stand or fall on this one," he said. "If I am wrong on this, I think the Subcommittee would be justified in not taking my other cases too seriously." I have always been convinced that when he first talked about his "top espionage agent," he hadn't the slightest notion which unfortunate name on his list he would single out for this distinction. I also believe that he sensed almost immediately that he had made a rather foolish mistake in picking Lattimore. For although in the end he managed to create a good deal of doubt about Lattimore (who made some notable

151

contributions of his own in the way of creating doubt about himself), he could hardly, at the time, have chosen worse.* Lattimore wasn't a spy, he wasn't a State Department employee, and he wasn't a Communist—though at times, in the thirties and forties, he had been a stout fellow-traveler and an eloquent advocate of a view of Asia that accorded with the Communist view. He was a kind of academic and journalistic politician, and McCarthy was subsequently to stumble over a half- or quarter-truth when, having given up on the claim that Lattimore was a spy, he described Lattimore as "the chief architect of our Far Eastern policy." A generation of China hands in the State Department had read Lattimore for years and had been greatly influenced by his views.

But McCarthy had known nothing of this when he started out. He needed a spy to keep things lively in the Tydings Committee. Owen Lattimore was tapped. He was made the arch-arch-villain—"Alger Hiss's boss in the espionage ring in the State Department." McCarthy claimed he had witnesses queued up outside the Caucus Room to sustain this. A bedraggled collection of apostate Communists came in to

* And he could, from his point of view, have chosen much better. One of his 81 (or 66) was John Stewart Service, who was a bona fide State Department man, who had had a good deal of difficulty in security proceedings, and who had in 1945 admitted turning over government documents to *Amerasia*, a publication of unsavory reputation and one that followed the Communist line on Asian affairs. Service was not a Communist; he was, on the contrary, a highly regarded career diplomat, and his involvement in the *Amerasia* case was not as damaging as it at first appeared—since the documents were not secret. But the facts in his case could have been made to look, in 1950, much worse than those in the case of Owen Lattimore.

say lamely that although Lattimore was not their beau ideal of an anti-Communist partisan, they lacked any shred of evidence that he was a Communist spy or even a Communist. "Maybe in the case of Lattimore I have placed too much stress on the question of whether or not he has been an espionage agent," McCarthy said. But he was a "policy risk" and an architect. "I believe you can ask almost any school child who the architect of our Far Eastern policy is, and he will say 'Owen Lattimore.'" I remember what comic relief the line brought to the press gallery when McCarthy produced it in a floor speech on March 30. But as that spring wore on, the statement acquired a validity—a time did come when, if McCarthy's question had been posed to schoolchildren, many would have given McCarthy's answer.

☞ The whole affair was nasty and squalid and offered little in the way of comic relief. McCarthy debased the currency of discourse with bad and counterfeit tender, and Gresham's Law set in. And there was more nastiness. McCarthy soon found a way of spicing his disquisitions with sex. He had discovered that homosexuality was regarded as a factor in security judgments, and he worked this for what it was worth, which was quite a bit. It gave lesser demagogues, who realized that the Communists-in-government issue could never be taken from him, a corner of McCarthyism to work for themselves. A subcommittee of the District of Columbia Committee was set up to investigate "sexual deviates" (I believe this ugly phrase was invented at that time) in government. An early bulletin from this group told of reports it had

153

of a Russian scheme to lure "women employees of the State Department under their control by enticing them into a life of Lesbianism." The District Police set up a special detail of the Vice Squad "to investigate links between homosexuality and Communism." *

Nothing, though, was more embarrassing than the kind of replies McCarthy's victims felt themselves called upon to make. McCarthy accused them of being spies and Communists; if he was in error, it was, it seemed, their job simply to inform the Tydings Committee of this fact and to offer such evidence as they may have had that they were not. What many did was to supply wholly gratuitous information intended, apparently, to show McCarthy that they were men in possession of exactly the kind of virtues he should admire. It was not enough, in those days, for anyone to say that he wasn't a card-carrying Communist; many felt impelled to show that they were dues-paying Redmen or Epworth Leaguers or Lions. Haldore Hanson, an official of the State Department's Office of Technical Cooperation and Development, made public this chapter of his biography in his prepared statement before the Committee:

---

* The government never took the position that there were any links between the two. It dropped homosexuals from sensitive positions on the theory that they were uncommonly susceptible to blackmail. The theory, still held in Washington, is probably unsound. All sorts of practices, aberrant or otherwise, expose men to blackmail, and the classic instance, the real setup for blackmail, is the man, like McCarthy, with a weakness for gambling with borrowed money. The homosexual is no more vulnerable than the heterosexual who occasionally commits an excess of normality.

I was active in the YMCA from the age of ten. I went to YMCA summer camps and was President of the Hi-Y Club during my high-school years. From the age of twelve, I was a Boy Scout. I became an Eagle Scout, a Boy Scout Camp Counsellor, and served as Scoutmaster during my first year of college. I was active in the Presbyterian Church, of which all my immediate family were members. My father was a Sunday School superintendent. During my senior year in high-school, I was awarded a summer in Europe as a result of an essay contest sponsored by a boys' magazine. . . . By means of scolarships, a job waiting on table, and loans, I was able to finish my college education. . . . I was elected to Phi Beta Kappa. . . . I was a debater and on the track squad.

In New York, at the height of it all, the Secretary of State addressed the American Society of Newspaper Editors and explained that "There is no need for anyone to be defensive about the Department of State." It was a splendid body of men, including such figures as "George McGhee, of Texas, a former oil man . . . Willard Thorp, a former partner of Dun & Bradstreet . . . Paul Nitze of Massachusetts, a former partner of Dillon, Read," and so on. Not only was the defense humiliating to those who employed it, but it raised the delicate question of what the large sections of the population who had never been Eagle Scouts and might even have been in the bad graces of Dun & Bradstreet would do if attacked by McCarthy. Moreover, some of the defenses could be used to establish guilt by association. The Communists had always found excellent pickings among Eagle Scouts and college debaters, and they had done tolerably well among persons with impeccable business and family con-

155

nections. One of McCarthy's victims who never denied his Communist sympathies (though he was never in the State Department) was Frederick Vanderbilt Field, who could hardly have chosen more felicitous forebears. And Alger Hiss, a real Hi-Y sort, had been a debater, a track man, and the "best hand-shaker" in his class at Johns Hopkins.

☞ The Tydings Committee issued an interim report in mid-July. Before he saw it, McCarthy said it would be a "disgrace to the Senate." He confirmed his prediction a few days later by calling it "a green light for the Reds." The report said that McCarthy had imposed a "fraud and a hoax" on the Senate: "Starting with nothing, Senator McCarthy plunged headlong forward, desperately seeking to develop some information which, colored with distortion and fanned by a blaze of bias, would forestall the day of reckoning." The two Republican members—Lodge, of Massachusetts, and Bourke Hickenlooper, of Iowa—did not sign the report. They complained that the investigation had not been broad enough to warrant the issuance of a clean bill of health to the State Department, which was, in effect, what the majority report did.

There was a time, after the Tydings report, when it looked very much as if McCarthy had shot his bolt. The interlude was short and the appearance was deceiving, but there was a period—it was in the first desperate days of the Korean fighting—when Washington paid very little attention to McCarthy. I have good reason for recalling the time, for in it I had rather an odd and revealing experience with McCarthyism. When McCarthy first got under way with his "lists," a friend of mine in the government, a man whose work was delicate in the extreme, confided in me that he knew of one case that, if discovered, would lend a good deal of credence to McCarthy's whole campaign. The case, my friend said, was that of someone—I shall call him, McCarthy-fashion, X —he had known in the thirties. X had not been in the government then, but he had been a Communist; of this there was no doubt in my friend's mind, for X had tried to recruit him. There was also no doubt in his mind that X was an ex-Communist. However, X had not made his defection public (perhaps because his membership had not been public), and now he was in the government, and since McCarthy had raised enough hell about people who had never been Communists and had never been in the government, there was no telling what he could do with this one. My friend thought it best not to tell me who X was, for he felt it essential to the welfare of his agency to have nothing at all to do with the whole McCarthy affair.

The story was always at the back of my mind, and whenever, in that disagreeable spring, McCarthy would come out with a new batch of names, I kept wondering if X was among them, and when I chanced to see my friend, I would ask him. The answer was always, astonishingly, no.

Then came the time, after the Tydings report, when McCarthy was in a brief eclipse. One day, in the midst of it, I chanced to be in the Senate press gallery, and someone was handing out a speech McCarthy was shortly to make. He had a brand-new "case." "Documents"—stamped "FBI Confidential" or something of the sort—were stapled to the text. Most of my colleagues tossed the stuff aside; they were sick and tired of him, and for the time being they could indulge their contempt. I read it, though, and I had, immediately, the feeling that McCarthy might at last have come upon something and that perhaps he had come upon X. When he made his presentation, I went in and heard him through. Those of us in the Senate as he spoke made a small group—four or five Senators, six or seven reporters, and a few wilted midsummer tourists. The Senators were inattentive; the reporters were just attentive enough to get the material for one or two paragraphs, and the tourists were tired. But I had the feeling, sitting there and listening to McCarthy harangue a practically nonexistent audience, that he might be on the point of enjoying his first real success.

As soon as I could, I called my friend and told him I had a strong suspicion that McCarthy had found X. I gave him some of the details. He confirmed my suspicion. In the days that followed, though, McCarthy made nothing further of the case. His speech had attracted almost no interest. The wire services had given him only an inch or so, and the large dailies had either ignored the story or used the wire-service accounts. He plainly thought that he had no stronger a case than he had had with Dorothy Kenyon and most of the others, and, having bigger fish to fry, he dropped it.

It had occurred to me, however, that he might come back to it, and that if he did, it might be just the thing to rehabilitate him. Reluctantly—for it involved an intervention in politics, which is something that, as a correspondent, I had always sought to avoid—I took it upon myself to go to an official of X's agency and tell him my story, which was that I had good reason to believe that McCarthy's facts about X were essentially sound as to the past. I said I had also been given to understand that X had broken with the Communists, but that if the record didn't show this there could be trouble.

I made my point. And it turned out that X, in the course of the various security and loyalty checks he had been through, had chosen to conceal his Communist past—a choice that might allow of any one of several moral judgments, but one that, to his misfortune, exposed him to charges of perjury. He was advised that it would be necessary to reopen the case. Within a few days, he quit the government.

Here, then, was a potential triumph of McCarthy's, and McCarthy did not even know about it. X was about the closest he ever came to turning up a real Communist in government, and he died, I am sure, unaware that he had ever really come close.

☞ But perhaps he knew—as, I guess, few of the rest of us then did—that he could afford to be profligate. The people who were rallying about him didn't really care whether he was technically right or wrong about X or A or B or Z. In their judgment, it was a mere splitting of hairs to distinguish between a Communist, ex- or otherwise, and a liberal or internationalist in the government service. They were all dogs to be beaten with any stick, and McCarthy was

159

the first really handy man with a stick to have come along.

Moreover, he was putting the time of the "eclipse" to good use, beating far larger dogs than X. He had set himself the formidable task of putting an end to Millard Tydings' long career in the Senate, and he worked at it through the late summer. Tydings lost in the fall to John Marshall Butler, who was the beneficiary of large sums of money raised by McCarthy, of tons of anti-Tydings literature—featuring a faked picture of Tydings and Earl Browder tête-à-tête*— prepared by McCarthy's staff, and of the remarkable services of one staff member, Don Surine. Surine, once of the FBI, knew Maryland well, for he had been assigned to a narcotics-*cum*-prostitution case in Baltimore and had been so diligent that he had ended up sharing accommodations with one of the lady principals. Cashiered by Mr. Hoover, he found employment as an anti-Communist expert with McCarthy, and he figured in the Tydings business—at least according to sworn testimony before the Rules Committee's Subcommittee on

---

* Browder, the deposed head of the Communist Party, had been a witness before the Tydings Committee. He contributed, for what it was worth, the intelligence that he had never met Owen Lattimore. On a much earlier occasion, Tydings had had Browder cited for contempt of Congress. The two had never been photographed together, and the caption below the Butler campaign picture did note, unobtrusively, most unobtrusively, the contrivance. It read: "Communist leader Earl Browder, shown at left in this *composite* [*sic*—italics definitely added] picture, was a star witness at the Tydings . . . hearings and was cajoled into saying Owen Lattimore and others accused of disloyalty were not Communists. Tydings (right) answered 'Oh, thank you, sir.' Browder testified in the best interests of those accused, naturally." Natch—and the line given Tydings was really a jewel.

Privileges and Elections—when he took a hapless Baltimore printer on a ride through the suburbs. The printer, William Fedder, had taken a contract for half a million post cards recommending a vote for Butler. The trick for the printer was that they were not to be printed—but written by hand, presumably by Butler's hand. Fedder found a number of Baltimore housewives who knew how to write and were happy to be amanuenses to Butler. But their services ran into money—in fact, to approximately $11,000. Fedder wanted to be sure he would get the money. He asked Butler to give him a letter pledging eventual payment. Butler complied. The difficulty was that this letter constituted acknowledgment of a violation of Maryland law—which limited candidates to a maximum expenditure of $5,000. One pleasant evening, as the air was getting brisk, McCarthy's Surine took Fedder for a tour of Baltimore's environs that lasted until four in the morning and ended, in an all-night restaurant, with Surine persuading Fedder to sign a statement that Butler owed him nothing for the half-million forgeries. The Elections Subcommittee said it had been "a despicable, 'backstreet' type of campaign, which usually, if exposed in time, backfires." But it wasn't exposed in time to backfire, and it probably wouldn't have backfired anyway; Tydings was out, Butler and McCarthy in. And Scott Lucas was out, too. Whether or not McCarthy deserved much credit for the results, he got a lot of it, especially from Senators giving thought to their own re-election.

By fall, the eclipse was over, and there was not to be another before the total, final one in 1954. He scarcely let a

161

day pass without demanding the resignation of Dean Acheson or the impeachment of Harry Truman. He ran a noisy, sickening campaign to deny Senate confirmation as Assistant Secretary of Defense to Anna Rosenberg, a New York businesswoman of excellent reputation and extensive service in state and federal government, on the ground that she had been a Communist and might still be one. The ground was wholly false; some crackpot informants in New York had confused her with a woman of the same name who was living on the West Coast and had been at some kind of Communist literary gathering twenty years earlier. It scarcely seemed to matter. He had made the headlines; he made them almost every day that winter. At a party at the Sulgrave Club in Washington, he got into a fist fight with Drew Pearson, a newspaper columnist and broadcaster, who taunted him with questions about his pending difficulties with the state tax authorities in Wisconsin. The argument grew into a feud, and the feud grew into a libel suit, and the libel suit grew into reams of publicity.

For publicity, he had a talent unmatched by any other politician of this century. Or perhaps it was an instinct. At any rate, he knew what publicity was made of—the very texture of the precious stuff. He knew the newspapermen and how and when they worked and what they needed and when their deadlines were and what made a "lead," what made an "overnight," what made a "sidebar." He knew how to "top" or "blanket" a story unfavorable to him. One day in 1951, the Senate was discussing him and his defiance of the Subcommittee on Privileges and Elections. The debate was going against him—he had accused the venerable members of "stealing the taxpayers' money" by spending it on an investigation of him. He buried the story with a resolution calling for the continuation of the investigation and for an extension of it to Senator Benton, whose resolution to expel McCarthy had started the whole affair. He came out on top of Benton in the newspapers. And as William Evjue of the Madison *Capital Times,* perhaps the most distinguished of Wisconsin journalists, wrote, it was passing strange that a story on McCarthy frying chicken for some friends or a picture of McCarthy with a new broom (sweeping clean) on the Capitol steps should "top" a story on polls of Washington correspondents and political scientists rating him as the worst Senator in the Senate.

It may have been strange that the papers played it that way, but McCarthy always knew what he was up to. He knew, in his good days, how to make a story out of nothing, and he knew how to back into somebody else's story. The Korean War took the play away from him for a while, but he did not let himself be put aside when, at the height of the war, the nation's attention was fixed on the controversy over General MacArthur. He gave free rein to the Multiple Untruth in a speech which "documented," he said, General Marshall's role "as an instrument of the Soviet conspiracy." He could go even farther afield. When Nathan Pusey became President of Harvard University, he was ready with a comment: "I do not think Dr. Pusey is or has been a member of the Communist Party."

He knew how to get into the news even on those rare occasions when invention failed him and he had no unfacts to give out. For example, he invented the morning press conference called for the purpose of announcing an afternoon press conference. The reporters would come in—they were beginning, in this period, to respond to his summonses like Pavlov's dogs at the clang of a bell—and McCarthy would say that he just wanted to give them the word that he expected to be ready with a shattering announcement later in the day, for use in the papers the following morning. This would gain him a headline in the afternoon papers: "NEW MCCARTHY REVELATIONS AWAITED IN CAPITAL." Afternoon would come, and if McCarthy had something, he would give it out, but often enough he had nothing, and this was a matter of slight concern. He would simply say that he wasn't quite ready, that he was having difficulty in getting some of the "documents" he needed or that a "witness" was proving elusive. Morning headlines: "DELAY SEEN IN NEW MCCARTHY CASE—MYSTERY WITNESS BEING SOUGHT." He had no cause for concern if the whole thing turned out to be nothing, as so often happened. He had the headlines; "MCCARTHY" was becoming a more and more familiar arrangement of type and was engraved more and more deeply on the American mind.

The very sight of a newspaperman would set his mind going. Once—this was after the change of administrations—he ran into a pair of them idling along in the Senate Office Building. "You two looking for a story?" he asked, knowing full well that their answer would be "Sure, have you got one?" "Mmm," he said, "now let's see." The three walked along together, took an elevator to the basement, and boarded the

little subway that leads to the Capitol. McCarthy was thinking hard. Suddenly he lighted up. "I'll give you something,"
he said. "You can say that I'm going to subpoena Harry
Truman, that's what I'm going to do." He reached in his
pocket, where he always kept a wad of blank subpoenas,
and began then and there making one out for the former
President. "You're not serious, Joe; you can't be," one of
the reporters said. "The hell I'm not serious," McCarthy
said. "I'll have this filled out in a second." "What are you
going to subpoena him for?" he was asked. McCarthy tapped
his big skull with his fountain pen. "Oh, I'm calling him to
testify about Harry Dexter White, that's what I'm calling
him for."

Of course, it never happened—that is to say, Truman
never testified, but the story got into print, even though the
reporters to whom it was given were angry about the system
that required them to publish "news" they knew to be fraudulent but prohibited them from reporting their knowledge of
its fraudulence. In time, what appeared to be the suscepti-
bility of the press to McCarthy was held to be the cause of
his lamentable successes. Why did the press publish this liar's
lies? McCarthy knew the answer: it was not because pub-
lishers in general wished to circulate his mendacities or even
because he had achieved a glamour that made him irresistible
to readers. It was because he had achieved a high elective
office, because what he said counted for something (in fact,
a great deal, as time went by) in the affairs of this nation,
and because there was always the possibility that there *was*
a mystery witness or that he *would* force Harry Truman to

testify. "McCarthy's charges of treason, espionage, corruption, perversion are news which cannot be suppressed or ignored," Walter Lippmann once wrote. "They come from a United States Senator and a politician . . . in good standing at the headquarters of the Republican Party. When he makes such attacks against the State Department and the Defense Department, it is news which has to be published." It was also, of course, news that a United States Senator was lying and defrauding the people and their government. But— in large part because McCarthy was a true innovator, because he lied with an unprecedented boldness, because he invented new kinds of lies—even those newspapers that were willing to expose him found that they lacked the technical resources.* If he was to be called a liar, someone had to call him a liar. The American press was simply not set up so that it could

* The New York *Times* once looked back upon its own coverage of a McCarthy investigation and acknowledged that it had done its readers a great disservice, though an unavoidable one. Reporting developments from the only possible source, the investigators, it ran such headlines as ROSENBERG CALLED RADAR SPY LEADER; RADAR WITNESS BREAKS DOWN: WILL TELL ALL; MONMOUTH FIGURE LINKED TO HISS RING. The *Times* admitted that there turned out to be no truth in any of these stories, but it explained that it had seen no alternative to publishing them. "It is difficult, if not impossible, to ignore charges by Senator McCarthy just because they are usually proved false. The remedy lies with the reader." To many people, this was rather like saying that if a restaurant serves poisoned food, it is up to the diner to refuse it. Yet the *Times* was, I believe, essentially right, for I suspect there is no surer way to a corrupt and worthless press than to authorize reporters to tell the readers which "facts" are really "facts" and which are not. Certainly in those countries where this is the practice, the press serves the public less well than ours does.

feature a "MCCARTHY LIES" story alongside a "MCCARTHY SAYS—" story. If his fellow Senators had been ready to challenge each mendacity, or if either of the two Presidents of his day had been willing and able to denounce him regularly, it would have worked. But that was not to be.

One of the many secrets McCarthy seemed to know (without, probably, knowing that he knew) was that the American press reflects the American mind and that the American mind, as Dwight Macdonald has said, is affected with "fact-fetishism." The fact has triumphed. Truths for most of us are only truths when they state conditions of demonstrable materiality. It was *not* a fact that Dorothy Kenyon worked for the State Department but it *was* a fact that McCarthy said that she did; to state the truth about her nonemployment by that agency was to state a fact in a negative way—really to assert that what was alleged to be so wasn't so. He seemed to understand this delicate point superbly, and he was able to see that the American mind could quite easily be bewitched by fraudulent "documentation," or demonstration, of fraudulent "facts," or "factual" frauds, and that, once bewitched, it would be very nearly impervious to the truths that happened to be truths, the facts that happened to be "facts," though negative in form.

And he knew something even more arcane and delicate—that we will take the symbols of the "established fact" for the fact itself. I had discovered this weakness in myself when talking to him of Malmédy. Examining his photostats and his onion-skin carbons of official correspondence, I had taken their relevance for granted; relevance had seemed somehow a

167

condition of their existence, and the "fact" that they were "facts"—*i.e.,* they existed, they could be seen with the naked eye, they could be held in the hand—had induced me to follow him quite a distance down his garden path. But of course they were not "facts," relevant or otherwise, but only symbols of factuality, and he knew it was characteristic of most Americans to make the mistake I had made. The characteristic is encouraged, if it is not developed, by our education and its emphasis on the acquisitive approach to data.

It sometimes seemed to me that he had elaborated an approach, based on this guilty knowledge, that was really a great satire, a gigantic spoof on the kind of scholarship in which the "fact" enjoys its ultimate triumph. The cream of the jest for this superb faker may have lain in the success he enjoyed in turning the devices of scholarship against scholars. Documents, documents, documents—he was always loaded with them. The bulging briefcase—the scholar's toolbox—became to him what snapping red galluses and a stream of tobacco juice were to the older Southern demagogues. He saw the possibilities of coming before the people with the dust of the archives clinging to him, and he was right. The true believers would twitch in ecstasy and skeptics would suffer the first tremors of belief when he held aloft a scrap of paper and announced that it was hot from the filing cabinets. It might be nothing at all or it might be grossly mislabeled. (In the post-Tydings period, there was seldom an appearance unmarked by his waving about a picture of a United

Nations employee named Gustavo Duran wearing the uniform, which had been his fifteen years earlier, of a member of the Spanish Republican Army. McCarthy described him as currently a State Department man and the uniform as that of "the Russian Secret Police." There is no instance known to me of anyone asking when members of the OGPU began to wear uniforms and pose for photographs.) He positively flaunted all the stigmata of the pedant: in the 101 pages of his *McCarthyism: The Fight for America* there are 314 meticulously numbered footnotes. Anyone who employed them to run down sources would have seen for himself how McCarthy butchered truth. He knew, though, that people don't run down sources, but are mightily impressed by being given the opportunity to do so. They take the symbol of the fact as proof of the fact.

And with it all, the principle of multiplicity was working for him. I recall an instance in which his "documentation" was challenged and he successfully invoked the other principle. He was on the Senate floor reading, he said, from a letter written by Owen Lattimore to a former colleague, Joseph Barnes. It was a most revealing "document," he maintained, and he said he would be glad to show it to any Senator. Several Senators thought that his excerpts had a very fishy sound, and the suggestion was made that he might be wrenching the meaning by obscuring the context. Not at all, said McCarthy—and made his offer to permit immediate inspection. To what must have been his astonishment, Senator Lehman accepted the offer and walked across the floor toward McCarthy's desk. "I yield no further," McCarthy said. And with excellent reason, for in truth he had not been quoting in context or out of context; he simply had *not been quoting at all*. He had simply invented, standing there on the Senate floor, lines that served his purpose at the moment and attributed them to Owen Lattimore. This became known only a bit later, when the letter turned up as part of a printed transcript. But by then he had said a good many more things, and there were few who troubled to compare his fictitious text with the actual one. "Who can keep track of them all?" Elmer Davis once wrote, apropos of McCarthy's lies and contradictions. "I have a stack of McCarthy's speeches two feet thick on my office shelf; but when he says something that stirs a vague recollection that he once said something very different, I seldom have time to run through his speeches. I can't afford to hire a full-time specialist to keep up with what McCarthy has said."

☞ On June 14, 1951, in midafternoon, McCarthy went to the Senate with a briefcase full of manuscript that would, he explained, be useful to the Senate Armed Services and Foreign Relations Committees, which had jointly undertaken, after President Truman's recall of General MacArthur, an investigation of American policy in the Far East. It dealt not with General MacArthur and not very much with Far Eastern policy, but with the career of the then Secretary of Defense, General of the Army George Catlett Marshall, of whom McCarthy said: "This is his plight:

I am in blood
Stepped in so far that should I wade no more,
Returning were as tedious as go o'er." *

It was, and is, an altogether extraordinary document—and not alone on the ground that it was the most daring and seditious of McCarthy's actions. It stands today as the most famous of his speeches, and yet it is, for reasons I shall attempt to explain, a speech to which no one ever listened and which very few have ever read.

Its celebrity came, in the first place, from its subject. In 1951, General Marshall was, as McCarthy correctly said, regarded by many of his countrymen as the "greatest living American." President Truman had described him in exactly these words. Those who agreed did not, one ventures to say, feel that General Marshall had accomplished larger or greater things than any other American. Among military men, Dwight Eisenhower and Douglas MacArthur were probably more highly regarded; among contemporary statesmen, Henry L. Stimson, who had died in 1950, had been more admired as a Secretary of State and as a Secretary of War. General Marshall had served with high distinction in military and civilian commands, but it was not so much what he had

* These lines from *Macbeth* seem to have been the only bit of Shakespeare McCarthy had ever heard of. He used them again in the Army-McCarthy hearings—on that later occasion to describe the persistence in evil-doing of Robert T. Stevens. Noting the second use, Michael Straight asked, "Was this in the deeper sense an allusion to himself?" I suspect that in some very deep sense—too deep, certainly, for me to fathom—this may have been the case. At any rate, I know of no sinner so quick to attribute his own sins to others.

done as what he was and what he symbolized that made so many stand in awe of him. He was, above all, a man of vast and palpable dignity. The dignity was in his bearing and in his entire mien, in his aloofness from controversy, in the silence with which he had borne disappointment and defeat and sorrow, with which he was well acquainted. He was the very image of the strong, noble, gentle Southern man of arms who could be no more dishonored by enemies and critics, if he had any, than the great progenitor of the tradition, Marshall's fellow Virginian Robert E. Lee. Like the Lee of Grant's remembrance, General Marshall had an "impassable face," and to look upon it was to repose trust in the man's purpose and integrity. In point of fact, no breath of scandal had ever touched him. No suggestion of misfeasance had ever been raised against him. If it could not be established by any of the customary measures that he was "the greatest living American," he was surely the least assailable American of his time. Or so at least it seemed on June 14, 1951, when Alcibiades, the mutilator of the images of gods and heroes, entered the Senate, loaded with "documents."

The Marshall legend did not, of course, awe McCarthy. He was willing at any time to profane any article of any faith. On two accounts, the Marshall legend invited his attention. For one, he had had his fill of small fry. For another, there was at the moment a contest of large figures that threatened to draw attention away from him and all his Owen Lattimores. The Army-McCarthy hearings, then three years in the future, were to attract more attention than the MacArthur hearings then in progress, but up to 1951, the Mac-

Arthur investigation, though it was not open to press or public, drew more attention than any of its time—more, perhaps, than any in American history up to that time. McCarthy had managed to get into the act by attending the hearings and emerging from the Senate Caucus Room every hour or so to give informal and wholly unauthorized briefings to the press. (It was the custom of the Committee to have portions of each session's transcript declassified by State and Defense Department authorities and then released to the press. McCarthy, though, was useful to the press because he "declassified" faster and more frequently than the government censors did.) But this was not enough. A briefing officer, even a volunteer one breaking the security of secret testimony in wartime, is not quite a central figure. Since the logic of his position put him on General MacArthur's side, he undertook the destruction of MacArthur's most formidable adversary.

He coolly decided not only to deny the great man his greatness, not merely to emasculate the symbol, but—of all things—to befoul the living man as a traitor, even an assassin. And he went about this in a most curious way. Millions of Americans became familiar with the most outrageous of McCarthy's lies about General Marshall, for they were cited time and time again to show that his audacity knew no bounds. I doubt very much, though, if many people ever read the text of the famous speech—despite the fact that it was subsequently issued, and widely circulated, as a book, under the title *America's Retreat from Victory: The Story of George Catlett Marshall.* As a matter of fact, I doubt very

much if McCarthy ever read it. This is not as absurd a suggestion as it may appear, for, actually, McCarthy, on June
14, 1951, did *not* deliver what has since become known
as his most famous speech. That afternoon, at the conclusion
of a brief discussion of the "increased expenditures of the
Committee on Expenditures in the Executive Departments,"
McCarthy obtained the floor. Very few Senators were on
hand, and before he could begin to speak, the Republican
leader, Kenneth Wherry, believing that McCarthy wanted an
audience, asked for a quorum call. McCarthy told him that
he did not at all desire an audience. "I have informed many
Senators," he said, "that in view of the fact that this speech
is approximately 60,000 words, I do not expect them to sit
and listen to it as I deliver it." Then he began to address a
chamber that at no time contained more than a dozen Senators:

> It is needless to tell you that this [the preparation of the
> speech] was a monumental task but one which I felt had to be
> done, for unless we understand the record of Marshall, it will
> be impossible . . . to foretell the next move on the timetable
> of the great conspiracy.
> I realize full well how unpopular it is to lay hands on the
> laurels of a man who has been built into a great hero. I very
> much dislike this unpleasant task, but I feel that it must be
> done. . . .

And he went on a bit, reading a review of the controversy
over Allied strategy in Europe in 1942 and 1943, when General Marshall had been Chief of Staff. Before he had gone
very far, William Langer, of North Dakota, interrupted to

congratulate McCarthy on "one of the most important speeches that has ever been made on this floor" and to express the wish that more Senators were on hand to hear it. McCarthy thanked the Senator from North Dakota but repeated his statement about not wishing to detain his colleagues with all this verbiage. "Certainly I do not wish them to miss the ball game this evening," he said. It was then a few minutes past five-thirty. And shortly after this colloquy, he decided that he would stop talking altogether and have the balance of the 60,000 words, or about 40,000, published in the *Congressional Record* as if they had been delivered on the floor. He departed the chamber, and, in five minutes or so, the Senators who remained cleared up a few items of executive business (receiving a message from the President on a tax convention with Switzerland and noting "sundry nominations in the United States Coast Guard," and the nomination of the Honorable Wayne Coy to the Federal Communications Commission).

What was printed in the *Congressional Record* as the text of McCarthy's speech is in several ways remarkable. In the first place, the body of the speech is not an attack on General Marshall's patriotism. It is a study of Allied high strategy with a good deal of emphasis on General Marshall's role. Nothing is plainer than that neither McCarthy nor anyone on his staff had anything to do with its composition. After receiving Senator Langer's congratulations, McCarthy modestly gave credit to his staff ("I believe most of them are in the gallery today. I salute them; they worked 18, 19, and 20 hours a day getting the document together"), but this is obvious poppycock, for the speech is the work of a scholar, or scholars, very much at home in diplomatic and strategic history and saturated in its language. None of the campus queens or former detectives on McCarthy's staff would have been capable of such an aside as

I am reminded of a wise and axiomatic utterance in this connection by the great Swedish chancellor Oxenstiern, to his son departing on the tour of Europe: He said, "Go forth my son and see with what folly the affairs of mankind are governed"

or

We may be sure that Stalin's didactic observations fell upon Marshall's ears with the authority of revelation.

Nor is the speech entirely the gutter attack on General Marshall it is generally recalled as being. At one point, its authors had McCarthy say of the General:

I do not propose to go into his motives. Unless one has all the tangled and often complicated circumstances contributing to a man's decisions, an inquiry into his motives is often fruitless. I do not pretend to understand General Marshall's nature and character, and I shall leave that subject to subtler analysts of human personality.

And at another, they had him quarrel with another of General Marshall's detractors, Freda Utley, who had expressed the view that Marshall, on his famous mission to China, had allowed himself to fall under the influence of the Communist diplomat Chou En-lai. The McCarthy text said:

I do not subscribe to Miss Utley's analysis of Marshall's state of mind. I do not regard him as the dupe of Chou En-lai.

176

The origins are not difficult to determine. It is a product of a school of revisionist historians who have in common the view that American diplomacy at least since the early thirties and into the early fifties was a failure because it failed to focus single-mindedly on Soviet power. Roosevelt was mistaken in recognizing the Soviet Union in 1933; wrong in aiding the Russians in 1941; wrong in seeking the total destruction of German and Japanese power in 1945; wrong in inviting the Russians into the Pacific war; wrong in insisting that Chiang Kai-shek hold his fire for the Japanese—wrong in very nearly all of his major decisions. The leaders of the school were Charles Callin Tansill and Stefan Possony of Georgetown University. Georgetown, was, and is, its headquarters, and there seems little room for doubt that McCarthy's speech was the work either of a member of the Georgetown school or of someone heavily influenced by it. It is, in fact, rather a creditable product of the school, whose point of view yields certain insights even for those who share very little of it. There was a case to be made against General Marshall; like a great many Americans of his time, he was unprepared for leadership in global strategy and global diplomacy. He was unable to see, as Winston Churchill, for one, could see, beyond the immediate conflict with fascism to the developing conflict with the Soviet Union and Communist China. This is only to say that while he served the republic well, he served it with somewhat less foresight than one can, with hindsight, wish he—and with him most of our war leaders—had shown.

The Marshall speech was a massive Multiple Untruth,

composed, for the most part, of a mass of historical truths—
tendentiously chosen, to be sure, and meanly organized, but
not more vicious than a good deal of what often passes for
history. Except for two or three interpolations by McCarthy,
it was scarcely even damaging. Yet it is no exaggeration to
say that it destroyed George Catlett Marshall—in the sense,
certainly, that it robbed him of the opportunity of giving
meaning to the rest of his life by the kind of service that was
made possible by an unsullied name. Whatever failings of
judgment and experience he might have had (and it can well
be argued that his were uncommonly few), his name and
reputation had lifted American spirits when he became Secretary of Defense in 1950—at a time when our arms were beleaguered and when the civilian directorate, under Louis A.
Johnson, could command no one's confidence. He stayed on
some months after McCarthy's strange oration, but in the
winter he resigned—to be succeeded for the duration of
Truman's term by the estimable Robert Lovett. McCarthy
had said there was blood on Marshall's hands, which was a
lie; but there was mud on his uniform, and no President (not
even one who would have told McCarthy to go soak his head
and would have celebrated Marshall from Milwaukee to
Chitamo) could ever again advance national unity by bringing George Catlett Marshall out of his melancholy retirement
in Leesburg. Such was the power of McCarthy's denunciations—a power that came from him, not from his unread
words—that almost no shock was produced when he later
said, defending his Senate speech, that Marshall "would sell

his grandmother for any advantage." Marshall was no longer unassailable. No one was.

In what remained of the Truman years, McCarthy was nothing but an engine of denunciation. Still without power except as a junior Senator from Wisconsin, he denounced and accused and blamed and insulted and vilified and demeaned. He was a pure delight now to the campaign committees, and the Republican organizations were in hot competition to have him come in with a load of documents on anyone who was giving them trouble. Approval came from high places. Robert Taft gave it out that in his opinion "the pro-Communist policies of the State Department fully justified Joe McCarthy in his demand for an investigation." (This had a trace of the Taft caution as well as a broad streak of the prevailing avoidance of reality. It wasn't the "policies" of the State Department that McCarthy had attacked. It was the men who made them, these and a lot who never made them. McCarthy never demanded an investigation of policies, and in fact there had been none. The Tydings investigation had been demanded—perhaps unwisely—by Democrats.) His tongue was wagging everywhere, and the response was gratifying:

When Joe McCarthy had finished Saturday night [the *Sun* of Spring Valley, Wisconsin, noted of a typical speech of the period], there were few skeptics in the jammed auditorium. We were in a position to witness perhaps 400 of the 700 in the audience. Only two remained seated. The rest rose as one person, clapping and cheering. Among them were four able Fort

Atkinson industrialists, two competent Fort Atkinson labor leaders, and half a dozen loyal Democrats.

The fewer the skeptics in a Fort Atkinson auditorium, the fewer the skeptics high in the party councils. This seems a principle of democracy. But he still had some critics in the party. Senator Margaret Chase Smith, of Maine, had, in 1950, drawn up an anti-McCarthy manifesto which became known as "A Declaration of Conscience"; she had as co-signers Edward Thye, of Minnesota; Irving Ives, of New York; George Aiken, of Vermont; Wayne Morse, of Oregon; and Robert Hendrickson, of New Jersey. (McCarthy was not mentioned, but it was he who outraged their consciences: "Certain elements of the Republican Party have materially added to [national] confusion . . . through the selfish political exploitation of fear, bigotry, ignorance, and intolerance. It is high time that we all stopped being tools and victims of totalitarian techniques . . . that if continued here unchecked will surely end what we have come to cherish as the American way." Etc.) But the critics thinned out, and those that remained were ineffective, and by the time of the 1952 Republican convention, McCarthy was in, solid and big. He was given a place on the program—a large place, and the chairman, Walter Hallanan, cued a wild and sickening demonstration by saying that he would give the delegates "Wisconsin's Fighting Marine," a man much maligned for his courage in "exposing the traitors in our government." "From the Halls of Montezuma" blared through the stockyards, and hordes of delegates sprang up with placards lettered "Acheson," "Hiss," and "Lattimore." McCarthy—

large enough now to be above the battle between Taft and Eisenhower and above the need to mention any active candidates—said that Douglas MacArthur was "the greatest American that was ever born";* that it was an awful thing that American wives and mothers must "go so deep into the valley of darkness and despair" because of the war Truman started for publicity purposes; and that he had documents to prove that the government was still loaded with Communists. (His "documents" for the Exhibition Hall were in scale; I remember them as about the size of a highway billboard— charts and graphs on the history of Communism, statistical tables, meaningless names. But they *were* enormous.) He was the hit of the convention.

And he came through it without making any commitments. The morning after Eisenhower's nomination, McCarthy was one of his callers at his Blackstone Hotel headquarters. "Are you pleased with the ticket, Senator?" one of us asked as he came from the candidate's suite. "I think Dick Nixon will make a fine Vice-President," he replied.

* In 1948, when there was a mild MacArthur boom, McCarthy favored Harold Stassen for the Republican nomination. MacArthur had lived in Wisconsin, and there was some native-son support for him. McCarthy wrote a "Dear Folks" letter to constituents, and in it said: "General MacArthur has been a great general. But he is now ready for retirement. . . . Twice before we have had Presidents who became physically weakened during their term of office, and both times it had very sad results. . . . General MacArthur would be much older than either of these two men [Franklin D. Roosevelt and Woodrow Wilson]. . . . Neither his first nor his second marriage, nor his divorce, took place in Wisconsin. . . . May I also extend to you my personal greetings and best wishes."

And he was off for the campaigns, his own and Eisenhower's. A group of capital-gains Republicans got up a kitty to put him on television to attack Adlai Stevenson, whom at one point McCarthy described as "Alger—I mean Adlai." It was a famous speech:

Tonight I shall give you the history of the Democrat candidate . . . who endorses and would continue the suicidal Kremlin-shaped policies of this nation. . . . Keep in mind that each item which I give you taken alone is a small part of [the] jig-saw-puzzle. . . . Stevenson's biography . . . states that [Archibald] MacLeish was the man who brought him into the State Department. MacLeish has been affiliated with . . . Communist fronts. . . . The Democrat candidate says: Judge me by my friends. . . . Alger Hiss and Frank Coe recommended Adlai Stevenson as delegate to a conference which was to determine our post-war policy in Asia. . . . I hold in my hand the official record of the series of lectures. . . . I hold in my hand a photostat of the *Daily Worker* of October 19, 1952. . . . While you may think there could be no connection between the debonair Democrat candidate and a dilapidated Massachusetts barn, I want to show you a picture of the barn. . . . Now let's take a look at the photostat of a document. . . . I hold in my hand copies of the ADA [Americans for Democratic Action] *World*. . . . In Detroit the other day the Democrat candidate made a statement that I had not convicted a single Communist. . . . While his statement is technically correct, its implication is viciously untrue. . . . Of course I have not convicted a single Communist. I am neither a judge nor a jury nor a prosecutor. . . . Now let us examine another piece of the jigsaw puzzle. . . . I hold in my hand—and you people in the television audience can see it—Docket #51-101, case of James F. McGranery, Attorney General vs. the Communist Party. . . . I hold in my hand the answer which J. Edgar Hoover gave. . . . We must have a Republican administration . . . and Congress. . . . [Then] we will have the power to help Dwight Eisenhower scrub and flush and wash clean the foul mess of corruption and Communism in Washington.

America, the Jesuit weekly, devoted two lengthy articles to getting at the truth behind a single sentence in the speech on Stevenson.

As a politician and a partisan, Stevenson could not be hurt as General Marshall was. His strength was not to be found in his lack of tarnish. McCarthy's speech doubtless hurt him, but nothing about it was more distressing than the fact that this flagon of poison was bought by men of power in the country and recommended for consumption by the party that was about to win control of the government; that and the fact that poison could be made of such ingredients.

☞ In Washington, in the fall of 1952, the Subcommittee on Privileges and Elections sat studying McCarthy's canceled checks and bank receipts. How had he come by deposits amounting to $172,623.18, and how had Ray Kiermas, his assistant, banked $96,921.18, and what had become of it all? How about the $10,000 from the Lustron Corporation? How about the Prince of Outer Baldonia? Pepsi-Cola? Seaboard Airline? The Subcommittee had been at this for a year, under three chairmen, none of whom had succeeded in getting McCarthy to come in and talk about Senator Benton's charges, which had occasioned all their pains. McCarthy kept in touch by mail: "Frankly, Guy," he wrote Guy Gillette, of Iowa, "I have not and do not intend to even read, much less answer Benton's smear attack." The Committee did not wish to be accused of discourtesy, so it issued no subpoena. As the Eighty-second Congress was dying, it got out a report that did not condemn him but—in a new genre for Congressional reports—only raised questions. ("Whether under the circumstances it was proper for Senator McCarthy to receive $10,000 from the Lustron Corporation. Whether Senator McCarthy used close associates and members of his family to secrete receipts, commodity and stock speculation, and other financial transactions for ulterior motives.") When the report was issued, McCarthy called it a "new low in dishonesty and smear." A few days after it was issued, his friend William Jenner took over the committee and the report became unavailable. For a while, its market value was about on a par with a Matisse litho.

McCarthy had been renominated by Wisconsin Republicans with fair ease. He toured the state with Eisenhower, who saved his praise of General Marshall for other states and who said he was, like the Senator, very much in favor of rooting out Communists. Eisenhower carried Wisconsin by 979,744 to 622,175. McCarthy carried Wisconsin by 870,444 to 731,402. McCarthy was low man on the state ticket. The figures are interesting, and I have no doubt they prove, as many Democrats argued, that the opposition to him was greatly underrated. He did generate opposition, and those who were most afraid of him often overlooked this fact. But silver linings are often wrapped in clouds, and in 1952 his *support* was the impressive thing. His opponent was a gifted

184

young man, Thomas Fairchild, with an admirable record in
Wisconsin public service—a strong contrast not only with
McCarthy's lying and bullying in national politics, but also
with his unsavory financial dealings, which, though not widely
publicized elsewhere, were well known in Wisconsin.

☞ On January 9, 1953, Senator John McClellan, of
Arkansas, who was to play a large role in the next phase of
McCarthy's career, submitted a report on his stewardship as
chairman of the Senate Committee on Government Operations in the Eighty-second Congress. It was a dull, substantial document describing committee action on proposals to
reorganize the Bureau of Customs and the Veterans Administration; on the provision of fidelity bonds for certain government employees; on transfers or conveyances of government
properties; on the settlement of federal accounts; and on
other routine and generally boring affairs. A relatively juicy
section of the report deals with the work of the Permanent
Subcommittee on Investigations, chaired by Senator Clyde
R. Hoey, of North Carolina. In the Eighty-second Congress,
it had fallen to Senator Hoey's lot to direct inquiries into
some of the more squalid activities of members of the Truman
administration in its last days. The Subcommittee had found
a Democratic National Chairman tampering with the Reconstruction Finance Corporation; an apparent swindle in the
sale of government-owned tankers; the over-the-counter sale
of postmasterships in Mississippi; and other such derelictions.
Both the Committee and the Subcommittee had broad man-
dates that were implicit in their titles, but it was the general

understanding of the Senate, which had seen them both develop from the Congressional reorganization planned by Robert La Follette in 1945, that they were to be primarily concerned with the hard, dry, substantive questions of administrative finance, procedure, and efficiency—and of legislative proposals to improve the performance of executive agencies.

Not to labor a rather small point, the chairmanship of the Committee on Government Operations, which fell to McCarthy in the Eighty-third Congress, was not the largest of plums, and it was a tribute to his imagination and inventiveness that he was able to make of it what he did. He astonished the administration and the Republican leadership in the Senate, and he may have astonished himself as well. After the election, he announced that he was through hunting subversives and would henceforth devote himself to exposing "graft and corruption." He may have thought so. Anyway, what had become of the issue now that the Republicans were in the saddle? The Eisenhower people and the Republicans in Congress thought that nothing was required but the tossing out of a few thousand Truman appointees and a close scrutiny of their replacements. The new President assured the country that he regarded this as a responsibility of the executive branch and that he intended to get at it without delay. There would, of course, be work for Congressional committees in reminding the country of how the Democrats had opened the gates to the enemy; two committees stood by for this assignment—the House Committee on Un-American

Activities, which had been hunting Communists since 1938, and the Senate Committee on Internal Security.

The day after the election, the Scripps-Howard newspapers interviewed McCarthy and were told that he planned "an entirely different role" for himself. "The picture has so infinitely changed," he said. "Now it will be unnecessary for me to conduct a one-man campaign to expose Communists in government. We have a new President who doesn't want party-line thinkers or fellow travelers. He will conduct the fight."

A month later, he was talking quite differently. "We've only scratched the surface on Communism," he said, and he promised that there would be no "slackening" on his part. But the Republican strategists appeared not to have heard this or not to believe it. They planned to take advantage of the atmosphere McCarthy had helped so greatly to create and at the same time to control McCarthy by directing his attention to other matters. I remember being told exactly this by Senator Taft early in January of 1953. When Taft felt smug about anything, he did not just grin like a Cheshire cat—he purred, too, and in time his whole face was suffused by the grin; he was all grin when he explained the fast one that had been pulled on McCarthy by the decision to give the Communist issue to Jenner, the new chairman of the Internal Security Committee, and Harold Velde, of Illinois, who was taking over in the House Un-American Activities Committee. Taft knew that McCarthy was dangerous, and while he had nothing but scorn for Jenner and Velde, he knew they were

187

men of modest abilities, and he felt he had engineered a brilliant coup by bottling McCarthy up in Government Operations, where he would spend his days studying reports from the General Accounting Office, and by letting the furor over Communism expire under the deadening touch of Jenner and Velde. "We've got McCarthy where he can't do any harm," he said. He went on to say that while he thought the Democrats had been too casual in their approach to Communists, he himself had never thought that Communists represented half as serious a menace as the Left liberals and welfare-statists. He wished to be able to do battle with them and not have the issue confused by talk about spies and saboteurs.

Taft died within six months, but he lived and was active long enough to see that he had miscalculated. What should always have been obvious to Eisenhower and Taft—that the demagogue cannot survive except as an oppositionist and the organizer of a flight from reality—soon enough became obvious to McCarthy. What nonsense to suppose that this man, known in all countries and spoken of in all tongues, would resign himself to poring over contracts for the sale of warehouses. Had he been the sensation of the Republican National Convention and the most sought-after campaigner merely to have Robert Taft, a three-time loser, relegate him to a committee looking into "motor pools and office furnishings"? The thought was ludicrous—there are no banner headlines in property conveyances. McCarthy could not function as part of a going concern; McCarthyism could have no future as a doctrine of assent. Why should McCarthy, who had reached the heights with no encouragement from Eisen-

hower and not much from Taft, care about the power or position of either of these leaders? He was in for six years; he
had survived Senator Benton's attempt to expel him from
the Senate; he had, in fact, attended to Senator Benton's expulsion by the voters of Connecticut.

He speedily set things up to suit himself. A glance at the
structure of the Committee he had inherited showed that the
pay-off was in the Permanent Subcommittee, which might,
with an aggressive-enough chairman, investigate just about
anything. He provided the Subcommittee with an aggressive
chairman—himself—and simply ignored the responsibilities
of the parent Committee. For that matter, he ignored the
responsibilities of the Subcommittee, too, and of course the
warrants of the unfortunate Jenner and Velde had, so far as
he was concerned, never been issued. Before the Eisenhower
administration and the new Congress were a month old, before John Foster Dulles had had time to hang the pictures on
the wall in his Foggy Bottom office, McCarthy was raising his
usual kind of hell in the State Department. He had a couple
of file clerks come before the Subcommittee to testify that
Departmental records had been rifled of damning evidence of
Communism and homosexuality. The personnel dossiers were
accessible to a large number of personnel, who could tidy up
their own records at will; therefore, the files were worthless.
It made a nice beginning—a solid foundation for what was
to come. How could Dulles go about the job of cleaning out
the State Department when the dirt had been swept from his
files? Plainly, the Secretary would need assistance, and, as
luck would have it, there was a man ready. Taft's bottle for

McCarthy had never been corked. McCarthy simply poured himself out.

Yet, in a manner of speaking, he was at that moment a genie ready for a genie's fate: to be stuffed back into the bottle. Nothing was more certain than that in the end the Eisenhower administration would be forced to confront his challenge. Even the sleepiest of governments must at some point respond to the threat of subversion. It may shelter McCarthys for a time because there seems more to be gained by doing so than by kicking them out; it may postpone the evil day because its leaders are repelled, as Eisenhower kept saying he was, by the thought of dirtying themselves and their offices in a gutter fight with gutter characters. But a confrontation has to occur—particularly when the subversive attacks such vital organs of the state as the armed services and the agencies of diplomacy.

It is arguable whether the confrontation with McCarthy came early or late—or just on time and in circumstances that might have been anticipated. It seems plain today, though, that when he determined to use the machinery of the Permanent Subcommittee, he stored up trouble for himself as well as for others and created the circumstances, which were probably unpredictable, for the confrontation. Until 1953, he had been, so to say, an independent operator. What he had done he had done for himself and by himself. He had had no staff to speak of, no loyalties except to himself.

In 1953, life became more complicated, and the complications led to a defeat, and the defeat led to ruin. He organized a staff; he involved others in his growing enterprise, and, thanks to the others, the enterprise came a cropper.

He hired Roy M. Cohn as Chief Counsel to the Subcommittee, and Cohn recruited G. David Schine as "Chief Consultant" (a bogus title, fully deserving quotation marks), and thereby hangs the tale of McCarthy's end. He may have been his own worst enemy, but if so, it was at one remove or two. It was Cohn and Schine to whom this lazy demagogue delegated the lion's share of the Subcommittee's work, and Cohn and Schine brought him low within a year.

☞ Cohn came first—appropriately, through the good offices of Walter Winchell, the professional gossip. He was a prodigy of sorts. The son of a judge who was a power in Democratic politics in Bronx County, he had completed at twenty the best kind of education New York City has to offer: the Fieldston School, Horace Mann Academy, Columbia College and Law School. At twenty-one, he was admitted to the bar and, certainly not hindered by his father's prominence in the Democratic Party, to the staff of the United States Attorney in New York. After an apprenticeship on narcotics and smuggling cases, he went into the then flourishing anti-Communist game. He had a hand in sending Julius and Ethel Rosenberg to the electric chair for stealing atomic secrets, in imprisoning thirteen Communist functionaries for conspiring to overthrow the government, and—after being transferred to Washington—in the indictment of Owen Lattimore for perjury. (In 1955, part of the indictment was dismissed. The rest

191

was later withdrawn.) Short and short-tempered, sullen in expression and manner, brutal in speech, Cohn reveled in publicity as McCarthy did, and he loved the hunt for its own sake. He once told Secretary Stevens over the telephone that although he didn't wish to be too rough on a particular witness —General Partridge, Chief of G-2—he couldn't promise to control himself. "I'm afraid once he gets up there [before the Committee], there will not be too much of a way to stop the thing," he said in a phone talk that was being monitored. "You might want a nice gentle fight, but once you get in the ring and start taking a couple of pokes, it gets under your skin." In all probability, Cohn's anti-Communism was somewhat less of a caprice and an improvisation than McCarthy's, for Cohn was Jewish and from New York, and at about the time he came to man's estate and participated in the Rosenberg prosecution, it seemed terribly important to many Jews not only to disassociate themselves from Jewish Communists, but to demonstrate a zealous and fiery anti-Communism. His Jewishness, indeed, was one of the things that qualified him for a part in the Rosenberg case—in which, by pre-arrangement, the entire prosecuting staff and the judge were Jews. But if Cohn's anti-Communism was more than a racket, the zest he displayed for assisting various agencies of government in decontaminating themselves seemed just as heavily freighted with self-interest as McCarthy's, though now and then of a somewhat different sort. When he felt that the Army was carrying justice and decency too far in treating his friend Schine as it would treat any other draftee, he minced no words in advising its civilian authorities that he would punish it (the word a number of Army people thought they heard him use was "wreck") on that account alone.

It was never too difficult to relate Cohn to McCarthyism. He had grown up in a political atmosphere. He had seen at close range the exercise of political power. Communism and anti-Communism contended for the souls of many of his schoolmates. His generation of young men interested in politics had tended far more toward a callous conservatism than toward what they regarded as the bleeding-heart radicalism of the thirties. But Schine was something entirely different. At twenty-six, he was a good-looking young man in the sallow, sleekly coiffed, and somnolent-eyed style that one used to associate with male orchestra singers, and there was some proof that the world was not completely on the skew-gee in the fact that the appearance of the "Chief Consultant" was not altogether deceiving. He had never been an orchestra singer, but he had at one time been a press agent for the Vaughn Monroe orchestra, and he had written and published two or three melancholy, ungrammatical ballads, one of which was called "Please Say Yes or It's Goodbye" and runs in part:

> Haven't found a good solution,
> There is only one way out.
> My heart is in a sad confusion,
> And I've got to end this doubt.
> So I'm asking you to tell me how things stand.
> A simple "yes" or "no" is all that I demand.

Schine had been brought up in wealth, which had come to his family through the ownership of the Schine Hotels and of a chain of motion-picture theaters. He had attended Phillips-Andover and Harvard College, where he had been remarkable as the owner of a Cadillac with a two-way telephone. He had dabbled in Hollywood a bit as well as in Tin Pan Alley. He had built up what he claimed, without serious contradiction, was a cigar museum that housed the largest and most varied collection of cigars in the world. In time, by some process almost impossible to imagine, he took up ideology, and even produced a commentary on it. Whenever his patron, McCarthy, or his chum, Roy Cohn, was asked about Schine's qualifications as chief consultant, the respondent would refer, with professions of great admiration, to a work called "Definition of Communism," by G. David Schine. This monograph ran to six pages and bore the colophon of the Schine Hotels—"Finest Under the Sun." In a couple of thousand deplorably chosen words, Schine managed to put the Russian Revolution, the founding of the Communist Party, and the start of the first Five-Year Plan in years when these events did not occur; he gave Lenin the wrong first name, hopelessly confused Stalin with Trotsky, Marx with Lenin, Alexander Kerensky with Prince Lvov, and fifteenth-century utopianism with twentieth-century Communism. Copies of this bedside treasury of wrong dates and mistaken identities and misunderstood principles were to be found in Schine Hotels, of which David's father had appointed him President and General Manager, from Miami to Hollywood. It was said to have been a copy found under a room-service menu in a hotel in Coral Gables or some such place that brought Schine and Cohn and McCarthy together.

A guest in the hotel read the pamphlet, was struck by its insights, sought out its author, introduced him to George Sokolsky, who introduced him to Roy Cohn, who introduced him to McCarthy, who hired him. At any rate, somehow or other it happened—he was hired, and as the whole Western world was soon to know, Cohn and Schine became great companions.

☞ Cohn and Schine—or, at any rate, Cohn, with Schine's encouragement—ran the Subcommittee in 1953. They had a sizable staff below them and McCarthy above them, but the strategies were theirs. When they came upon something good, McCarthy would come in for the kill, but as a rule he had to be told by them what to kill. Once, I recall, there was an announcement of an investigation of federal scholarship and academic-exchange programs. I went to the Capitol for the first hearing; it developed that the day's only scheduled witness had been taken ill, so Cohn asked McCarthy to announce an adjournment, which McCarthy did. The reporters, who had been in some confusion as to exactly which of the numerous programs was under investigation, gathered around McCarthy to find out. "What are you after, Joe—the Fulbrights, the Smith-Mundt fellows, or some of the others?" "It beats me," McCarthy said. "I thought they were all Halfbrights. Ask Roy. He thought this one up." I forget what Cohn said. The hearings never were resumed.

Cohn thought most things up. He started the Subcommittee off with an investigation of the Voice of America, which was then the stronghold and may in a sense have been the birthplace of the Loyal American Underground. Ever since the Tydings hearings, McCarthy had been throwing out hints about a network of true patriots within the government feeding him information. In his Senate speech on February 20, 1950, when he went through his "81 cases," he had said, "If it were not for some good loyal Americans in the State Department . . . I should not have been able to present this picture to the Senate tonight." And he was as defiant then as in 1954 about concealing identities. He said the State Department was trying hard to uncover these people, whose jobs "would not be worth a tinker's dam" if their names were made known, and he promised that "the Senator from Wisconsin [will never name] the government employees who may have helped him secure the information which he has presented to the Senate." There could not have been much truth in this. Why, when he was just a few days out of obscurity and perhaps soon to be returned to it, should anyone in the State Department have given him information? Besides, he had no information; his cases all had been in Congressional files for three or four years. If he had been given anything it could have been nothing more useful than the phone extension for the House Appropriations Committee.

Later, to be sure, as his power grew, he was fed information. People in the FBI were leaking to him frequently, and probably a few in the State Department and elsewhere. But the government did not become the "bloody sieve" that Stuart Symington called it until 1953. The Voice of America was the place where the underground was really organized and functioning. In its New York offices, there were said to be about thirty active members, and almost the first thing Cohn and Schine did was move to New York, where Schine had a suite in the Waldorf Towers. There they interviewed underground members, and there, later, they examined the people the underground had fingered. What they got from the underground was, of course, the most trivial sort of intelligence. Mr. A. hadn't liked a book all anti-Communists were supposed to like. Miss B. had neglected to marry Mr. C., with whom she lived. Mrs. D., on the religion desk, was really a freethinker. Though Mr. E., who denounced Stalin daily in Russian, talked like an anti-Communist, he had been a Communist as recently as 1929, and perhaps his conversion was a fake. Mr. F., the engineer who chose the sites for some new Voice transmitters, was said by some engineers to have chosen poorly, and possibly his idea had been to put them in poor locations so that no one would ever hear the broadcasts. Mr. G., supposedly a specialist in Papuan affairs, had written several scripts that had greatly offended Papuan anti-Communists, and if he weren't a Communist, why should he go on this way? It was all pretty much on that level, and it had to be, for the plain fact was that the Voice of America, like most government agencies at that time, had been combed through and shaken out and fluoroscoped and leeched, and if any Communists remained, they were so well hidden that the sort of people who were in the underground would never find them—unless, of course, some of those in the underground *were* Communists, which was not altogether out of the question. Anyway, it appeared to be pretty poor stuff. But Cohn and Schine accepted it gladly and worked wonders with it, proving once again that part of the magic of McCarthyism lay in its Luther Burbank touch with humble and unpromising materials. Working with nothing but a mass of trifling, unrelated, and mostly negative facts, it could produce whole fields of Shasta daisies. By the time Cohn and Schine and McCarthy and the television cameras were through, they had toppled most of the Voice leadership, forced the administration to disown it, sown despair and confusion throughout the ranks, and scandalized a good many foreigners who had been in the habit of listening to it. And in Boston, an unnerved engineer who had been involved in the siting of a Voice transmitter killed himself; later, there was competent testimony to the effect that there was nothing wrong with the locations.

For pure destructiveness, the investigation of the Voice was a triumph, and it was impossible to escape the conclusion that destruction was all that the investigators had sought. Often, officials who had been accused of nothing at all and were only eager to save their divisions from being ruined by the testimony of wounded or embittered or nutty subordinates sought to explain their fears and hopes. They found the investigators supremely uninterested. Causes and reasons and explanations and extenuating circumstances simply bored them. They were frank to say that all they wanted was circumstantial evidence of malfeasance. Accomplishment was none of their business. Once a group of Voice executives went to the Schine suite to argue that their agency was serving the country well and that no mistakes it had made should be used to discredit it before American and world opinion. "This committee isn't set up to show that agencies are doing what they're supposed to do," Roy Cohn said. "Our job is to find the weak spots." It was pointed out that the impression the hearings gave was that there were nothing but failures—and willful failures at that, probably the work of Communists. "We just aren't concerned with what you do most of the time," Cohn said. "It's the mistakes that interest us."

The Voice of America investigation came to an end in late March of 1953. It was never completed. It just stopped—its largest possibilities for tumult had been exhausted, and it trailed off into nothingness. Then, suddenly, Cohn and Schine turned up in Paris—on Easter Sunday, April 4—and were off on a historic adventure. It was marked from beginning to end by comedy—and at the end by devastation in the International Information Administration, by bitterness and anguish in every American embassy in Western Europe. This was no joke, but the trip was. Europe laughed its head off. In the basic circumstance, there was the ready-made plot for a gorgeous farce: two young Americans —a study in contrasts, like Laurel and Hardy or Rosencrantz and Guildenstern, with names memorably mated and advantageous for puns and rhymes—madly, preposterously bent on the ideological purification of the greatest government on earth. And there were such familiar fixtures of low comedy as a female secret agent who had once been the toast of Vienna, a contretemps that involved a platoon of diplomats involved in a search for a missing pair of pants, and an altercation—denied by the principals but believed by newspapermen and, in any case, firmly fixed in legend—in which Schine chased Cohn through a hotel lobby, swatting him over the head with a rolled-up magazine. The British correspondents who followed them quickly began chanting, "Positively, Mr. Cohn! Absolutely, Mr. Schine!" The pair spent forty hours in Paris, sixteen in Bonn, nineteen in Frankfurt, sixty in Munich, forty-one in Vienna, twenty-three in Belgrade, twenty-four in Athens, twenty in Rome, and six in London.

What was it all about? After a time, it turned out to be about books in I.I.A. libraries, but the interest in books was probably minor at the start. The expedition had been set up only a few days in advance, and the purpose of it was so obscure that everywhere the travelers touched down they gave a different account of why they were traveling. In Paris, they said they were looking for inefficiency in government offices overseas. In Bonn, they said they were looking for subversives. Asked in Munich which it was, Cohn explained that it was both. "Efficiency," he said, "includes complete political reliability. If anyone is interested in the Communists, then he cannot be efficient." Back home, on "Meet the Press," he said he didn't consider himself competent to judge performances abroad and had gone only to look into "certain things."

In Rome, a new angle came to light. McCarthy, in Washington, had told the press that they had been sent abroad to bring back a report on the amount of money that had been spent "in putting across the Truman administration" in Europe. This was news to Cohn, but he was equal to it. "We haven't heard about that," he said, "but anything the chairman of our committee says, if he said it, goes with us."

They had no purpose beyond McCarthy's continuing one of free-style, catch-as-catch-can harassment. For this the trip was unnecessary; its victories could have been enjoyed without any traveling at all. The book-burning was not a consequence of the trip; the State Department had begun to pulp, ignite, and donate to charity the offending volumes the moment it learned that McCarthy had developed bibliographic interests. By the time Cohn and Schine got to the libraries, most of them had been thoroughly bowdlerized; what remained to be done scarcely required their attentions. In terms of McCarthyism's own economy, the trip was wholly unnecessary.

Nevertheless, it was richly productive of mischief. Cohn and Schine were a pair to be laughed at, but they made a bitter jest, for they moved about under a crazy-quilted panoply that unmistakably bore, among other devices, the Great Seal of the United States.

They were simply on the prowl for anything they could turn up by talking with underground members or fellow-travelers—and with any Europeans who might have tidbits. They employed a woman named Hede Massing, the former toast of Vienna and, in her post-toast life, the wife of Gerhart Eisler, a Moscow agent, and herself a former Communist spy in Washington, to give them the benefit of her observations of American government employees in Europe. And they

201

hired a jobless German politician named Hermann Aumer (he had lost his Bundestag seat when it became known that an oil company had paid him 22,000 marks to vote for an increase in gasoline prices) to brief them on the American High Commission in Germany. (Aumer later said his main work had been to prepare a memorandum on anti-McCarthy articles appearing in German newspapers that might be receiving American subsidies.)

Cohn's and Schine's dealings with persons such as Aumer and Hede Massing were for the most part conducted in private. What made the trip a sensation was the public behavior of the travelers, which was observed and recorded for posterity by as many journalists as are normally assigned to such eminences as kings, presidents, and Rita Hayworth. Even their exchanges with hotel clerks were taken down. They had a standard and characteristically tasteless joke for hotel registrations. Asking for adjoining rooms but insisting that the accommodations be separate, one or the other would explain to the generally uncomprehending room clerk, "You see, we don't work for the State Department."

Vienna was a typical way station for the investigators. They arrived there by plane from Munich on Friday evening, April 10. (Hede Massing had been at the airport to see them off, and as Cohn and Schine went up the ramp, Cohn shouted down, "So long, Hede. If anything goes wrong, get in touch with Joe!") They stayed in Vienna all day Saturday and into Sunday afternoon. The total elapsed time was forty-one hours, which was slightly above the par of twenty-eight.

Three and a half hours were devoted to the labor of inspections, surveys, and talks with government officials. Two and a half hours were spent in press conferences. They held their first immediately upon landing. Cohn denied the story about Schine having hit him on the head. "A pack of lies," he said. He then went on to give the routine talk about their inquiry, pointing out that the visit to Austria was unique in that they had no reports of American subversion in that country. "We are not trying to get anybody here," he said. At noon, they met with the Ambassador for twenty minutes. *Au courant* with diplomacy and psychological warfare on that particular frontier, they went shopping. Schine visited a tobacconist and picked out some unusual cigars for his cigar museum. This was followed by a latish lunch with American officials, after which they went back to their hotel, leaving it in midafternoon for a tour of the spacious Soviet Information Center. Here, their interest, which, reporters said, had been noticeably lagging, perked up. According to one account, Cohn and Schine, "speeding through the cards, discovered that the authors Agnes Smedley and Theodore Dreiser, among others, were represented in the Soviet collection. An American escorting officer, pointing out other books on the open shelves, showed them that Mark Twain was also represented. Then the party headed for the U.S. Information Center, three blocks away, to study the files for the presence of such authors as had been spotted in the Soviet's card catalogue down the street.

The full inspection of books and periodicals lasted just a bit less than thirty minutes. Right after it, Cohn and Schine held their second Vienna press conference. The reporters

203

asked, politely, how a combination of ignorance of the subject and half-hour inspections could possibly enable them to form reasonable judgments of government operations in Vienna. They airily explained that they were supplementing what they had seen and learned with information gathered from reliable "Austrian sources." The press was unable to learn the identity of the Austrian sources; some of its members wondered by what feats of magic they had managed to see any Austrians, since their only known visitor was a German newspaper writer and they had visited no one. They are still wondering.

On Sunday morning, the travelers went out to the airport and said farewell to lovely Vienna, and two days later flew back to McCarthy.

I was working in Europe a few months after Cohn and Schine left, covering much the same territory they had covered, and I had a chance to see what they had wrought. Actually, not many people had been fired as a result of their trip. The most notable victim, probably, was Theodore Kaghan, who had been a Public Affairs Officer in the United States High Commission for Germany. A witness at the Voice of America hearings had called him a "pseudo-American," and it had come out that in the thirties he had shared an apartment in New York with a Communist. He might have survived these scandals if he had not described Cohn and Schine as "junketeering gumshoes" to a newspaperman during the tour, and he might have survived even this if the State Department had not been in such a panic to get rid of him. He was eased out speedily, and so were a few others, but what really damaged the whole American complex in

Europe was the shame and anger of the government servants who had witnessed the whole affair. I must have talked with a hundred people in Bonn, Paris, Rome, and London who told me their resignations were written, signed, stamped, and ready for mailing or delivery. Some did not really want to resign; others planned to, and were simply waiting until they could find other jobs or make the necessary arrangements for getting their families out. No one, probably, could estimate the number of people whose departure could be traced to this affair, and surely no one could estimate its effect on morale. Morale sank very low—so low, indeed, that I was surprised to note, among government people in Europe, a willingness to denounce McCarthy in extravagant language and to ridicule Cohn and Schine. This was most unlike Washington at the time, and the explanation I was given was that very few people cared any longer whether they held their jobs or not.

☞ Cohn and Schine had worked together six months and had been back from Europe two months when Schine was officially advised that the United States Army required his services. This was early in July, and by the following April, the entire country found nothing more absorbing than an investigation centering on Schine's efforts to serve his country in other ways and on the efforts of others—notably McCarthy, Cohn, and the Secretary of the Army, Robert Stevens—to accommodate him. Of these three, McCarthy was perhaps the most unwilling collaborator. It was never entirely clear what McCarthy felt about Schine. At first he had welcomed him to his merry company. Why not? Schine was agreeable. He owned hotels in delightful places. He had the Waldorf Towers suite—a nice place for executive sessions. Moreover, Roy Cohn, who was invaluable, liked Schine enormously. McCarthy sometimes said Schine was the greatest expert on Communism he knew. But McCarthy said that about a lot of people, and when Roy Cohn began fretting himself about Schine's Army life and giving more and more time to it, McCarthy began, understandably, to look upon Schine as a pain in the neck. Once, when Schine was in service and Cohn was trying to have the Army put him on some kind of duty with the Committee, McCarthy telephoned Robert Stevens and said, according to the notes of a monitored telephone call introduced at the hearings:

I would like to ask you one personal favor. For God's sake, don't put Dave in service and assign him back on my committee. . . . He is a good boy but there is nothing indispensable about him . . . it is one of the few things I have seen Roy completely unreasonable about. . . . Roy was next to quitting the committee. He thought I had gone back on the committee.

But McCarthy did not talk Cohn out of his unreason— possibly he never tried—and Cohn devoted himself, on the one hand, to making life easy for Schine and, on the other, to making it rough for the Army. It was Cohn's rage that led to the affairs of Major Peress and General Zwicker and the Fort Monmouth investigation and the Army-McCarthy hearings in which the whole series of messes was disclosed. It was

Cohn's loyalty to Schine and McCarthy's to Cohn that led to decline and eventual fall.

☞ "In the late spring of 1954," Michael Straight wrote in *Trial by Television,* a vivid account of the hearings, "there occurred in Washington one of the most extraordinary dramas in recent history." He might have said more. Nothing remotely like the Army-McCarthy hearings had ever been seen in American history. As a spectacle of a political character enacted before an audience, there has never anywhere been anything to match it. The audience alone was almost beyond belief—upward of 20,000,000 at a time, or not much less than the population of the entire country just before the Civil War. The hearings ran for thirty-five days, or 187 hours on television, and several times 20,000,000 saw long stretches of it. Unlike the onlookers at most political spectacles, this audience had not been shanghaied. The compulsion to look—or, in the jargon of the medium, "to view" —came from the drama itself. Television, by the easy admission it gives to easy entertainment, has enormous power to distract, but no deliberate or commercial distraction, conceived and executed by professionals at great cost, has ever gripped the attention as this interminable, plotless, improvised, amateur production did in early 1954. Hundreds of thousands saw every hour of it.

The hearings were extraordinary in form. In fact, they were not really "hearings" at all—though certain investigative procedures were followed. Karl Mundt, the ranking Republican after McCarthy, assumed the chair, rapped for order now and then, directed the counsel to get information, and used all the platitudes he had absorbed as a champion boy orator and as a Senator. Ray Jenkins, a veteran defender of moonshiners and husband-shooters in Tennessee, who was the Subcommittee's special counsel and turned out to be a special pleader for McCarthy, elicited the general testimony on the Subcommittee's behalf. But just about there the resemblance to hearings ended. The rest was ordeal, combat, theater, duel, confession, catharsis, the testing of wills—all accomplished through a flood of talk about matters that would not have involved the principals at all if they had not involved a man whose challenge was anything but trivial. It was this challenge that was being faced in ways that at first seemed stupid and pitiful and later seemed, to some at least, a kind of institutional adaptation, a new organ generated by a free but troubled society to meet a new condition of existence.

The hearings were never really *about* Cohn and Schine, or Major Peress or General Zwicker, but in the course of them their stories were told. Schine got his draft call, and immediately he and Cohn began to high-pressure the Army. The Army considered the source and made no complaints. Cohn and Schine had gone to work for an immediate commission on General Miles Reber, the Army's chief of legislative liaison and a man accustomed to demands from Capitol Hill. The Army counsel, Joseph L. Welch, questioned him.

WELCH: Were you actually aware of Mr. Cohn's position as counsel for this Committee?

208

REBER: I was, Mr. Welch.

WELCH: Did that position . . . increase or diminish the interest with which you pursued the problem?

REBER: . . . I feel that it increased the interest.

WELCH: Disregarding the word "improper" influences or pressure, do you recall any instance comparable to this in which you were put under greater pressure?

REBER: . . . I recall no instance in which I was put under greater pressure.

Cohn wanted Schine to have a commission right away—no fuss about filling out forms or establishing qualifications. The matter went to the Army Chief of Staff and on to the Secretary of the Army and on to the Secretary of Defense. Two colonels were assigned to explore the possibilities for helping Schine. The possibilities simply did not exist. General Walter Bedell Smith, Undersecretary of State and a former military aide to the President, was asked if he could do anything to break out of channels. Perhaps Schine could be put in Central Intelligence. Allen Dulles, the director, was sought out. Something could probably have been arranged somewhere, somehow, but there was Schine's draft board and the Selective Service people to think of. Hell would break loose if the thing turned into a draft scandal.

Cohn and Schine had the thought that the Army might use Schine as an assistant to the Secretary. Schine asked the Secretary to drop up to the Waldorf Towers suite; the Secretary was pleased to do so. They talked together a while, and Schine asked if Stevens would care to see Senator McCarthy

209

holding an investigation—of the Army, as chance would have it—in the federal courthouse at Foley Square. Stevens thought that would be nice. Schine summoned his Cadillac. Jenkins brought out further details:

JENKINS: Was anything said to you . . . with reference to preferential treatment to be accorded Schine?

STEVENS: Well, Mr. Schine and I had quite an interesting talk in the car riding downtown.

JENKINS: Will you relate what the conversation was, Mr. Secretary?

STEVENS: Well, the conversation was along the line that I was doing a good job in ferreting out Communists.

JENKINS: Was that your statement or his?

STEVENS: That was Mr. Schine's statement. . . . He thought I could go a long way in this field. And he would like to help me. He thought that it would be a much more logical plan for him to become a special assistant of mine.

JENKINS: Than to do what?

STEVENS: Than . . . to be inducted into the Army.

There was nothing for it but for Schine to allow himself to be drafted. Cohn received assurances, though, that the matter would not be dropped there and that efforts would be made to allow the Army to avail itself of Schine's remarkable knowledge and experience of Communism, which was—was it not?—the enemy. Schine found himself a member of Company K at Fort Dix, in New Jersey. At the hearings, the company commander, Captain Joseph Miller, said that Schine stopped him on their first barracks encounter:

Private Schine asked me—or rather told me—that if I ever wanted to make a little trip to Florida that he knew a Colonel Bradley—but here I cut him off in the middle of a sentence.

Captain Miller had a stern sense of duty and a poor sense of Schine's importance. But he was to learn. Schine went A.W.O.L. He was released from drill to make or accept 250 long-distance calls. Word was getting about that he had certain things going for him in Washington. And he did. He got passes on all weekends and holidays throughout his basic training, which may have been basic but wasn't in his case training. One rainy day, Captain Miller found Schine sheltered in a truck while the rest of Company K was on the firing range. Schine said he was studying logistics and other things. He added, according to Miller, that "his purpose was to remake the military along modern lines."

In time, Cohn did succeed. Schine was virtually detached from the Army and returned to service with the Committee. The hearings were replete with stories of other interventions and other concessions. Many people found them shocking, and they were, but worse was to come. Efforts to obtain special treatment, to avoid unpleasant duties, to goldbrick—this is all somehow a traditional feature of life in an armed democracy. What was far more of an outrage was the revenge that Cohn and McCarthy took on the Army: the fuss over Major Peress, the humiliation of General Zwicker, and the near destruction of the Fort Monmouth installation. It may be that in McCarthy's case revenge was not the spur. His interest in Schine was only an aspect of his need for Cohn

But he did need daily victories, and Cohn—seeking Schine's liberation from basic training—led him to the Peress case and from that to General Zwicker and thence to Fort Monmouth,* and he got some victories.

☞ The Army-McCarthy hearings were first conceived as an essay in mediation. McCarthy had called Zwicker in for an accounting on the Peress affair and had mocked and tormented an honorable officer. The Secretary of the Army attempted to protect the General by saying he would not allow him to testify again. Egged on by the Vice-President, the Republicans on the Subcommittee had summoned Stevens to a luncheon with McCarthy and had got the Secretary to agree to have Zwicker testify. The Secretary read the fine print and was sick at heart. Some journalists got from John Adams, the Army counsel, a chronology of events and published it. McCarthy made countercharges. The Subcommittee moved in and arranged a confrontation, though this was no part of its business or, for that matter, of the Senate's. The Senate has no powers of this sort. (It does have certain judicial functions —to try impeachments and judge its own members.) Nor is it empowered to find facts for their own interesting sake or to referee arguments between public officials. The Army said that McCarthy and members of his committee had used

---

* It cannot be overlooked, though, that McCarthy held an ancient grudge against the Army. His tactics in the Malmédy investigation bore a striking resemblance to his tactics in the 1953 and 1954 investigations.

"improper" methods in attempting to get preferential treatment for Schine. McCarthy said that the Army had been holding Schine as a "hostage" in order to force him to abandon his investigations.

Broadly speaking, our system, up to 1954, had functioned by entrusting the judgment of such abuses as were charged—provided, of course, they were not legally actionable—to public opinion. If exposure did not cause them to come to an end, then the electorate would in time have its chance to sit as a jury. Senate intervention was a distinct novelty.

Yet it seemed to me at the time, as it does now, that three things of value were accomplished by the hearings. In the first place, McCarthy was stopped from further acts of destruction for the duration of the hearings. In the second place, the fact that he was a seditionist was made manifest to the entire country, so that only those tolerant of sedition (a very considerable number of Americans) could remain tolerant toward him. In the third place, a Senate opposition was forged; three Democrats and one Republican on the Subcommittee had no choice but to appear as antagonists. (I am not implying that they would have failed their responsibilities if a choice had been theirs.) Beyond all this, there was a kind of aesthetic dividend: a man named Joseph Linden Welch, a proper Bostonian from Iowa, the son of an English housemaid and a Jack Tar of the Royal Navy, was provided an opportunity, which he seized, to pose against the Americanism that Fulton Lewis, Jr., said was a synonym for McCarthyism an Americanism compounded of love of country,

213

a decent respect for the opinions of mankind, and an adherence to the tradition that esteems the public uses of fairness, reason, compassion, wit, and love.

The hearings on Schine stopped the hearings on Fort Monmouth. McCarthy was quick to recognize this. He asked the Secretary of the Army sixteen times if the Department of the Army wished the investigations discontinued; Stevens did, of course, but, as a loyal member of the Eisenhower team, he was unwilling to concede that anything done by Congress could be contrary to the national interest. Sixteen times the Secretary answered evasively. But McCarthy knew the score, and on the seventeenth try he gave it:

McCARTHY: Now can you tell us today whether or not you wanted the hearings at Fort Monmouth suspended?

STEVENS: I wanted them suspended in order that the Army could carry out the hearings themselves and stop the panic that was being created in the minds of the public on a basis that was not justified by the facts.

McCARTHY: How did you finally succeed in getting the hearings suspended?

STEVENS: How did I succeed?

McCARTHY: Yes; they are suspended as of today. How did you succeed?

STEVENS: They aren't suspended as far as I know.

McCARTHY: Bob, don't give me that. You know that the hearings were suspended the day you or someone filed your charges against Mr. Cohn, Mr. Carr, and myself. . . . Let's not be coy.

McCarthy was entirely right. The Fort Monmouth hearings were stopped, and from almost any point of view except

McCarthy's this was all to the good.* (It was to the good even from the point of view of those who were ready to concede that investigation might be justified, for McCarthy was not really investigating, but was merely asserting that employees who had not been finally cleared under existing security procedures were certifiable subversives.) More than that, the whole enterprise of McCarthyism was suspended for the duration of the hearings—and, as it was to turn out, for a good deal longer. The mere commotion and hubbub of the Army-McCarthy hearings delayed the whole process of erosion, which had seemed very far advanced by the spring of 1954.

The hearings established before most of the nation the fact that McCarthy himself was an enemy of the established order. This came out in a number of ways but in none more vividly than in the colloquy with Joseph Welch over the information contained in the purloined letter from J. Edgar

---

* In the perspective of 1959, it appears more vital than ever. Russian progress in missile development increases the need for effective warning systems, and ours, as of this writing, is not as effective as it needs to be. An intercontinental ballistic missile fired from Soviet territory would take about thirty minutes to reach this country. It takes twenty minutes for the countdown on the best of these we have in various stages of development. This leaves ten minutes for detection, the elimination of ambiguities, and the making of the decision to retaliate—which, under existing law, requires Presidential approval. The elimination of ambiguities is far from easy. A flock of geese could be mistaken for onrushing missiles by our radar; a bombardment of aluminum foil might thoroughly confuse us. The Fort Monmouth people were working on these problems, among others, and their work was clearly essential to the national interest.

Hoover to G-2, which had been turned over to McCarthy by one of his fellow seditionists. McCarthy was on the witness stand, under solemn oath and under examination by the special counsel to the Army:

WELCH: Senator McCarthy, when you took the stand you knew of course that you were going to be asked about the letter, did you not?

MCCARTHY: I assumed that would be the subject.

WELCH: And you of course understood that you were going to be asked the source from which you got it?

MCCARTHY: . . . I won't answer that. . . .

WELCH: Could I have the oath that you took read to us wholly by the reporter?

MUNDT: Mr. Welch, that doesn't seem to be an appropriate question . . . it's the same oath you took.

WELCH: The oath included a promise, a solemn promise by you to tell the truth and nothing but the truth. Is that correct, sir?

MCCARTHY: Mr. Welch, you are not the first individual that tried to get me to betray the confidence and give out the names of my informants. You will be no more successful than those who have tried it in the past.

WELCH: I am only asking you, sir, did you realize when you took the oath that you were making a solemn promise to tell the truth to this Committee?

MCCARTHY: I understand the oath, Mr. Welch.

WELCH: And when you took it, did you have some mental reservation, some Fifth or Sixth Amendment notion that you could measure what you would tell?

MCCARTHY: I don't take the Fifth Amendment.

WELCH: Have you some private reservation when you take the oath that . . . lets you be the judge of what you will testify to?

216

McCARTHY: The answer is that there is no reservation about telling the whole truth.

WELCH: Thank you, sir. Then tell us who delivered the document to you?

McCARTHY: The answer is no. You will not get the information.

WELCH: You wish then to put your own interpretation on your oath and tell us less than the whole truth?

McCARTHY: . . . you can go right ahead and try until doomsday. You will not get the names of any informants who rely upon me to protect them.

WELCH: . . . will you tell us where you were when you got it?

McCARTHY: No.

WELCH: Were you in Washington?

McCARTHY: The answer was I would not tell you.

WELCH: How soon after you got it did you show it to anyone?

McCARTHY: I don't remember.

WELCH: To whom did you first show it?

McCARTHY: I don't recall.

WELCH: Can you think of anyone to whom you showed it?

McCARTHY: Oh, I assume that it was passed down to my staff most likely.

WELCH: Name the ones on your staff who had it.

McCARTHY: I wouldn't know.

WELCH: You wouldn't know?

McCARTHY: No.

WELCH: Would it include Mr. Cohn?

McCARTHY: It might.

WELCH: It would, wouldn't it?

McCARTHY: I said it might.

The hearings created an image of the destructive personality, a figure apart, in a way, from the recalcitrant witness

217

Welch tried to examine. McCarthy was not merely above the law in refusing to name his informants; he was above, or outside, any system of order, of fair play, of decency, or even simulated respect. It was for him to throw the sessions into confusion whenever he chose and for others to make no effort to apply the tests of germaneness or truthfulness. "I get awfully sick and tired," he said, "of sitting down here at the end of the table and having whomever wants to interrupt in the middle of a sentence"—and a few minutes later, in the middle of someone else's sentence:

> McCARTHY: Mr. Chairman.
> MUNDT: Do you have a point of order?
> McCARTHY: Call it a point of order or call it what you may, when counsel for Mr. Stevens and Mr. Hensel [Struve Hensel, counsel for the Department of Defense] and Mr. Adams makes a statement . . . do I have a right to correct it or do we find halfway through my statement that Mr. Welch should not have made his statement and therefore I cannot point out that he was lying?

The three Democrats on the Subcommittee—John Mc-Clellan, Stuart Symington, and Henry Jackson—had, in the late summer of 1953, refused to participate in any of its affairs on the ground that McCarthy had usurped certain functions that belonged to the group as a whole. Their basic complaint was that he hired staff members without consulting any of them; they said they would take no part in hearings until he agreed to mend his ways. He did not of course mend his ways; he merely said, early in 1954, he would do so. Had his been an ordinary subcommittee, the defection of the entire minority would have effectively disabled it. But it was not an ordinary subcommittee—it had been, in that period, an instrument of blackmail, and from the point of view of the institutions and human beings it damaged, it mattered very little whether or not the Democrats were sitting in on its deliberations. The blackmailing had gone on before they left, and it continued after they left. This is not to say that the Democratic withdrawal was a useless and feeble gesture of protest. In the atmosphere of 1953, it took courage to offer McCarthy any kind of resistance, and as things stood in those days—with the White House as terrified by him as the most vulnerable Senator*—the three Democrats took about the only kind of action that was consistent with a sense of their own welfare. Their withdrawal, however, did not alter the fact that McCarthy moved where he wanted without visible resistance.

This came to an end with the hearings. Before 20,000,000 people, there was no choice for the Democrats but to resist, at whatever cost. This man, after all, had accused their party of presiding over two decades of treason. More than that, he was testing each of them individually. The drama derived its tension from the greatest of all sources: the conflict of human spirits. The great audience was far more interested in the players and their relationship one to another than in the

---

* The White House did protest when a member of McCarthy's staff, J. B. Matthews, wrote an article in the *American Mercury* charging widespread subversion among the Protestant clergy, and it would have protested again if McCarthy had said that God himself was a Communist or even if he had desecrated the American flag on the Capitol steps.

larger conflict of ideas and institutions. Every face was a study, every voice a revelation of the man from whom it came. On camera, McCarthy was not the genial assassin who might be encountered in the corridors. He snarled, and he roared, and if peace with honor was possible (Mundt, Dirksen, and Henry Dworshak, of Idaho, held that it was), it was to be had at the heavy risk of having to acknowledge tarnishes. The Democrats could not so much as toy with the idea of accommodation, for McCarthy missed no opportunity to make an issue of party.

At one point, in the dispute over the FBI document, McClellan said that the issue was "whether a Senate subcommittee is entitled to gain by theft what it cannot legally obtain by subpoena." McCarthy accused McClellan of trying to railroad him into jail. "I'm asking no such thing," McClellan said. "I don't care. . . . No one's afraid of you out any more than in." This was not strictly the case; the time to stop fearing him was not yet at hand, and the fear of many reasonable men at the time was great enough to lead them to believe that the country would be far better off if a way could be found of jailing him. (For the rest of that year, the Department of Justice was under heavy pressure to seek his indictment for violation of the espionage laws.) But McClellan had breathed scorn and defiance, and from that moment on the spell was broken, not only in the Subcommittee but in the Senate. This is not to say that McClellan, Symington, and Jackson were from that moment on models of valor and eloquent defenders of the faith. They still, sometimes, appeared to be models of discretion and uncertain of what their faith

220

was. They vied with McCarthy for the honor of being the toughest Communist-fighter ("I can be as hard as anyone in rooting out Communists," McClellan said), and they competed with the Republicans in a kind of slavering praise of the Federal Bureau of Investigation, an agency deeply involved in some of the worst of McCarthy's offenses, and of its director, J. Edgar Hoover, who more than anyone else knew what a fraud McCarthy was and who was the one man who might have dared at any time to pit his reputation against McCarthy. But the Democrats did have their moments of strength and truth and eloquence, and if John McClellan had spoken with bravado when he said he knew no fear of McCarthy on either side of prison bars, Stuart Symington spoke his feelings of the moment when, having been accused of cowardice by McCarthy, he looked at the breeder of tumult and said:

You said something about being afraid. I want you to know from the bottom of my heart that I am not afraid of anything about you or anything you've got to say any time, any place, anywhere.

The hearings ended on June 17, and two and a half months later the Subcommittee made public four reports. The Republican majority said that the Department of the Army had failed to establish its charges against McCarthy and that McCarthy had failed to exercise sufficient discipline over his staff. The Democrats said that McCarthy had behaved improperly and had been encouraged by Stevens' pusillanimity. One Republican, Charles Potter, of Michigan, filed for himself the opinion that McCarthy had behaved badly, and another, Everett Dirksen, said that he failed to see improprieties by McCarthy or his staff. The reports were of little interest or significance. Long before they were written, it was evident that the hearings had led to a new situation. McCarthy had not been crushed, but he had suffered a major defeat. He no longer owned a subcommittee. The Fort Monmouth investigations had not only been suspended—they had been killed. Roy Cohn had won no friends, and it was clearly out of the question that he should remain in Washington. In August he resigned and went back to money-making in New York; if the country was to be saved from Communists, it would be saved without his assistance. The reports released on September 1 dealt with problems that now belonged to the ages.

Because the hearings were inconclusive—as in the very nature of the case they had to be—the problem had to make its way, eventually, to the committee of the whole. No one could any longer maintain that it was up to the Wisconsin electorate alone to judge McCarthy. On July 30, while the Subcommittee members were still trying to decide what to say about McCarthy and the Army, Ralph Flanders introduced on the floor a resolution of censure based on McCarthy's contempt of the Senate, his contempt for truth, and his "habitual contempt for people." There was prolonged debate, and on August 2, the Senate voted, 75 to 12, yet another inquiry. It authorized the creation of a Select Committee to consider charges and report to the Senate on Resolution 301:

Resolved, that the conduct of the Senator from Wisconsin, Mr. McCarthy, is unbecoming a member of the United States Senate, is contrary to Senatorial traditions, and tends to bring the Senate into disrepute.

The Vice-President, following consultation with the majority and minority leaders, named to the Select Committee some carefully selected and indisputably Senatorial Senators. (The theory of a "select" committee is that its members represent not their states or other legitimate interests, such as those of the nation, but the Senate of the United States and nothing else. Normally, they are chosen for ceremonial functions, such as attending funerals or glad-handing itinerant kings.) The Republican chairman, Arthur V. Watkins, was a Mormon elder from Orem, Utah, a gaunt patriarch who, it was soon discovered, could play variations on the crack of doom with a chairman's gavel. His party colleagues were Frank Carlson, of Kansas, and Francis Case, of South Dakota, and the three Democrats were Edwin C. Johnson, of Colorado, John C. Stennis, of Mississippi, and Samuel Ervin, Jr., of North Carolina. With the possible exception of Ervin, a new man at the time and a Southern jollifier and storyteller in the Alben Barkley tradition, they were not a sparkling lot—on the contrary, they were dim, conspicuous for their inconspicuousness, and a good many people hastily concluded that the Senate was throwing the lion into a den of lambs.

Without Watkins, the Committee might well have been eaten by McCarthy. But Watkins, though in former days he

223

had given no sign of taking offense at McCarthy's outrages, decided early that he was going to conduct a fair and sober hearing—and he must have known that this would be fatal to McCarthy. "In general," he announced when the Committee held its first session on August 31, "the committee wishes it understood that the regulations adopted are for the purpose of insuring a judicial hearing and a judicial atmosphere, as befits the importance of the issues raised. For that reason and in accordance with the order the committee believes to be the sentiment of the Senate, all activities which are not permitted in the Senate itself will not be permitted in this hearing." This, apparently, was his way of saying that while it might be all right to foul the atmosphere of regular committees—those, for instance, considering the defense of the republic and its relations with other sovereign powers—with the sooty gases given off by cigarettes, cigars, and pipes, the rule of a committee weighing alleged affronts to the dignity of the Senate would be NO SMOKING. This was utterly without precedent; so was his ruling that the opening statement McCarthy had prepared and the Committee had examined before the hearings was in large part "not material and relevant to the issues in this hearing." For what was irrelevant, Watkins was saying, was nothing less than McCarthy's assertion of the view that "this country and its institutions [are] in imminent peril of destruction by international Communism." Maybe this was so, and maybe it was not, but the peril of the country could not be held a reasonable justification for acts that tended to bring the United States Senate into disrepute. Anti-Communism was all very well in its place, but it could not be a refuge for a scoundrel whose behavior was unbecoming a Senator.

Despite the ruling as to relevance, Watkins, in what he made plain was a gesture of charity, allowed McCarthy to read his statement, and it was immediately plain that he wanted to avoid censure if he possibly could. McCarthy accepted the privilege demurely, and began to read an apologia that was his first known attempt at largeness of spirit and moderateness of expression:

This is a serious matter to me and I think to the country. It weighs heavily on me, and I would like my feelings known, in broad outline at least. . . . I was late, Mr. Chairman—we were all late, although I daresay some of us were earlier than others. . . . I have carried on my part in the fight as best I know how. . . . It has been said that I am the cause of disunity in the country and in my party. There is disunity, and perhaps my activities have been part of the cause. . . . But now it is urged that I be censured. I would be untruthful if I agreed that my accusers were not affected by ulterior political considerations.

The noble-Roman rhetoric was the work of L. Brent Bozell, a young Yale man of flagrant gentility who had written, with William F. Buckley, Jr., *McCarthy and His Enemies* and had joined McCarthy's staff about the time Roy Cohn left. The Committee listened courteously but with no discernible manifestation of approval or disapproval as McCarthy struggled with the alien tempo and the sometimes startling vocabulary of his unfamiliar script. Once he read "spacious" where he should have read "specious," paused, aware that something was wrong, shrugged an authentic McCarthy shrug, and went on gamely. The instant he finished, Watkins made a crisp announcement: "Now we proceed to a consideration of the matters which the committee deemed of first importance in connection with these hearings."

There were five categories of these matters of importance to the Committee: one, contempt of the Senate and its committees; two, encouragement of lawbreaking by government employees; three, the unauthorized receipt and use of classified documents and information; four, abuse of Senate colleagues; and, five, the affair of General Zwicker.

The Committee had retained, as its special counsel, E. Wallace Chadwick, a former Pennsylvania Congressman, who, in his somewhat less ingratiating way, was as Dickensian a type as Joseph Welch. Chadwick was a frail, bent man with the look of a disappointed schoolmaster—one who might have put in a lifetime teaching Greek to dunces and come to the conclusion that it had not been worth it. His approach was to read to the Committee every word of a huge anthology of McCarthyana compiled by him and tending to bring McCarthy, if not the Senate, into disrepute. Every affront McCarthy had given a colleague, every seditious and defiant remark in the course of committee hearings, the whole of the Zwicker exchange—it was all there, and Chadwick read it as if every gross phrase made him feel like retching; it was all so painful that McCarthy's lawyer, Edward Bennett Williams, interrupted to say that he and his client would gladly stipulate the authenticity of Chadwick's documents. This would save time as well as anguish. Senator Watkins rejected the proposal. He said that if a need for "economy measures" arose, he would reconsider Williams' suggestion, but that until such a time, counsel would go on reading. Two possible explanations of the chair's ruling offered themselves. One was that Watkins saw some positive, and perhaps purgative, value in assaulting the ear of the Committeemen with McCarthy's entire repertoire of impudence and defiance; the other was that the chairman was trying to make the hearings as boring as persistence and ingenuity could possibly make them. Watkins was not eager for publicity. ("Let us get off the front pages and back among the obituaries," he told reporters at one stage. "That would suit us fine.") Chadwick read on until his voice was exhausted; then an assistant, Guy de Furia, took over.

Edward Bennett Williams had agreed to serve as McCarthy's counsel on the condition that McCarthy not try to be his own advocate. He was to be on his best behavior: no interruptions not approved by Williams, no insults to the Committeemen. McCarthy agreed, and by and large he kept his word. Watkins helped him keep it, for on the few occasions when he did scream "Point of order" or "Mr. Chairman," the gavel came down with the force of a headsman's ax. (On one occasion, he was heard to say that it was "the most unheard of thing I ever heard of," and it probably was.) Thanks to Williams, McCarthy came close to winning an acquittal from the Committee. Williams conceived a *tu quoque*, or you're-another, defense that was formidable in most respects. When McCarthy's offenses were considered one by one, it turned out that there were very few for which no Senatorial precedent could be found. Had he been inexcusably arrogant and bullying in his treatment of General Zwicker? Indeed, he had been—and to many others besides —but he was not the first man to abuse his power in this way. Williams found an instance, only a few days before the censure hearings, in which Prescott Bush, of Connecticut, had been accused of similar discourtesies in the course of a one-man hearing on public housing. Why not censure Bush along with McCarthy? Had McCarthy given out classified information? He had, but he was not alone in this; a member of the Select Committee, Edwin Johnson, had, only a few years back, been widely criticized for giving out classified facts on hydrogen weapons on a television program. Had McCarthy called Senator Flanders "senile"—yes, but Senator Flanders had compared McCarthy with Hitler; which is worse, to be senile or a Hitler? It was true that McCarthy had urged government employees to give information directly to him whether or not some "bureaucrat had stamped it secret," but was this so different from the action of Watkins himself in signing a committee report that urged "employees in the executive branch . . . to turn over to committees of Congress any information which would help the committees in their fight against subversion"?

There were differences, of course. McCarthy was everlastingly doing those things that other Senators did now and then—and sometimes, as in the case of Senator Johnson, did inadvertently. And there was a difference between Flanders' comparing McCarthy with Hitler, whom McCarthy often seemed to be emulating, and McCarthy's abuse of dozens of Senators. It was the whole pattern and meaning of Mc-

Carthy's career that seemed to cry out for censure—and that could never, of course, be censured. In the end, the Select Committee urged that the Senate voice its disapproval of him on just two counts: his contempt, in 1951 and 1952, of the Subcommittee on Privileges and Elections and his abuse, in 1954, of General Zwicker. It submitted a 40,000-word report explaining its recommendations and explaining its failure to recommend censure on other grounds. (It said, for example, that McCarthy's remarks about Flanders were "highly improper" but that they did not constitute grounds for censure because they were "induced by Senator Flanders' conduct in respect to Senator McCarthy.") The report was received, and a debate on the motion was scheduled. It had to be put off because McCarthy took to the hospital, but in time it was held, and on December 2, 1954, 67 of his colleagues voted for and 22 against an amended version of the Committee's resolution. The Zwicker count was dropped on pretty much the same grounds as the Flanders count: Zwicker had provoked McCarthy into provoking Zwicker. A new count was added—abuse of the Watkins Committee. The resolution itself tells the story. Here is the text:

Resolution Relating to the Conduct of the Senator from Wisconsin, Mr. McCarthy

Section I: Resolved, that the Senator from Wisconsin, Mr. McCarthy, failed to cooperate with the Subcommittee on Privileges and Elections of the Senate Committee on Rules and Administration in clearing up matters referred to that subcommittee which concerned his conduct as a Senator, and affected the honor of the Senate and instead, repeatedly abused the members who were trying to carry out assigned duties, thereby obstructing the constitutional processes of the Senate, and that the conduct of the Senator from Wisconsin, Mr. McCarthy, is contrary to Senatorial traditions and is hereby condemned.

Section 2: The Senator from Wisconsin (Mr. McCarthy) in writing to the chairman of the Select Committee to study censure charges (Mr. Watkins) after the Select Committee had issued its report and before the report was presented to the Senate charging three members of the Select Committee with "deliberate deception" and "fraud" for failure to disqualify themselves; in stating to the press on November 4, 1954 that the special Senate session that was to begin November 8, 1954 was a "lynch party"; in repeatedly describing this special Senate session as a "lynch bee" in a nationwide television-radio show on November 7, 1954; in stating to the public press on November 13, 1954 that the chairman of the Select Committee (Mr. Watkins) was guilty of "the most unusual, the most cowardly thing I've heard of" and stating further: "I expected he would be afraid to answer the questions but didn't think he'd be stupid enough to make a public statement"; and in characterizing the said committee as the "unwitting handmaiden," "involuntary agent," and "attorneys in fact" of the Communist Party and in charging that the said committee in writing its report "imitated Communist methods—that it distorted, misrepresented, and omitted, in its effort to manufacture a plausible rationalization" in support of its recommendations to the Senate, which characterizations and charges were contained in a statement released to the press and inserted in the *Congressional Record* of November 10, 1954, acted contrary to Senatorial ethics and tended to bring the Senate into dishonor and disrepute, to obstruct the constitutional processes of the Senate, and to impair its dignity; and such conduct is hereby condemned.

McCarthy had followed his attorney's advice through the hearings, but he had cut loose later, and the resolution showed whose ox had been gored. When the resolution had at last been voted upon, the Vice-President noted that it did not "censure" McCarthy but "condemned" him, and the Mc-Carthyites took solace—God knows why—in that. There were newspaper reports that Nixon had, by a few swift, concealed strokes of the pen changed the title from "To Censure the Senator from Wisconsin, Mr. McCarthy." Nixon denies this. It hardly seems to matter. McCarthy was not ungracious. "I wouldn't exactly call it a vote of confidence," he said, "but I don't feel I've been lynched."

 *Last Days*

McCarthy had not been lynched, but he was finished. He was no longer a threat to anything, no longer a serious force in American politics. This can be boldly asserted with McCarthy in his grave and the recorded history of these last years as an infallible—or, at any rate, an unchallengeable—guide. But it was also clear to some people at the time, particularly to people who knew and understood and observed McCarthy. One of this number was the Vice-President, who had not only been at the center of things, but who had an informing touch of McCarthy in himself. Nixon never resumed his role as a peacemaker and he advised the President that peace was no

232

longer necessary. He called on Eisenhower one day to notify him that the boil had been successfully lanced. Emerging from the interview, he told reporters that he had reminded the President of the old saying "You must not strike at a king unless you can kill him." McCarthy had struck, and the king had survived, and Nixon, or some Bachelor of Arts on his staff, had come up with an aphorism to convert a sound hunch into a principle.

It had the ring of truth, but it wasn't really true. Not, at any rate, in the free world, where there are no Bastilles or Lubiankas. Failure to achieve success the first time, or the second or third, does not doom revolutionists. (Assassins are doomed, as a rule, whether they succeed or not.) Even in Russia, the enemies of czarism struck at the czars and the system several times before their efforts were crowned with the awesome success of 1917. Indeed, defeat seems almost an essential ingredient of victory, a necessary preparation for it, and there is scarcely a great mass leader—from Hitler at one end of the moral spectrum to Gandhi at the other—whose history does not tell of a half-dozen or so phoenix-like ascents from ashes far grayer and colder than those from which McCarthy might have risen in 1954.

His defeats were bad enough, but they left him with much. He was free. He had all his rights. He had not lost any of the appurtenances of power. He was still a member of the United States Senate. He was out of favor with the Board of Governors, but he had never really been in its favor. There have always been powerful Senators who weren't well thought of in the club. His contract with the Wisconsin electorate had

233

four years to run, and if the state leaders of the party were to have any say in the matter, it would be renewed. He had his seniority in the Senate and all his committee assignments. In the 1954 elections, the control of Congress had passed to the Democrats, and he had lost his chairmanship, but that is how the game is played, and not much of the blame for the party's losses could be attributed to him. Before the elections, Herbert Lehman and Ralph Flanders had tried to have the Senate take his chairmanship away. The Senate refused to do it. After the elections, Clifford Case, of New Jersey, proposed to the Republican leaders that McCarthy be removed from the Government Operations Committee and allowed no part in any Senate investigation. The proposal was rejected, as everyone knew it would be. Exactly half the Senate Republicans—and by and large the more influential half—had voted against censure, and in the face of this, not even the Democrats were in a mood to deprive him of any of his perquisites. On the contrary, if McCarthy had really slipped, it was sound Democratic strategy to hang him prominently around Republican necks.

He had not slipped with his following. His performance in the Army-McCarthy hearings had been revolting to a good many Americans, and the polls were showing a sharp decline in the number of people who thought well of him (50 per cent at the start of the year), but this was not crucial. What knowledge does the demagogue have if it is not a knowledge of the people's inconstancy? After all, he plays upon it all the time. Those who were truly followers—McCarthyites— had been thrilled by his part in the hearings. They admired ranting, and their man had shown once more that he was a Caruso among ranters. In and of themselves, the events of 1954 did not cost him, so far as anyone knows, a single true friend. Lieutenant General George Stratemeyer had organized, just before the censure debate got under way, a Committee of Ten Million Americans Mobilizing for Justice, with Rear Admiral John G. Crommelin as "Chief of Staff." All of the old militants rallied around, and on the day of the censure vote, a protest petition said to bear 1,000,816 signatures was delivered to the Capitol in a Brink's armored truck. There was no reason to believe it was phony. In New York, on November 29, the Committee held a mass meeting. Thirteen thousand McCarthyites, give or take a few curiosity seekers, showed up screaming "Who Promoted Peress?" and roaring approval when told that while the Peresses of this world go marching on, "we soothe the injured feelings of a crybaby general." McCarthy was praised by the Committee officers, by Admiral William E. Standley, a former ambassador to Russia; the Governor of Utah, Bracken Lee; Mrs. Grace Brosseau of the Daughters of the American Revolution; Alvin M. Owsley of the American Legion; Charles Edison, the inventor's son and a former Governor of New Jersey; and many others. The Hortonville High School Band had been flown in from Appleton to play "On Wisconsin," and a blues shouter named Billy Hamm said he was going to "shake, rattle, and roll" for the perishing republic. He did, with audience participation. McCarthy couldn't make it; he was just out of Bethesda with his arm in a sling and readying himself for the debate. Jean McCarthy was there, as was Roy

Cohn, who beamed on the 13,000 and said, "Joe McCarthy and I would rather have American people of this type than all the politicians of the world."

People of this type McCarthy never lost. Whatever their weaknesses, they were not summer soldiers, and among them McCarthy was, if anything, stronger and nobler in defeat and, as they saw it, martyrdom than he had been before. It took a kind of beleaguered spirit to believe what he had been saying—to credit his endless talk about plots and conspiracies —and to the beleaguered the blows that rained upon him in 1954 were proof only of the enemy's power and of his courage in giving chase to what, at the New York rally, Admiral Standley had called the "hidden force" in the United States government.

Indeed, in death he seemed to have an even securer place in the affections of his supporters than he had had when he was at the peak of his powers. Though I wrote of him a good deal while he lived and was formidable, and never wrote flatteringly, I first encountered the full wrath of the Mc-Carthyites in 1958, when I published an account of the last days of his life and an estimate of his character for *Esquire*. Then the furies descended. I have half a file drawer full of suggestions that I walk into the Atlantic Ocean until my hat floats, that I ask God's forgiveness for my acts of desecration, that I buck for the next Stalin Prize, and so forth. While he lived, I never knew such vituperation. For some of it, the institutional part, I tend to make a heavy discount. The house organ of the American Legion sought to discredit

236

my testimony by painting me as a hardened sinner; a church publication, *Our Sunday Visitor,* sought to discredit the forum, *Esquire,* in which my attempt at explanation appeared. But what impressed me was the volume of letters from terribly anguished men and women who would not stand idly by while McCarthy's name was dishonored. The letters were ugly, threatening, in many cases vile. Yet they bespoke a love for the man which, though it was doubtless a form of self-love, was not entirely without a power to be affecting. Three hundred subscriptions, or a lot, to *Esquire* were canceled, and this was a tribute. "There are heroes of evil as well as of good," La Rochefoucauld wrote, and McCarthy was surely a hero—the only one, I should think, since Franklin D. Roosevelt.

☞ McCarthy was finished in 1954 not because he had suffered wounds of a kind no demagogue could survive, but because he had suffered wounds that a particular demagogue named Joseph R. McCarthy could not survive. And these were quite real. If he had not lost status (as distinguished from stature) in the Senate, he had lost, momentarily anyway, the power to panic that august body. Sixty-seven members, or two-thirds-plus in that day, had voted for censure at the close of a year that had opened with only William Fulbright willing to cast a vote of record against him. And six months later, when McCarthy proposed the last resolution that was to bear his name (an attempt to embarrass the President at the Geneva conference by insisting he introduce the question of

237

freedom for the satellites), it was rejected 77 to 4. Issues raised by McCarthy or involving him were at last being discussed on their merits.

The White House became a tower of strength. After the censure vote, the President called in the Cato of the Wasatch, Arthur Watkins, to "congratulate him," as the President's press secretary put it, "for the splendid job he did." It was a gratuitous gesture (the time for praise and encouragement was earlier, and this suggested that Watkins was a fine hanging judge), but Eisenhower's boldness now knew no limits. Before long, the news was out, via Mary Jane McCaffree, Mrs. Eisenhower's social secretary, that Senator and Mrs. McCarthy had been stricken from the White House list of the socially acceptable; alone among Congressional couples, they would not, after January 1955, be eligible for invitations to state dinners and receptions. This was supererogation. Could daring and hurt be carried further? They could be, and they were. Where once McCarthy had written his own ticket in the State Department and the Department of the Army, he was now rebuffed even by the Post Office. He proposed a man named Thomas Miller for postmaster of Appleton, and Arthur Summerfield, the Postmaster General, who two years earlier had pleaded with Eisenhower to accept McCarthy, and show some joy in the acceptance, said primly that Miller was "unsuitable" because he had once been a gambler and a bootlegger. McCarthy sought to retaliate. He tried to rouse the Senate against the appointment of Paul Hoffman to the United Nations General Assembly. But the President, who in 1953 had promised to make no more appointments displeasing to McCarthy, showed no signs of remembrance or concern. Reporters asked James Hagerty if the President had seen McCarthy's brief against Hoffman. "Yeah, we read it," Hagerty said.

McCarthy was, then, in certain difficulties with constituted authority. Demagogues often are. It is a condition in which they can find much cause for rejoicing, but one sensed, in late 1954 and early 1955, that McCarthy had suffered a kind of interior collapse. He had never had a vision of the future, but he had looked to each day for its fresh prodigies. It was no longer so.

☞ In the two and a half years that remained of his life, he made only a few spiritless, irresolute attempts at a comeback. Now and then, he would get the Senate floor to announce a late finding (for example, that John Foster Dulles had set a hundred and fifty men to censoring the Yalta papers) or to push a campaign of some sort (put Douglas MacArthur in charge of all foreign policy). But he seldom spoke with much force, and in Washington no one was paying much attention. When he got the floor, Senators would drift from the chamber to the cloakroom or to other business. The Vice-President would summon some freshman Senator to take his place in the chair, and Lyndon Johnson, the new Majority Leader, would leave some junior Democrat behind to observe the proceedings and be on guard against a sneak play. At the announcement of a McCarthy speech, the reporters in the press gallery would see a chance to catch a bite, to exchange gossip, or to find out what Lyndon Johnson was up to. Handouts from McCarthy's office would land in the waste-baskets, and the group that had called itself "the goon squad"—the dozen or so correspondents who for nearly five years had been assigned to covering his every move and recording his every word—was disbanded. For a time after the censure, he had continued to be news, and if he had resumed the offensive, he would have continued to be news. But no one was willing to pay a full salary to a man who did nothing but tail a Senator from Wisconsin who was becoming a jackstraw once again.

From time to time, he could be seen shambling (or lurching, for he was drinking a lot more and holding it less well) down the corridors of the Senate Office Building, en route to some committee room where photographers and reporters had been sighted. There was no Roy Cohn scurrying along at his side, no bodyguard; the bearers and retainers and attendants were gone, and he was pretty much alone with Ray Kiermas, who had been with him from the start. Arrived at a hearing room, he might circle it three or four times—scowling, peering, grinning with effort—to draw the photographers' atten-tion. It wasn't of much use. Mostly, they ignored him, and if, for old times' sake, they focused on him (for the photographers had liked him and had been much in his debt), their editors filed the pictures—perhaps with a thought to a Where-Is-He-Now? story in a few years' time. He got free television time every so often, generally on some panel or television show with a low Trendex rating, and used it to call Paul Hoffman "a throwback on the human race," Sherman Adams "a pinhead," or Harold Stassen "one of the most contemptible politicians of our era." It was the old language, but in another voice and mood.

For a while, he tried statesmanship. He was led to this enterprise by some of the Rightist eggheads who had supported him as a scourge of the Communists—most notably by L. Brent Bozell, who had provided the Ciceronian rhetoric of the censure hearings. In one period, early in 1956, McCarthy had Bozell write some meaty speeches on foreign and military policy, and some of these were quite good. One, on April 25, described with remarkable prescience our lag in missile development and the diplomatic consequences of that lag; it may well have been the year's most prophetic speech. But talking about missing missiles didn't make the headlines that talk about hidden Communists had made. (There, indeed, was the rub, and part of the reason why missiles are still in short supply.) Under Bozell's tutelage, McCarthy voted to give the Air Force $960 million more than the President had thought necessary. But it all got him nowhere, and after a time he felt as silly as he looked in a toga.* He threw it aside.

He made a pass or two at the farm vote. In the administra-

---

* The alliance with the high-brow reactionaries could never have come to much anyway. I talked with Bozell one evening in 1956 and asked him how he felt about McCarthy as a conservative. "Terrible," he said. Bozell said he continued to like and admire McCarthy but that he was hurt by the discovery that McCarthy wasn't a conservative at all. He could not be brought to repudiate the welfare state and was becoming, in fact, more and more like a Left liberal in domestic affairs—favoring more public housing, more social security, more federal subsidies of all sorts.

241

tion and in Congress, there were arguments over whether agricultural price supports should assure 85, 87.5, or 90 per cent of parity. McCarthy said it was all a lot of cheap-skate talk, and came out first for 100 and then for 110 per cent of parity. This was a promising line for a demagogue down on his luck; historically, at any rate, there has never been anything quite so good for a necessitous politician as becoming a friend to farmers. It would have been a plausible role for McCarthy, whose style owed a great deal to agrarian radicalism, and it is conceivable that a noisy advocacy of the cause of the sowers and reapers of America might have helped him rise from defeat in 1955 or 1956. It could have been nicely combined with Communists in government and anything else he wished—free silver, justice to the white-collar workers, labor fakery, anything. But although he voted and talked as a farmer's friend, he didn't stick to the business of making political capital of it. He had always had difficulty in staying with anything, but in those declining days, his powers of concentration were feebler than ever.

In the 1956 election, he played hardly any role at all. He did not attend the San Francisco convention of his party that year, and the convention was the duller for his absence. He did not campaign. After the censure vote, he had made a "public apology . . . to the American people" for having supported Eisenhower in 1952. He had been grievously in error, he said, for believing in 1952 that Eisenhower was anti-Communist. More than that, he thought, after the President's heart attack, that it would be "unkind" to ask him to run again. He said he thought that either J. Edgar Hoover or

Herman Welker would make a good Republican candidate. No Hoover or Welker booms materialized. In the 1956 campaign, there was no one to suggest that Adlai Stevenson was a fellow-traveler, and there was astonishingly little talk of how many Communists the administration had thrown out. (The Vice-President, who did most of the campaigning, took not a leaf from McCarthy's book. "Give 'em Heaven," the President had instructed Nixon as he took off on his first tour, and Nixon did just that: "Folks, Eisenhower is a great man, just remember that, and the Eisenhower program means a cleaner, finer, more moral America.") After the election, when John McClellan, who had taken a leaf or two from McCarthy's book, was getting high on the front pages by making life miserable for Dave Beck, the boodling head of the International Brotherhood of Teamsters, McCarthy tried to get into the act—now by championing the Fifth Amendment labor skate, now by bullyragging him. But he didn't work at it. He would come into the Caucus Room late, interrupt a line of questioning with questions of his own, many of which were incoherent, and after twenty minutes or so walk out in an almost trancelike state. He was vastly dispirited.

He was sick a lot of the time and frequently hospitalized, as a rule for the treatment of ailments that were either obscure in their nature or deliberately made obscure to the public by the attending physicians. Had the censure debate really been delayed because of his hospitalization for what Dr. George Calver, the Capitol physician, called "traumatic bursitis"? Visited in the hospital, McCarthy said he had undergone surgery to have some pieces of glass removed from his elbow.

243

(The story was that a Milwaukee admirer had shaken hands with uncontrollable vigor, pumping McCarthy's arm so hard that his elbow cracked a glass-topped table and absorbed some of the top.) But the hospital doctors, questioned by reporters, said there had been no surgery at all. It was always that way—mixed up. There was endless talk of back trouble, leg trouble, liver trouble, prostate trouble, lung trouble, heart trouble, herniated-diaphragm trouble, and—always—bottle trouble. In Washington, it was widely assumed that many of the visits were for the purpose of having the booze drained off. But he *was* sick. He would run alarmingly to fat, then he would grow gaunt. He lost forty-one pounds in a few weeks —by his and his doctors' accounts, and there was no reason to doubt them. He looked ghastly. Not even his closest friends knew for certain what was wrong, though some thought they did. ("He also suffered extraordinary pain because of his herniated diaphragm," George Sokolsky wrote. "Once I gave a little dinner for McCarthy. His pains came on. His suffering was unbelievable, and that night he had to be taken to the hospital. It was his herniated diaphragm, and he was operated on for it.")

There have been descriptions of him as having spent his last years in an unbroken alcoholic stupor. These descriptions are inaccurate. He had always been a heavy drinker, and there were times in those seasons of discontent when he drank more than ever. But he was not always drunk. He went on the wagon (for him, this meant beer in place of whisky) for days and weeks at a time. The difficulty toward the end was that he couldn't hold the stuff. He went to pieces on the second or third drink. And he did not snap back quickly.

Still and all, he did not devote his life to drinking. He was never a sot. Even in his last days, he was as busy as the average Senator and a lot busier than many. And he had a private life: he and his wife adopted a baby, Tierney Elizabeth, and he was a devoted father. When he was fit, he spent a lot of time with his friends. He went deer hunting in the Wisconsin woods.

He became increasingly interested in money. He had always cared deeply about it but he had liked getting rid of it as much as getting hold of it. Now he wanted to keep it. He spent less on horses and poker. He pored over the market news—a soybean type once more. He developed, friends said, an obsession with security. He began thinking in terms of a quiet, cozy, nonpolitical old age. "Jean and I have enough money for a small cattle-spread in Arizona," he said. "I might open a law office for friends and neighbors." He knew people who told him they knew the money game. On their advice, he took some fliers in oil and uranium and made a sizable fraction of a million on paper. His advisers egged him on. Visions of sugarplums danced in his head. He had gone on the wagon—no more bourbon, only beer—and was all investor. Then some of the people who had been going along for the ride decided they had gone far enough. They quit while they were ahead and while McCarthy was in Wisconsin and, for the moment, not keeping up with his portfolio. (He had hit a deer with his car. The car was wrecked. He waited for delivery of a new one in a town without a ticker.) When he got back to Washington, he discovered that he had sustained heavy losses—not on paper, but in legal United States tender. He fell off the wagon in a heap and never got on again.

This was very close to the end, and some at least among his friends believe that he died with an unbearable sense of betrayal in his financial adventures.* Others, it is only fair to say, believe otherwise. "He was discouraged," George Sokolsky wrote. "He regarded himself as betrayed. He particularly felt that he was betrayed by Vice-President Nixon, whom he had always trusted." It is conceivable that he felt himself betrayed on every hand. Men in his straits generally do feel that way.

On April 28, 1957, he was admitted to the Naval Medical Center at Bethesda, Maryland, where he had been on many earlier occasions. Mrs. McCarthy said he had gone there for the treatment of a "knee injury"—a recurrent theme in McCarthy pathology and presumably connected with the leg injury sustained during the Equator-crossing. The press thought he was being dried out again. He was put in the neurological section. The Navy doctors announced that his condition had been diagnosed as "peripheral neuritis," which is an inflammation of the nerve ends farthest from the central nervous system and is often associated with advanced alcoholism. McCarthy had, it was announced, been ill at home

---

* There are several tales of these adventures, but they cannot be gone into without involving many living persons.

for several weeks, and hospital spokesmen on this occasion said that his condition was "very serious." On May 2, at 6:02 P.M., one hour after the last rites had been administered by the Center's Roman Catholic chaplain, he died, with his wife at his bedside. It was more in fondness than in derogation that an old member of the "goon squad" pointed out that he had made it "just in time for the seven o'clock news," which had always been his favorite time for uncovering a new master spy, for blistering Sherman Adams, or for telling Eisenhower to watch his step. The first bulletins gave no cause of death. Those that followed spoke of "acute hepatitic infection" and "hepatitic failure." Some reports, among them *Time* magazine's, interpreted this to mean that he had cirrhosis of the liver, an affliction which turns that most mysterious of organs into something the consistency of damp sawdust and ends its production of bile. The commonest agent for the transformation is alcohol. Did he, in the Victorian phrase, "drink himself to death"? One way or another, he probably did, but probably not in the usual, or Victorian, way. It is conceivable that years of drinking had led directly to cirrhosis, but the suddenness of his death suggests another possibility. He had had hepatitis, that chic malady formerly known as jaundice (its principal symptom), and for a victim of this disease, alcohol, even in small quantities, is poison.

The chances are that his last drinking bouts, which were begun after he had got the bad news about his investments and which were said to be formidable, were fatal. Either way, liquor and the liver had something to do with it. And he was dead.

247

☞ The obituary writers had a difficult time, and most of them took the easy way out. They said he was a "controversial figure" but that surely he had "believed" in what he was doing. The most eloquent and truthful obituary was spoken through tears by a woman whose husband had known and liked him despite a vast contempt for his public role. This man came home late in the evening of May 2 and found his wife sitting by the radio and weeping—not in unalloyed grief, as it turned out, but in grief and anger. She had, she explained, listened to every news report. "They've all said the same thing," she cried out, "and they're all wrong, wrong, wrong. They all hated him, but they had to find a saving grace for their damned broadcasts, so what have they given him— sincerity. Nuts. Each one has said, 'At least he was sincere —he believed in what he was doing,' when that was the one goddamn thing *no one* could say about him." She went on, in lachrymose eloquence. "He was a stinker. He was never 'sincere'—Christ, what a laugh. He never thought of *believing* in what he was doing. There wasn't much good you could say of him, except that he was generous to his friends and a few of us couldn't *help* liking him. No one has said that, and no one will—ever. Only this junk about his being 'sincere.' The poor bastard."*

---

* One broadcaster—a seven o'clock man—did not dwell on his sincerity. This was Edward R. Murrow, and he has a vivid memory of handling the story. "I got the bulletin shortly before I went on the air," he recalls, "and I knew it was a moment to strike not a single false note—in unmerited praise or mean dispraise. I think I have never

☞ At Jean McCarthy's request, there was a funeral in
the Senate Chamber, in addition to the one in St. Matthew's
Cathedral. He was the first Senator in seventeen years for
whom such a request had been made; the last had been
William E. Borah, a noble old Idaho windbag and an insurgent in the tradition from which McCarthy had borrowed
much. It was at once a moving and a mawkish affair. Of
politicians in general, it may be said that they are among the
most charitable and forgiving of human beings. McCarthy
had these virtues at least, and those who feared and despised
him knew this well. Alexander Wiley, whom McCarthy had
sought to retire in 1944, announced the death and recited
McCarthy's history, complete with all the McCarthyite myths.
Two bitter antagonists, Mike Mansfield, of Montana, and
Wayne Morse spoke with no trace of untimely condescension
or bitterness. Not as much could be said for the Chaplain of
the Senate, the Reverend Frederick Brown Harris, who
turned out to be quite intensely political:

Now that his lips are silent in these days of destiny, when the
precious things we hold nearest our hearts are beset by subtle
dangers such as have never before been faced, may the ancient
admonition of God's holy word be heard and heeded with a new
alertness by those who guard the nation's ramparts: "If the
watchmen upon the walls see the enemy advancing and give not
the warning, then the blood of the people shall be required of the
watchmen's hands." [How inapposite, one thought, the apposite

been more objective in reporting anything. Yet in the morning I found
myself upbraided by hundreds for callousness, gloating, and fraudulent
compassion."

may be.] And so this fallen warrior, though dead, speaketh, calling a nation of freemen to be delivered from the complacency of a false security and from regarding those who loudly sound the trumpets of vigilance and alarm as mere disturbers of the peace.

The flag-draped coffin was put on a military transport plane —with his friend the late Herman Welker and two reporters aboard—and flown to Appleton. The airborne wake was provisioned as the best wakes generally are. There was no talk about the prophet being without honor except, etc. Grief was held at bay over—literally over—McCarthy's dead body.

On May 7, services were held at St. Mary's Roman Catholic Church in Appleton. He was buried in that church's cemetery, which is on a bluff overlooking the Fox River.

☞ When he died, the true believers cried murder most foul. This is what true believers always do. They said, as one might have expected them to, that the Reds, the Truman-Acheson Democrats, the bleeding hearts, the Ivy League eggheads, the Eisenhower Republicans, Americans for Democratic Action, the Army Department coddlers of Communists, the Adams-Brownell clique, all of the forces of darkness, subversion, and betrayal had come together to crush this patriot and had succeeded in breaking his great heart. The obituary language was often unlovely. The McCarthyite publisher William Loeb of Manchester, New Hampshire, said that a gang led by "the stinking hypocrite in the White House" had "worn down [McCarthy's] adrenal and other glands." And a house organ of his Texas friends, the Fort Worth *Southern*

Conservative, said, "Joe McCarthy was slowly tortured to death by the pimps of the Kremlin." Others were less violent and less clinical. "And it was the vote of censure," Fulton Lewis, Jr., who was probably something other than a true believer but who knew their language, said, "that started Senator McCarthy on his long slow death. From then on, he had no will to live." And George Sokolsky, another authorized spokesman for the stricken McCarthyites, said, "He was hounded to death by those who could not forget and could not forgive."

He had died, then, of a broken heart, brought on by contemplation of a broken crusade. This, of course, would have been said if he had been struck by lightning or bitten by a rabid dog, but the known subjectivity of the judgment does not make it false. We know that the will to live is a necessary condition of living. Life may endure for a time when it is gone, but when it is challenged by disease or the ravages of time or a heedless mode of existence, it may hang on desire and not much else. There is reason to suppose that McCarthy's distress toward the very end had more to do with a broken bankbook and shattered dreams of a cattle spread than with a broken crusade, but that scarcely matters. The crusade, such as it was, had ended for him two years earlier, and with it had ended the thirst for glory that was to be replaced by a yen for Arizona and a few cows and lawbooks. Maybe it was the degeneration of the dream that led to death—or to the drinking that in turn led to the degeneration of the dream and from there to death. Whether drinking was a primary or a secondary cause of his untimely passing, he

251

could have held onto life a bit longer by not drinking, and he elected to drink.

☞ To acknowledge this much, though, is to raise a whole series of questions about McCarthy. Why was he undone by the events of 1954? What was his heart made of that it should shatter so easily? In the face of his collapse, can one sustain the claim that he was a great demagogue, a great seditionist? What, after all, had been so terrible about the events of 1954? To be scorned by the respectable, disowned by Eisenhower, written off by Nixon, denied patronage by Arthur Summerfield, halfheartedly censured by sixty-seven Claghorns and Throttlebottoms, deplored by a few more newspapers—why should any of this have mattered? What kind of demagogue was it who would not say "tough beans" when the Eisenhowers said they wouldn't have him to dinner any more? What did it all matter? The faithful were all about— waiting for a rallying cry, an order to regroup and resume the offensive, convinced that they were in the twenty-first year of treason. Their leader was young, and vigor was his when he needed it.

If he had been a Hitler, he might have burned down the Senate. Being McCarthy, he had hired a lawyer and sought an acquittal. (True, he did not want acquittal badly enough to compromise for it, but the question is why he should have wanted it at all.) He buckled before respectable and official opinion. He shared its view that he didn't have much of a future, and it was the sharing of the view that was fatal. He might have regarded his repudiation as a kind of emancipation; had he done so, he could have struck out on his own, and there is really no telling what he might then have accomplished.

Instead, he died because he could not lay off liquor. This, too, is odd. Historically, it is unheard of that the leader of a crusade should die in this fashion. Normally, such men, the demonic and the saintly alike, are ascetics. Their dreams of power or glory are headier brews than anything fermented or distilled. To realize their intoxicating but nontoxic dreams, they will give up anything. It is quite impossible to imagine Hitler dying from an overdose of schnapps because he had bad news from his broker. Normally, demagogues are like lovers and poets; they simply do not acknowledge rejection and repudiation. Juan Perón, thrown out of his own country and later a refugee from his place of refuge, continued to inflame his followers and to stir things up in half a dozen countries.

Essentially, I believe, the explanation lies in the fact that McCarthy, though a demon himself, was not a man possessed by demons. His talents as a demagogue were great, but he lacked the most necessary and awesome of demagogic gifts —a belief in the sacredness of his own mission. A man may go a long way in politics—particularly in democratic politics —without much in the way of convictions, but to overcome adversity he needs the strength that can be drawn either from belief in an idea or from a sense of his own righteousness. If he has no convictions, he can scarcely draw courage from them.

It was the lack of conviction that made McCarthy at once a more vulnerable and a more interesting human being than any of his followers or imitators. The conviction he lacked was an absurd thing. He was somewhat the better for not having it—as we were the better for the fact that he sought glory more than power. The glory drive is always less dangerous because it is more easily frustrated. It is selfish, or selfseeking, in the narrowest sense, and it makes defeat and humiliation a personal affair. A discouraged politician with no deep sense of mission can go off with his reveries of peace into the Arizona desert, but a man possessed could never do so, for he knows that his dreams and his demons could not follow him. "Faith in a holy cause," Eric Hoffer has written, "is to a considerable extent a substitute for the lost faith in ourselves." If McCarthy ever had faith in a holy cause, he lost it early (or acquired it very late, too late to do him any good), and he reposed all trust in himself and in the tumult he knew himself capable of creating. He was a cynic, and while cynicism is never admirable, it is better for the world when a man as able as he was is contemptuous of morality than when he is aflame over a vicious and destructive morality. The one McCarthy employed was vicious and destructive, but it never set him afire, though it did burn others.

 *Those Days*
Seen from
These Days

McCarthy was faulted by his own unbelief; he may have been strengthened by it, too, for cynicism opens up certain possibilities even as it closes others. But suppose, briefly and for the sake of argument, that demons had possessed him; suppose, too, that his lust for power had equaled the trust he put in tumult; suppose that by more careful management he had averted the defeats of 1954—or that his desire had carried him beyond them; suppose, in other words, that he had combined with his matchless ability to bring out the worst in the American mind the resoluteness and endurance of the mass leader who also follows himself—what, then, might have been his and the American future?

If it is possible to conceive of a more resolute McCarthy, then it is possible to conceive of greater damage to the republic. He came upon the scene at a moment that could hardly have been more opportune, and throughout his five great years most of the auguries were favorable. In that time, as in this, there were no authentic national heroes and few authentic leaders; since the death of Franklin D. Roosevelt, there had not been a really commanding figure in American public life. Harry Truman had grit and substance, but he was not cast in a heroic mold. Dwight Eisenhower had been trained as a hero, but he was only a general. Below the summit, there were Robert A. Taft, who was splendid in many ways but was too starchy for most people, and Adlai Stevenson, who was also splendid but was not starchy enough. There was Douglas MacArthur, who was pompous and elderly, and there was George Catlett Marshall, who was elderly and was destroyed by McCarthy.

I cannot easily conceive of circumstances in which McCarthy, either faulted as he was or freed of his disabling weaknesses, could have become President of the United States or could have seized the reins of power on any terms. To visualize him in the White House, one has, I think, to imagine a radical change in the national character and will and taste. The nation that chose blandness in 1952 and 1956 would almost surely have found McCarthy indigestible as President. It could accept him as a Senator or as a hell-raiser in or out of the Senate; we seem, in this epoch, to like a tranquillizer in the White House and dexedrine in the Congress. But in the power game, it isn't all or nothing, as McCarthy proved. Having gone as far as he did, it seems clear that he might— had he been a bit more sturdily constructed and a bit more serious about himself—have gone a great deal farther. By building more carefully, he might have exerted a still greater influence over whoever did hold the reins of American power. If history had been co-operative—continuing or increasing the tensions and anxieties and misconceptions on which he thrived—changes in the country's temper might have come to pass that would have made possible a successful bid for power.

The truth is that lack of experience makes it difficult for us to judge the possibilities of a national demagogue. For a nation that has known a good deal of mob rule and that— in its devotion to public liberties—makes mobs quite easily accessible to demagogues, we have had, I think, remarkable good fortune in having had so little trouble. There has, of course, been a good deal of demagogy in our politics—for there is a bit of what H. L. Mencken called "the pumper-up of popular fears and rages" in every democratic politician— but, historically, not many men have succeeded, even briefly, in trampling the Senate underfoot or crushing and confound-ing the generals and commanders. In the nineteenth century, there were some formidable demagogues, but in this century, despite increased opportunities and competition, there have been, aside from McCarthy, few who enjoyed any success that is likely to be remarked upon in the future. In 1954, Reinhard H. Luthin, a specialist in such affairs, published a book entitled *American Demagogues—Twentieth Century*. It contained studies of nine men and one husband-and-wife team—James E. and Miriam Ferguson, or "Pa and Ma" Ferguson, who cut some disorderly capers in Texas forty years ago, each having been governor of the state at one time or another. On Luthin's list were James M. Curley, of Massachusetts; Theodore Bilbo, of Mississippi; William Hale Thompson, of Illinois; William H. Murray, of Oklahoma; Frank Hague, of New Jersey; the Fergusons; Eugene Talmadge, of Georgia; Vito Marcantonio of New York; Huey Long; and McCarthy. (He might have added the Reverend Charles E. Coughlin, but presumably did not do so because Father Coughlin never sought or held public office.) It makes, when one reflects upon it, rather a cheering list. Except for McCarthy and Huey Long, they were all provincial figures. None was influential much beyond the borders of his state; some—like Thompson and Hague, who were mayors, and Marcantonio, a Congressman—were of influence mostly within municipalities. (Marcantonio, who ran as a rule on the Republican ticket and unfailingly followed the Communist line, had no personal following outside the Harlem and East Harlem districts in Manhattan.) Furthermore, it is open to question whether all these people really qualify as demagogues by any acceptable definition. Some were only rascals, which is something else again, and some were genuine cranks. At any rate, McCarthy and Long are the only impressive ones in the lot; for the rest, both the evil and the good they did is interred with their bones.

But if I am right in thinking we have been, by and large,

lucky, there is no assurance that our luck will hold. There may be several ways of accounting for the fact that McCarthy was our first and only national demagogue, but one factor that cannot be overlooked is that he came along at a time when we were more a nation than we have ever been before, at least in the political sense. The New Deal, World War II, and the Cold War "nationalized," as E. E. Schattschneider has put it, American politics. Up to thirty years ago, it was only now and then (generally in times of economic stress) that even the domestic policies of the federal government impinged noticeably on the lives of most Americans. As for foreign policy, when we had any, it was a matter of almost complete indifference to all but a handful. There was very little that either a true stateman or a demagogue could say that would bring responses from every part of the country. Aspirations and anxieties could be exploited by politicians, but not very often by politicians dealing with national and international issues.

It is quite the other way about now. Today it is often difficult to see what difference it makes who is governor or mayor or what their policies are. State and municipal governments administer necessary services and public utilities, but they are less capable of having "policies" than they formerly were, and, in any case, "policies" are likely to be heavily influenced by the federal government, which props up the states with federal aid for almost everything of importance and which thus exercises a great deal of leverage. Federal tax policies, farm policies, labor policies, relief policies, education policies—all these and more matter increasingly to the

259

private citizen. And foreign and military policy matter more than any of the others. It matters so much, indeed, that it was the central reality from which McCarthyism fled. Where one finds fanaticism taking a political form nowadays, it is not over currency or labor or anything domestic (with the exception of race), but over foreign policy.

And beyond all this, there is the "nationalization" that has come about through communications. Radio made a national audience possible, and television has converted the audience into onlookers, from coast to coast.

☞ McCarthy showed that there could be a national demagogue, and it seems to me clear that, had he been a somewhat different sort, his daily prodigies need not have ended in 1954. We cannot know how far he might have gone with them, though I for one am fairly convinced that he had to stop somewhere short of what might, in American terms, be held the ultimate triumph. We can attempt to estimate, though, how much he was able to accomplish, and we can have, in retrospect, some kind of appraisal of our defenses against the threat he posed.

Among those who thought McCarthy and McCarthyism both an ugly threat and a large one, I tend more than most to be impressed by the power he contained within himself and by the power of the resistance to him, and I am sure that my view on both scores will be heavily discounted by others. The opposite view on both accounts was well and concisely expressed by a young scholar and journalist, Karl E. Meyer, of the Washington *Post,* who has thought much and written

on the whole question. He was kind enough to send me some
of his materials, and in an accompanying letter he wrote:

It was a disquieting voyage into the recent past to sort through
the papers and glance at the headlines of that incredible time
when the institutions of society seemed to crumble before the
attacks of a man who believed in essentially nothing. I hope
your book will throw some light on *why* American society appeared so vulnerable to an adventurer armed mainly (so it seems)
by the timidity of his victims.

This book, I fear, throws little light of the sort he asks, for
although I recognize this view as one held by many people I
respect and admire, I do not share their view of the period.
I could not, for one thing, say that the "institutions of society"
crumbled before him or even seemed to do so. I believe, as I
have written, that his impact on many institutions was enormous and is still to be seen, like shell holes in a fortress wall.
It is one thing, though, for a structure to bear the visible
marks of a powerful assault and quite another to "crumble,"
and I am aware of no institutions of any value that disin-
tegrated or fell apart. Nor can I bring myself to agree that
McCarthy was armed mainly "by the timidity of his victims."
He forged some of his own arms and borrowed others, and he
struck with great power.

Some of his victims were timid, some were not. And some,
too, including not a few of the least timid, were themselves
very vulnerable. Of course, McCarthy, once he began to learn
the tricks of his sordid trade, was often careful to choose
victims who were either timid or vulnerable or both. Since
the truth about a man or an institution was no concern of

261

his, he had an almost unlimited choice of victims, and when he could he chose the easy ones and passed over the difficult ones.* But it was surely not the "timidity" of George Catlett Marshall that made him notable among victims. It was the audacity of Joseph Raymond McCarthy.

Some, to be sure, McCarthy could not ignore. Being a seditionist and attempting to exploit particular grievances, he had no choice but to oppose whoever was President and whoever was Secretary of State. He had, indeed, to set his face against the United States government and the myriad institutions that make it up. Some of its institutions he damaged a great deal, others not so much, and still others not at all. In some places the damage has mostly been repaired. American diplomacy, which was most gravely injured, seems to have recovered its

---

* I take this as proof that he was also armed with shrewdness. In 1953, he summoned to the star chamber James A. Wechsler of the New York *Post,* and hounded him for hours on end about his connections with the Young Communist League at Columbia College twenty years earlier. The pretext for calling Wechsler was that one or two of Wechsler's books were in government libraries overseas, but it was altogether plain that what McCarthy was really up to was an investigation of unfriendly journalists. The member of McCarthy's staff in charge of this particular campaign was the late Howard Rushmore, whose peculiar odyssey had led him from the job of movie critic of the *Daily Worker* to Hearst's New York *Journal-American,* to McCarthy's staff, to the editorship of *Confidential,* to suicide in a New York taxicab in 1958. Rushmore advised me that the plan was to call a number of other New York journalists after Wechsler's testimony and that I could expect to be one of those called. However, Wechsler proved to be neither timid nor vulnerable. He gave McCarthy as good as he got. McCarthy, who had plenty of other things to do, fired Rushmore and left the New York journalists alone.

esprit, which does not mean that it has increased in wisdom. Nothing can be done about the time and the opportunities lost, wasted, or misused during the time in which he led the great flight from reality, but at least it has become possible once again to discuss American policy in the light of the national interest rather than in the light of how McCarthyism would respond. This is not to say that policy can in every case be *formulated* without regard to irrelevancies. There never has been such a time, and if, for example, there seemed today to be more profit than loss in granting diplomatic recognition to the satellite government of East Germany, the chances are that, for domestic reasons, we could not take the profit. This may be lamentable, but it isn't novel. And it is nothing like the situation five years ago, when rational discourse was impossible for many men involved in our diplomacy. There have always, in this and other countries, been hindrances to policy that were quite apart from wisdom or unwisdom, but what was so hideous when McCarthy was about was that debate was so often foreclosed. If, today, a State Department expert on Germany or China wished to argue the case for recognition before a Congressional committee, he could do so with no more than a normal—and on the whole healthy—amount of concern over his own career.

If the morale of the foreign service has largely been restored, not as much can be said for the government's scientific enterprises, where the good will of men of a highly individulistic and morally uncompromising sort has always been needed, and still is. And Congressional investigative procedures still bear the heavy mark of McCarthy's influence; it

263

continues to be the habit of many committees to examine American citizens not for the purpose of gaining useful information but for the purpose of tainting their characters before public opinion. McCarthy invented the whole technique of questioning at length witnesses he knew would take the Fifth Amendment, and since his departure other Congressmen have competed for the uncommunicative and have sought to establish new world's records for the number of Fifth Amendment claims they could get from a single witness. McCarthy's records have all been shattered.

I am trying only to make the point that what we have is a mixed bag, that matters vary a good deal from one aspect of government and politics to another. I am sure that one could, without too much effort, prove a lowering in the whole tone and temper of political debate as a consequence of our experience with McCarthyism. At the same time, it seems to me essential to deplore only what is deplorable and even to note instances of good flowing from evil, if there are any such. I believe that at least one agency of government was actually strengthened by the malaise of the McCarthy years. Protected by the Constitution, by the vital force of a great tradition, and by the strength and character of its own members, the United States Supreme Court took judicial notice of the rents McCarthy was making in the fabric of liberty and thereupon wrote a series of decisions that have made the fabric stronger than before. McCarthy provided the court with one of its finest hours. It is doubtful if the mixed bag contains very many plums, but there is at least this one.

☞ Those of us who have been educated in the twentieth century habitually think in sociological terms, whether or not we have had any training in sociology. Observing a phenomenon like McCarthyism, we almost automatically dismiss from our minds the notion that a single human being could have much to do with it, even though it bears his name. Obviously, it was a product of "forces"—not of a single living creature. "McCarthyism was a by-product of the Cold War," Joseph and Stewart Alsop wrote. "McCarthyism is *both* a movement supported by certain vested-interest elements and a popular revolt against the upper classes," Talcott Parsons, a real sociologist, explained. "McCarthyism is the revenge of the noses that for twenty years of fancy parties were pressed against the outside window pane," Peter Viereck wrote—thus describing the first nose revenge since *Cyrano de Bergerac*. And there were many similar explanations. Walter Lippmann and Arthur M. Schlesinger, Jr., saw it as a resurgence of the isolationism of the thirties. Samuel Lubell saw it as an attempt to punish those whom many Americans held to be responsible for a whole host of rights and wrongs, going back to our intervention in World War I. Richard Hofstadter felt that the roots went back to the Midwestern and Southern populism of the last century. In a famous television review of McCarthy's career, Edward R. Murrow summed up what was common to all these analyses: "Cassius was right: 'The fault, dear Brutus, is not in our stars but in ourselves.' "

Not for a moment do I doubt the merit in each of these

explanations, to all of which my brief summaries do injustice. I am sure that many others could be added to them. When a demagogue finds a grievance or a fault, he exploits it. That is the nature of the beast. But what strikes me about them all is that they leave Joseph R. McCarthy out of the picture altogether. In each, he is only an instrument, a voice, a symbol—or an ailment within us. Perhaps he was, but in that case one is at a loss to know why McCarthyism waited so long to come alive and why it seemed to die—or at least to become greatly enfeebled—when McCarthy succumbed to despair. The grievances and discontents were all there before he came along, and I assume that most of them persist to this day. Others before him had sought to exploit the "forces" he exploited, and some had enjoyed a certain amount of success; others are attempting to exploit them today—and, indeed, one often sees manifestations of "resurgent McCarthyism," a term which may come in handy someday for some other movement. It would be odd if none of this were to be seen. Life and history go on, and nothing ever dies completely. But assuredly the fevers of McCarthyism subsided in 1954, and most of us knew it and felt it.

It is possible, of course, to say that the McCarthy years were only a rather dramatic episode in a broad and continuing historical movement. In *Rededication to Freedom,* Benjamin Ginzburg, who was associated a few years ago with the Senate Judiciary Committee's Subcommittee on Constitutional Rights, argues this case and argues it well. "These things," he says, speaking of some of the changes since 1954, "mark the passing of the McCarthy phase of the pres-

266

ent-day antilibertarian movement." He cites innumerable abuses of civil liberties over the past few years, many cases of the hounding of government employees and private citizens for their private views and eccentricities, and the continuing nonsense in most of our loyalty and security procedures. The line of argument seems to me of a piece with saying that the fault is in us, not in our stars. No one in his senses would say that McCarthy invented antilibertarianism; Mr. Ginzburg's "present-day movement" is itself only a phase of a greater one. The point about McCarthy is that when he was on the loose we passed through a time when the "movement" threatened to become a great tide. The fault, we must surely know, was always in ourselves, but he was close to being a genius in bringing it out. Nietzsche had an answer to this kind of reasoning. "Here," he wrote, "is a hero who did nothing but shake the tree when the fruit was ripe. Do you think that was a small thing to do? Well, just look at the tree he shook." It was quite a tree, and it took quite a man to shake it as he did.

The ripest and most fragile fruit fell and were bruised. The Truman administration was falling of its own weight in 1950. The Eisenhower administration (if I may work my way quickly out of Nietzsche's metaphor) took office with a debilitating conviction that it is the constitutional duty of an executive branch to respond to the will of the people by never opposing the legislative branch. The Senate, filled with a terror which may have been moral cowardice but was certainly understandable to anyone who can sympathize with the politician's indulgence in discretion, could not deal with him until he threatened the absolute outrage of destroying military morale in a time of military crisis. The civil servants were frightened because, without protection from the White House or the Congress, they were wholly defenseless.

He shook the entire tree, not just the political limbs. Many of the nonpolitical limbs proved weak. The world of mass entertainment—Hollywood, television, and much of the press —cracked badly. Motion-picture and television scripts were often studied by learned men to make certain they contained nothing offensive to McCarthyism. Sometimes projects were abandoned because it was feared that the whole conception was offensive to this man and his hordes. Performers even down to deodorant demonstrators were now and then cashiered as "disloyal" or as "security risks." The world of advertising—which is closely linked to the world of mass entertainment if in fact it is not one and the same thing— was similarly asthenic, and it often spread the affliction. Vice-presidents in charge of "internal security," commonplace in Rockefeller Center and Hollywood, turned up in breweries, brokerage houses, and casket factories.

It was insane, looney, and ghastly, but it did not mean that the free human spirit had collapsed. Hollywood has always been a hotbed of conformity, and advertising is always ready to ride with any hounds. By their very nature, these institutions yield before external pressure; it is, in fact their substitute for inspiration. The difference between art of even the lowest order and mass entertainment is that one is created by internal pressure and the other by external pressure. (The latest complaint is that the mass media are under the influence

268

of the "teen-age market," and if this is a less sinister influence, it is not necessarily less corrupting.) And the sections of the press that capitulated were mainly those that function more to provide public entertainment than public enlightenment.

Other institutions showed up much better. Most of organized religion opposed McCarthy vigorously. Despite the inroads he made among working people, organized labor never ceased to criticize him. Here and there a college or a school board did something absurd in response to the atmospheric pressures generated by McCarthyism, but by and large American education resisted. Powerful sections of the press were always hostile. The New York *Times,* the New York *Herald Tribune,* the Washington *Post,* the Cowles newspapers, the Knight newspapers, the Luce publications—all were anti-McCarthy. And so were many influential journalists with readers in all parts of the country: Walter Lippmann, Joseph and Stewart Alsop, Doris Fleeson, Marquis Childs, Drew Pearson, Thomas L. Stokes. And on radio and television there were, in the ranks of his critics, Edward R. Murrow, the late Elmer Davis, Quincy Howe, Martin Agronsky, Edward P. Morgan. If I may inject yet another purely personal note, I may say that as a practicing journalist in those years, writing on political subjects for the *New Yorker, Harper's,* and other magazines, I never felt under any compulsion to say anything but what I believed to be the truth about McCarthy and McCarthyism. I got a good deal of disagreeable mail, but I owned a capacious wastebasket, and that took care of the correspondence.

Senator Joe McCarthy

☞ On his seventieth birthday, November 20, 1954, Norman Thomas, a devoted champion of liberty and decency, observed the approaching end of McCarthy's great period and expressed a generally sanguine view. "In spite of all this [McCarthy, McCarthyism, and other noxious growths of other days], there has been," he said, "a saving common sense about our democracy. . . . [The] end has always been victory for comparative reason and decency. The struggle against demagoguery scarcely fits the St. George-against-the-dragon myth. . . . Our democratic St. George goes out rather reluctantly with armor awry. The struggle is confused; our knight wins by no clean thrust of lance or sword, but the dragon somehow poops out, and decent democracy is victor."

It was that way in 1954, certainly, and there could be a principle embodied in Norman Thomas's pooped dragon. McCarthy may have suffered an interior collapse because he sensed futility. He may have been himself an unknowing victim of the truth or the myth of our saving common sense. It is possible that McCarthy actually believed John McClellan when John McClellan said he wasn't afraid of McCarthy. The reluctance of the American St. George may have been contagious, and McCarthy may in the end have been a reluctant, as well as a fatigued, dragon. I do not think this conflicts with the view that he was flawed by his inability to believe what he was saying. The cynic may know sooner than other men when he is licked, and McCarthy may well have felt—without having reasoned, for I do not believe he often reasoned—that though great prodigies may still have been possible for him, the effort to gain them would require that life's blood which no cynic likes to yield.

However that may be, we are faced with the fact that he gave the tree one hell of a shaking. It did not fall, and he did, but we cannot put aside our memories of the day when 50 per cent of the people had a "favorable opinion" of this bully and fraud and another 21 per cent had "no opinion" of him. There must be grave risks in any open society, Learned Hand has said, and William James might have added that the grave risks make life worth living. McCarthy offered a powerful challenge to freedom, and he showed us to be more vulnerable than many of us had guessed to a seditious demagogy— as well as less vulnerable than some of us feared.

Author's Note I have tried to acknowledge all major sources, including my own memory, at appropriate places in the text. Where no source is indicated, it may be assumed that I am drawing on the public record or discussing matters that are part of it.

Here and there, I have adapted passages from work of mine that originally appeared in the *New Yorker, Esquire,* the *Reporter,* or my own *Affairs of State: The Eisenhower Years,* published by Farrar, Straus & Giroux.

I have the customary debts to others, among them Herbert Block, Aimee Buchanan, Charles Clift, James Donovan, Robert J. Donovan, Clay Felker, Harold Hayes, Philip Horton, Don Irwin, Murray Kempton, Murrey Marder, Earl Mazo, Mary McCarthy, Mary McGrory, Thomas McIntyre, Karl E. Meyer, Leonard Miall, Edward R. Murrow, Lee Nichols, Philip Potter, George Reedy, Eleanor Rovere, Arthur M. Schlesinger, Jr., William Shawn, William V. Shannon, Merriman Smith, Alvin Spivak, Robert G. Spivack, William S. White, Edward Bennett Williams, and Page Wilson.

R.H.R.

New York
April 20, 1959

Index

Acheson, Dean G.: McCarthy accuses, 6, 11; injuries suffered from McCarthy, 12–13; effect of McCarthyism on, 14; mentioned, 59, 128–129, 132, 162, 180
ADA *World*, 182
Adams, John, 212, 218
Adams, Sherman, 240, 247
Advertising: fear of McCarthy, 268–269
Agronsky, Martin, 269
Aiken, George D., 180
Alcorn, H. Meade, 120
Algren, Nelson, 48
Allied Molasses Company, 106
Alsop, Joseph and Stewart: description of McCarthy headquarters, 143–144; mentioned, 52, 87, 265, 269
Amerasia, 152n
America, 183
American Committee for Cultural Freedom, 145n–146n
American Demagogues—Twentieth Century, 257–258
American Democrat, 20n, 45
Americanism, 51
American Legion, 236–237
American Mercury, 219n
Americans for Democratic Action, 63
American Society of Newspaper Editors, 155
America's Retreat from Victory: The Story of George Catlett Marshall, 173
Anderson, Jack, 81
Antilibertarianism, 266–267

Anti-Semites, 141, 141n
Apostles of Discord, 141n
Appleton State Bank, 107
Aristophanes, 4, 45
Army-McCarthy hearings: McCarthy's tactics at, 25–32, 58–60, 205–222; mentioned, 39, 46, 172
Arundel, Russell, 106–107
Aschenauer, Rudolph, 112n
Atkinson, Brooks, 8–9
Augustine, Saint, 71
Aumer, Hermann, 202

Baldwin, Hanson, 29
Baldwin, Raymond, 37, 111, 114, 117
Barkley, Alben, 223
Barnes, Joseph, 169
Beck, David, 243
Benton, William: resolution for McCarthy's expulsion, 36, 37; mentioned, 163, 183, 189
Bilbo, Theodore, 258
Block, Herbert: coins phrase McCarthyism, 7
Bohlen, Charles E., 33
Boileau, Gerald, 94
Bozell, L. Brent: statement on McCarthy, 22; writes speeches for McCarthy, 225, 241, 241n
Bradley, A. C., 73
Brewster, Owen, 135
Bricker, John, 65
Bridges, Styles, 32
Brosseau, Mrs. Grace, 235
Browder, Earl, 160, 160n
Buckley, William F., Jr.: statement on McCarthy, 22; 225
Burnham, James, 22

273

Bush, Prescott, 228
Business: fear of McCarthy, 268–269
Butler, John Marshall, 160–161
Byrd, Richard E., 50n
Byrne, Emmet, 65n
Byrnes, James F.: letter used by McCarthy, 54, 124–125

Calhoun, John C., 5
Calver, George, 243
Carlson, Frank, 223
Case, Clifford, 234
Case, Francis, 223
Castro, Fidel, 48
Catholic Youth Organization, 49
Central Intelligence Agency: threat to investigate, 47–48
Chadwick, E. Wallace, 226–227
Chamberlain, John, 22
Chiang Kai-shek, 32, 177
Chicago *Tribune*, 124, 126
Childs, Marquis, 269
China, Communist: Acheson and Marshall statements on, 14
Chou En-lai, 176
Churchill, Winston, 10, 177
Civil Service Commission, 25
Clark, Mark, 47–48
Clay, Henry, 5
Coe, Frank, 182
Cohn, Roy M., 31, 40, 52, 59, 235–236, 240; *see also* Cohn and Schine
Cohn and Schine: investigation of Voice of America, 191–199; trip to Europe, 32, 199–205; and Army-McCarthy hearings, 206–222
Cold War, 259, 265
Communism: McCarthy discovers, 4, 6, 55, 122–123; McCarthy's use of, 19; real threat of, and McCarthy illusion, 40–43; Schine's ideas of, 194–195
Communists: McCarthy's campaign speeches against, 41–42; McCarthy's war against, in State Department, 54, 119–140, 145–159; McCarthy's cynicism about, 72; and La Follette's defeat, 103–104; and the Malmédy case, 112n; investiga-

tion of Voice of America, 195–199
Confidential, 262n
Congress: damage done to investigative agencies by McCarthy, 263–264
Congressional Directory, 93n–94n
Congressional Record: McCarthy quote from, 81–82, 81n–82n; publication of speech on General Marshall, 175–176; mentioned, 109
Congress of Industrial Organizations, 104
Constitution of the United States, 5
Cooper, James Fenimore, 20n, 45
Coughlin, Charles E., 20, 258
Coy, Wayne, 175
Crommelin, John G., 235
Crucial Decade, 80
Cultural and Psychological Traits of Soviet Siberia, 31
Curley, James M., 258

Daily Worker, 104, 182, 262n
Davis, Charles, 143
Davis, Elmer, 170, 269
Declaration of Conscience: author and signers of, 180
Decter, Moshe, 145n–146n
Definition of Communism, 194–195
De Furia, Guy, 227
Demagogues: McCarthy's gift as a national demagogue, 3, 252–271; characteristics of, 19–20, 43–44, 188, 234; definitions of, 45–46; some provincial demagogues, 257–258
Democracy, 45
Desmond, Frank, 125–126
Dever, Paul A., 13
Dewey, Thomas E., 120
Dies, Martin, 135
Dirksen, Everett, 26, 220, 222
Distinguished Flying Cross, 95
Divorce cases: McCarthy record in, 91–92, 121
Dollar's Worth of Housing for Every Dollar Spent, 108
Douglas, Paul, 13
Dreiser, Theodore, 203
Dulles, Allen, 209

Dulles, John Foster: and Scott Mc-Leod, 32–33; joint statement with McCarthy, 34; mentioned, 12, 189, 239

Duran, Gustavo, 169–170

Durocher, Leo, 65

Dworshak, Henry, 220

Eastman, Max, 22

Eberlein, Michael, 84–87

Eddy, Loyal, 92n

Edison, Charles, 235

Education: and McCarthyism, 269

Edwards, Willard, 124

Eisenhower, Arthur, 18

Eisenhower, Dwight D.: held captive by McCarthy, 5; and General Marshall and McCarthy, 15–16; shares power with McCarthy, 29, 32–34; churchgoing of, 71; Mc-Carthy's wire to, 129–130; McCar-thy's after-nomination call on, 181; tours Wisconsin with McCar-thy, 184; notified of McCarthy's political end, 232–233; turns against McCarthy, 238–239; Mc-Carthy apologizes for support of, 242–243; Nixon campaigns for, 243; character, 256; mentioned, 29, 51, 171, 180, 183, 186, 247, 252

Eisenhower, Mrs. Dwight D., 238

Eisenhower administration: McCar-thy's effect on, 5, 11–12, 14–18, 219, 219n; dismissals of Federal employees, 17–18; and the prob-lem of McCarthy, 190; character of, 267

Eisler, Gerhart, 201

Elizabeth II, 10

Ervin, Samuel, Jr., 223

Esquire: reaction to article on Mc-Carthy in, 236–237

Euripides, 45

Evjue, William, 163

Fairchild, Thomas, 185

Far Eastern Policy Investigation, 170–179

Faubus, Orval, 35n

Fedder, William, 161

Federal Bureau of Investigation: McCarthyites in, 25, 196; men-tioned, 160, 221

Ferguson, James E. and Miriam, 258

Field, Frederick Vanderbilt, 156

Flanders, Ralph: resolution to cen-sure McCarthy, 222–223; men-tioned, 55, 110, 228, 229, 234

Fleeson, Doris, 269

Foreign Operations Administration, 33

Foreign Policy: McCarthy's impact on, 5, 12–13, 262–263; McCarthy's pressure on Marshall and Ache-son, 14; McCarthy and the Korean armistice, 15

Fort Monmouth Investigations, 206, 211, 212, 214, 215n, 222

Fort Worth *Southern Conservative*, 250–251

Friendly, Alfred, 128n

Fulbright, William: and McCarthy, 34–35; and Orval Faubus, 35n; mentioned, 237

G-2, 25, 39–40

Gallup Poll: on McCarthy, 13, 23

Gandhi, Mohandas, 48, 233

Geneva Conference, 237–238

Georgetown University, 177

Gillette, Guy, 183–184

Ginzburg, Benjamin, 266–267

Goldman, Eric F., 80

Gold Star Mothers, 49

Gomillion, Otis, 92n

Government employees: dismissals of, 17–18; reason for support of McCarthy, 27n, 268

Government Operations Committee: under McCarthy's chairmanship, 24, 186–205; invented by La Fol-lette, 99; McCarthy's removal from, proposed, 234

Greatest Man in the World, 49n–50n

Greek Shipping Interests: McCarthy agreement with, 33–34

Greenspun, Herman, 68n–69n

Griffith, Thomas, 53

Guerard, Albert, 47

Hagerty, James, 239
Hague, Frank, 258
Hallanan, Walter, 180
Hamm, Billy, 235
Hand, Learned, 271
Hanson, Haldore, 154–155
Harper's Magazine, 128n
Harris, Frederick Brown, 249–250
Harsch, Joseph C., 18
Hendrickson, Robert, 180
Hensel, Struve, 218
Hickenlooper, Bourke, 156
Hiss, Alger, 42, 152, 156, 180, 182
Hitler, Adolf: compared with Mc-Carthy, 17–19; mentioned, 48, 233
Hoey, Clyde R., 185
Hoffer, Eric, 254
Hoffman, Paul, 238–239
Hofstadter, Richard, 265
Hollywood: fear of McCarthy, 268–269
Homosexuality, 68, 153–154, 154n
Hoover, J. Edgar, 150, 183, 215–216, 221, 242–243
Hoving, John, 63
Howe, Quincy, 269
Hughes, John Emmet, 18

Intellectuals, 22
International Information Administration: Cohn's and Schine's investigation of, 32, 40, 199–205
Irish Americans, 21
Ives, Irving M., 180

Jackson, Henry, 218, 220
James, William, 271
Jenkins, Ray, 208, 210
Jenner, William, 56, 184, 187, 189
Johnson, Edwin C., 223, 228
Johnson, Louis A., 178
Johnson, Lyndon, 239–240
Johnson, Samuel, 71, 86
Jones, James, 48
Jonkman, Bartel, 146

Kaghan, Theodore, 204
Kempton, Murray, 55
Kennedy, John, 13

Kenyon, Dorothy, 147, 158, 167
Kerensky, Alexander, 194
Kerouac, Jack, 48
Khrushchev, Nikita, 44
Kiermas, Ray, 37–38, 183, 240
Kohlberg, Alfred, 142
Korean War, 15
Kraus, Charles H., 122

Labor: and McCarthyism, 269
La Follette, Philip, 98, 101
La Follette, Robert M., 5
La Follette, Robert M., Jr.: defeat by McCarthy, 5, 98–104, 120; mentioned, 186
Lamont, Corliss, 31, 42
Langer, William, 175
Laski, Harold J., 65n
Las Vegas *Sun*, 68n–69n
Lattimore, Owen: McCarthy charges against, 151–153, 169; mentioned, 140, 160n, 172, 180, 191
Lawton, Kirke, 31–32
Lee, J. Bracken, 235
Lee, Robert E., 172
Lehman, Herbert, 134, 169–170, 234
Lenin, Vladimir I. U., 48, 194
Lewis, Fulton, Jr., 7, 142, 213, 251
Lewis, John L., 105
Liebling, A. J., 65n
Life, 105
Lindbergh, Charles A., 50n
Lindner, Robert, 70n
Lippmann, Walter: on McCarthy, 166; on Acheson, 12–13; mentioned, 265, 269
Lodge, Henry Cabot, Jr., 13, 156
Loeb, William, 250
London *Times*, 10, 31
Long, Huey, 20, 69n, 258
Lovett, Robert, 178
"Loyal American Underground": people in, 25–27; birthplace of, 195–196; mentioned, 42
Lubell, Samuel, 21, 265
Lucas, Scott, 36, 133–134, 161
Luce, Henry, 73
Lustron Corporation: and Mc-Carthy, 38, 108, 121, 183–184
Luthin, Reinhard H., 257–258

Lvov, Prince, 194
Lyons, Eugene, 135–136

MacArthur, Douglas, 12, 101, 163, 181, 181n, 239, 256
MacArthur hearings, 170–179
Macbeth: McCarthy's quotation of, 170–171, 171n
MacDonald, Dwight, 167
MacFarland, Ernest, 36
MacLeish, Archibald, 182
MacMurray, Howard, 104
McCaffree, Mary Jane, 238
McCarthy, Bridget Tierney, 79–80, 86
McCarthy, Jean, 235, 246, 249
McCarthy, Joseph R.: impact and power, 4–19, 28–37; Senate investigation of, 37–39, 222–231; as a national demagogue, 45–50, 255–257, 260–271; character, 48–65, 71–74, 252–257, 260–262, 270–271; drinking habits, 52, 244–245, 247, 251–252, 253; campaign for judgeship, 53, 87–89; psychiatrists' views on, 66–70; physical condition, 69–70, 243–244, 246–247; early life, 77–84; birth and death dates, 79; emergence as a Republican, 85–86; judgeship and military service, 89–98; campaign for the Senate, 98–104; early days in the Senate, 104–118; attack on Communists in the State Department, 119–140, 145–159; interest in money, 141–144, 245–246; talent for publicity, 162–170; attack on General Marshall, 170–179; and Army-McCarthy hearings, 205–222; loss of power and interior collapse, 232–243; death, 247, 251–252; obituaries, 248, 248n–249n; funerals and wake, 249–250
McCarthy, Tierney Elizabeth, 245
McCarthy, Timothy, 79
McCarthy: The Man, the Senator, the "Ism," 81
McCarthy and His Enemies, 22, 225
McCarthy and the Communists, 145n–146n

McCarthyism: beginning and definitions of, 7–9, 13, 40–44, 265, 270; and Roy Cohn, 193; magic of, 198; subsidence of, 266; mentioned, 136, 215
McCarthyism: The Fight for America: quotation from, 75–78; mentioned, 8, 169
McCarthyites: persons and contributions, 20–27, 141–145; loyalty of, 234–237, 241n; statements on McCarthy's death, 250–251
McClellan, John: report of, 185; at Army-McCarthy hearings, 220–221; mentioned, 218, 243, 270
McCormick, Robert R., 142
McGhee, George, 155
McGranery, James F., 182
McLeod, Scott, 32–33
McMahon, Brien, 133, 148
Madison *Capital-Times,* 121, 163
Malmédy investigation, 111–118, 121, 167, 212n
Mansfield, Mike, 249
Mantle, Mickey, 65n
Maragon, John, 106, 111
Marcantonio, Vito, 258
Marciano, Rocky, 51
Marine Corps: McCarthy's service in 93–98, 108, 108n–109n
Marquette University, 84
Marshall, George Catlett: statement on Communist China, 14; Eisenhower's would-be defense of, 15–16; McCarthy's attack on, 170–179; mentioned, 109, 163, 184, 256, 262
Marx, Karl, 194
Massing, Hede: and Cohn and Schine, 201–202
Matthews, J. B., 219n
May, Ronald W., 81
Mencken, H. L., 257
Meyer, Karl Ernest, 104n, 260–261
Military Affairs Committee, 112n
Miller, Joseph, 210–211
Miller, Thomas, 238
Milwaukee *Journal,* 63, 93, 121
Moeur, Kelly, 77
Monroney, A. S. Mike, 99

Morgan, Edward P., 269
Morse, Wayne, 180, 249
Morton, Johnny, 77
"Multiple Untruth": description of, 109–110; McCarthy's use of, 123–134, 163–170, 177–178; power of, 136–140
Mundt, Karl: at Army-McCarthy hearings, 207–208; mentioned, 29, 34, 135, 220
Murphy, Arnold F., 94
Murray, William H., 258
Murrow, Edward R., 248n–249n, 265, 269

National Press Club, 61n, 105
National Review, 22
New Deal, 259
New Leader, 135
New Yorker, 109
New York *Herald Tribune*, 9, 24, 269
New York *Journal-American*, 262n
New York *Post*, 57, 126, 262n
New York *Times*, 8, 29, 126, 166n, 269
Nitze, Paul, 155
Nixon, Richard M.: statement about Communists, 18; view of McCarthy, 135; McCarthy's statement on, 181; and meeting of Stevens and McCarthy, 212; changes Senate resolution against McCarthy, 231; attitude toward McCarthy in 1954, 232–233, 252; campaigns for Eisenhower, 243; mentioned, 223, 239, 246

Orestes, 45
Organization Man, 51
Our Sunday Visitor, 237
Owsley, Alvin M., 235

Parsons, Talcott, 265
Partridge, Richard C., 31, 192
Pàscal, Blaise, 148
Pearson, Drew, 162, 269
Pegler, Westbrook, 124
Pepsi-Cola Corporation: and McCarthy, 38, 106–107, 121

Peress, Irving, 39, 42, 44, 206
Perón, Juan, 253
"Politics of Loyalty: From La Follette to McCarthy in Wisconsin, 1918–1952," 104n
Pope, Alexander, 40n
Possony, Stefan: and McCarthy speech on Marshall, 177
Potter, Charles, 221
Press: and McCarthy, 137–140, 162–169, 173; fear of McCarthy, 268–269; newspapers hostile to McCarthy, 269
"Prince of Outer Baldonia," 106–107, 111, 183
Profiles in Courage, 13
Progressive Party, 101
Psychiatrists: views on McCarthy, 66–70
Purple Heart, 95
Pusey, Nathan, 163

Quaker Dairy Company case, 90–91

Rahv, Philip, 43
Rankin, John, 135
Rape of the Lock, 40n
Rebel Without a Cause, 70n
Reber, Miles, 208–209
Reconstruction Finance Corporation, 38
Rededication to Freedom, 266–267
Religion: and McCarthyism, 269
Republican campaign (1952): McCarthy's part in, 180–185
Republican campaign (1956): McCarthy during, 242–243
Republican Party: and McCarthyism, 14, 21
Reston, James, 27n
Revolt of the Moderates, 21
Riggs National Bank, 144
Roberts, William A., 122
Roman Catholics: and McCarthy, 21, 122
Roosevelt, Eleanor, 18
Roosevelt, Franklin D.: views of revisionist historians on, 177; character, 256; mentioned, 11, 36, 181n, 237

Rorty, James, 145n–146n
Rosenberg, Anna, 162
Rosenberg, Julius and Ethel, 191–192
Roy, Ralph Lord, 141n
Rushmore, Howard, 262n

Sabath, Adolph, 54, 124–125
Schacht, Hjalmar, 18–19
Schattschneider, E. E., 259
Schine, G. David, 32, 40; *see also* Cohn and Schine
Schlesinger, Arthur M., Jr., 265
Schuh, Matt, 107
Science: damage done to scientific enterprises, 263
Scripps Howard Newspapers, 187
Seaboard Airline Railroad, 38, 183
Sedition, 25–27, 45, 213, 262
Senate: fear of McCarthy, 34–39, 161, 267–268; censure resolution, 56–57; insecurity of Senate seats, 100–101; McCarthy speech about Communists in State Department, 130–134; reaction to Wheeling speech controversy, 135–136; problems confronting, during McCarthy hearing, 148–149; investigation of McCarthy, 183–184, 223–230; loses fear of McCarthy, 237–238
Service, John Steward, 152n
Shakespeare, William, 171n
Shannon, William, 126
Smedley, Agnes, 203
Smith, Margaret Chase: anti-McCarthy manifesto of, 180
Smith, Walter Bedell, 209
Smurch, Jack, 49n–50n
Sokolsky, George: and Cohn and Schine, 195; statements about McCarthy, 244, 246, 251; mentioned, 124
Soviet Information Center (Vienna), 203
Soviet Union: real threat of, 40–41; views of revisionist historians on American policy regarding, 177; Russian missile development, 215n
Spring Valley (Wis.) *Sun*, 179–180

Stalin, Joseph, 44, 194
Standley, William E., 235, 236
Stassen, Harold E., 18, 33–34, 240
State, Department of: McCarthy's attacks on, 6, 54, 119–140, 145–159, 169; efforts to counteract McCarthyism, 12; McCarthyites in, 25, 196
Stennis, John C., 223
Stevens, Robert T.: abdication to McCarthy, 28–32; McCarthy quotes *Macbeth* on, 171n; and Cohn and Schine and Army-McCarthy hearings, 205–222; mentioned, 44, 49, 192
Stevenson, Adlai: statement on McCarthy, 9–10; McCarthy's speech on, 182–183; mentioned, 49, 243, 256
Stimson, Henry L., 171
Stokes, Thomas L., 269
Straight, Michael, 171n, 207
Strandlund, Carl, 38, 111
Stratemeyer, George, 235
Sugar Rationing: McCarthy crusade against, 38, 106–107, 110
Summerfield, Arthur, 238, 252
Supreme Court, 264
Surine, Don, 160–161
Symington, Stuart: at Army-McCarthy hearings, 220–221; mentioned, 27, 74, 196, 218

Taft, Robert A.: approval of McCarthy, 179; miscalculation about McCarthy, 187–190; mentioned, 5, 33, 72, 101, 107, 109, 135, 136, 142, 180, 256
Talmadge, Eugene, 258
Tankersley, Mrs. Garvin, 142
Tansill, Charles Callin: and McCarthy speech on Marshall, 177
Television: and Voice of America investigation, 198; and Army-McCarthy hearings, 207, 219–220; McCarthy "shows," 240–241; and demagogues, 260; fear of McCarthy, 268–269
Ten Million Americans Mobilizing for Justice, 235–236

Texans, 22, 142–143
Thomas, J. Parnell, 135
Thomas, Norman, 270
Thompson, William Hale, 258
Thorp, Willard, 155
Thurber, James, 49n–50n
Thye, Edward J., 180
Tobey, Charles W., 106–107, 110
Tobin, Maurice, 13–14
Trial by Television, 207
Trotsky, Leon, 194
Truman, Harry S: denounces Mc-Carthy, 12; mentioned, 15, 76, 78, 120, 150, 162, 165–166, 170, 171, 256
Truman administration: McCarthy's effect on, 5, 11–14; mentioned, 185, 267
Twain, Mark, 203
Tydings, Millard: defeat by McCarthy, 36, 146n, 160–161
Tydings Committee: investigations of, 145–159; mentioned, 75, 140, 179

United Automobile Workers, 104
United Mine Workers, 105
United Nations, 132
Utley, Freda, 176

Valentine, Dan, 128–129
Van Straten, Henry J., 145
Van Susteren, Urban P., 92
Velde, Harold, 187, 189
Veterans of Foreign Wars, 13–14
Viereck, Peter, 265
Vincent, John Carter, 143
Voice of America: investigation of, 195–199; mentioned, 40, 132

Waist-High Culture, 53
Walsh, Edmund A.: inspiration of McCarthy's war on Communists, 122–123
Warren, Earl, 23
Washington *Evening Star*, 95

Washington *Post:* on McCarthy and the Eisenhower administration, 14–15; mentioned, 9, 128n, 260, 269
Washington *Times-Herald*, 142
Waters, Mrs. Agnes, 141n
Watkins, Arthur V.: personality, 223–224; congratulated by Eisenhower, 238
Watkins Committee: hearings on McCarthy, 56, 223–230
Wayne, Hummer & Company, 145
Webster, Daniel, 5
Wechsler, James A.: statement on McCarthy, 57–58; heckled by McCarthy, 262n
Weiss, Carl A., 20
Welch, Joseph Linden: at Army-McCarthy hearings, 46, 59, 208, 213, 215–218; mentioned, 226
Welker, Herman, 57, 242–243, 250
Werner, Edgar V., 87–89
Wheeling *Intelligencer:* quotation of McCarthy's speech, 125–126, 134
Wheeling speech: read into *Congressional Record,* 81–82, 81n–82n; genesis of, and effect, 123–134
Wherry, Kenneth, 135, 136, 174
White, Harry Dexter, 11, 165
White, Lincoln, 129
Wiley, Alexander, 39, 97–98, 249
Williams, Edward Bennett: before Watkins Committee, 226–228; mentioned, 56
Wilson, Woodrow, 13, 181n
Winchell, Walter, 191
Wisconsin *State Journal*, 98
Wisconsin State Tax Department· McCarthy tax evasion, 121
Woltman, Frederick, 55, 127
World War II, 259

Yalta papers, 239
Young Communist League, 262n

Zwicker, Ralph, 30, 39, 44, 49, 206, 212, 226, 229